Halas, Hef, the Beatles, and Me

Jack Mabley

CONTEMPORARY
BOOKS, INC.
CHICAGO ▪ NEW YORK

Copyright © 1987 by Jack Mabley
All rights reserved
Published by Contemporary Books, Inc.
180 North Michigan Avenue, Chicago, Illinois 60601
Manufactured in the United States of America
International Standard Book Number: 0-8092-4792-5

Published simultaneously in Canada by Beaverbooks, Ltd.
195 Allstate Parkway, Valleywood Business Park
Markham, Ontario L3R 4T8 Canada

Contents

FOREWORD
by James R. Thompson, Governor of Illinois...........v

PREFACE..vi

THE CRAFT OF JOURNALISM...........................1
Trapped in the Champaign Police Station. How to Report a Fire. On Writing Columns. Yes, Virginia, There Is a Hapless Maroon. The Green Chair. Hazards of a Reporter. The Man in the White Raincoat. Mismanaging the News. How to Stay Out of Jail.

MY KIND OF TOWN....................................25
The Friendliest City in the United States. Cocktail Party for the Press. Ding. Sid's Junction. Cats. The Bartender's Side. Garbage. Don't Say the Word *Beatles*! Urban Legends.

CITY HALL AND OTHER URBAN PECULIARITIES....43
Mayors from Kennelly, Martin, to Washington, Harold. Campaign Idiocy. There Goes the Judge. Don't Believe the Crowd Estimates.

TO YOUR GOOD HEALTH............................56
Live to Be 102. Sugar Blues. Listen to the Doctor. Smoke.

THE FORGOTTEN CHILDREN........................65
Forgotten Children . . . and Adults.

SHORTS...73

THE GOOD OLD DAYS................................78
A New House for $6,500. Shine Your Own Shoes. Rationing. On Alley Picking and Other Fun Things. GM—72 to 7⅝. Baked Bean Sandwiches and Bread Pudding. The Good Years?

BEYOND THE CITY LIMITS 94
The Suburban Curse. In the Boondocks. The Johnnie Gann Chronicles. Dessert with Jackie O. A Visit to Sun City. Motels. "Take It Off!" A Ride in Hitler's Mercedes. God's Many Voices. The Springfield Tapes. The Best State.

PEOPLE 120
A Talk with Saul Bellow. The Ultimate Hedonist. George Halas. Stanley Yankus. Jane Addams. Seeking the Magic of Billy Graham. The Least Interesting President. Heroes. The Happy Brain. More People: Nelson Algren, J. Edgar Hoover, Everett McKinley Dirksen, Andrew Greeley, Dick Cain.

COMMIES, ANTI-COMMIES, AND NAZIS I HAVE KNOWN 148
The Russians Have Come. The Entertainer. Nazis.

PERSONAL 156
I Lose a Friend. Blessings. Merry Christmas. Ed Lahey. The Numbers Game. Animal Tales. At War with Nature.

MORE SHORTS 170

FACES IN THE CITY 174
Urban Dialogues. The Garbageman. Party at Hef's Pad. Big Mama. The Checker.

HOME LIFE 186
The Woman in the Home. The Father as a Pal. The Sound and the Fury. Do It Yourself—at Your Own Risk.

THE WAR ZONE 196
Ike on War. The Bomb. Sneaky Ways to Start a War.

POOPERY 203
&%$#@*?>{*%!~#@!!!!!! The Power of the Mind. Are Good Manners Out of Style? Movies Were Better than Ever. The Service Man's Dream. Should the Old Be Allowed to Vote? AC/DC, Heavy Manners, and Skankin' Lizard. The Best Years. The Ultimate Salesman. The Importance of Being Number One.

THE SPORTING LIFE 219
Good Sports, Bad Sports. Let 'Em Drink Beer. In the Cubs' Locker Room. High Five. Playing Football Without a Helmet. Learn from Losing. Boxing Should Be Abolished.

THE 1968 DEMOCRATIC CONVENTION 234
The Riots. Julie, Rennie, Abbie, and Tom. The Power of Aum.

LOOKING AHEAD 241
Looking Back to the Future. The Lost Tribe. The Land of Plenty. Second Career.

Foreword

Illinois journalism has created some giants and Jack Mabley easily stands in that select group of men and women. His stories and columns have informed, entertained, and educated generations of Illinoisans.

Before I became Governor, Jack had long championed the cause of our state's mentally ill and developmentally disabled. The columns he wrote about the Dixon Mental Health Center led directly to long overdue improvements at one of the state's largest mental health facilities.

When I became Governor, it was apparent that the Dixon facility had outlived its long usefulness. In several trips to Dixon to determine its fate, I walked those grounds with Jack when it was 10°F below and 95°F in the shade. I eventually made the decision to close the facility and it has since become one of our state's finest medium-security prisons.

But there were some profoundly developmentally disabled patients at the old Dixon facility who could not be moved out of the area. We built a new developmentally disabled facility at Dixon, and I thought it was only fitting that we name the new building after the person who had been these patients' friend and unofficial guardian for so long.

And that's why I was proud to name that new building the Jack Mabley Developmental Center.

James R. Thompson
Governor of Illinois
June 1987

Preface

When I was a columnist and editor on Chicago newspapers I was asked a number of times why I didn't write a book. My answer was I didn't want to write a book. Six columns a week and tending to editors' jobs I simultaneously held took all my time. And I was never a big fan of reprinted columns.

If I wanted to get anything off my mind, I had a column a day to do it.

When I left the *Chicago Tribune* in 1982, I went into the business of corporate communications. In the course of this business I acquired two Macintosh computers and a laser printer. This book became inevitable. With the Mac it is easy to write and edit, to revise and rewrite and delete and add and correct and augment. I did my business work on it and had time left over. The book just started to roll out.

I saved a copy of every story and column I've written since I've been paid to write. A lot of them have relevance today. The material in many has some historical value. Events of a decade and two and three ago take on a new significance—or less significance—with time.

For instance, one of my first assignments after I got back from

World War II was to cover meetings of the atomic scientists at the University of Chicago, who reluctantly decided they had to abandon their academic shelter and try to save the world from the horrors of the monster they created. If they hadn't initiated the antinuclear movement I wonder if we'd be here today.

With time George Halas grows in stature and J. Edgar Hoover shrinks. When I covered the Beatles I wondered what the kids saw in their music.

When you're living through history—the Great Depression, World War II, Vietnam, the youth rebellion, the presidential scandals, a port disaster that took five hundred lives, a scientific revolution—you don't have full appreciation of their significance or place in history. One of the pleasant surprises of age is the time to look back and sort things out, to gain perspective and to appreciate what you've gone through. I went through marvelous and exciting and challenging and terrible times.

When I was doing a daily column I never tried to write what I thought most people wanted to read. This common denominator approach is responsible for much of the mediocrity in the mass media. The evidence is on your television tube every night.

I write about things and people that interest me. Because I have rather plebeian tastes and lifestyle many people could identify with my ideas and misadventures, and the column had a high readership.

This is not a book of reprints. I have taken events and opinions and ideas I've written about in the past thirty years and presented them from a viewpoint of the late eighties.

One of the chapter titles is "Poopery." This is a new word and requires some explanation. It is the contribution of Mayor Harold Washington. During his second campaign, Washington, who is a magniloquent orator, and has a pixie sense of humor, kept using a word in his extemporaneous speeches which reporters interpreted as *poopery*. At least it sounded like *poopery*.

This led to no end of jollity in the columns and commentary about whether the honorable mayor was talking about some activity involving pooper-scoopers and the necessity of keeping the parks and sidewalks clean, or whether some more obscure meaning lay behind the word.

Finally the mayor was asked. No problem. His word is spelled *potpourri*.

The preferred pronunciation in my *Webster*'s is pō-poo-rē, secondary, pät-poor-ē. So Washington had been pretty close to the proper pronunciation, except he dwelt a little too long on the first syllable.

It means a mixture of dried flower petals with spices, kept in a jar for its fragrance.

The secondary definition is "a medley, miscellany, or anthology" or "a combination of incongruous elements."

Which is a reasonably close definition of this book. But please don't call it poopery.

The Craft of Journalism

Trapped in the Champaign Police Station

The Champaign, Illinois, police arrested eight men in a raid on three gambling joints the night of March 31, 1938. The *Daily Illini*, the student newspaper which I edited, exposed the places, which ran blackjack, craps, numbers, poker, and horse bets. "The games are fixed and the people who run them are riffraff," we told our readers.

The heat from our campaign brought the raids. We also stated that prostitution and gambling can't be carried out without high visibility, and any police force that doesn't see such crimes is either stupid or crooked.

The Champaign police did not like me. The sheriff of Champaign County, who was friendly with me, advised me to carry a gun.

I went to the police station after the raid to get the story. When I finished getting names and bail and charges, I turned to leave.

The station had, and probably still has, three exits. At each of these exits stood a large, ugly man, staring at me. Like three Jack Palances.

"Sergeant, these three guys are trying to intimidate me," I told the desk sergeant. "How about a squad car to take me back to the office?"

The desk sergeant smiled. "You're dreaming, kid. Anyway, we only got one squad running and they're out on a robbery call at the city electric wagon."

I phoned our city desk. "Look, I'm trapped in the police station. Round up the five biggest guys you can find and take a cab down here."

Ten minutes later the Illini Rescue Party walked hesitantly into the police station.

They were led by a sophomore reporter named Dudley, who weighed 110 pounds. His troops were two small freshmen who were probably wondering what this had to do with higher education.

The rescue party in toto didn't weigh as much as one of the intimidators.

We marched out the door and scrambled into the cab.

My education was rounded out. I was ready for Chicago journalism.

How to Report a Fire

Several months after I went to work for the *Chicago Daily News* the Norris grain elevators in South Chicago exploded and burned. Because I was the only reporter available in the newsroom early in the morning, I was sent to the scene.

I drove until I heard sirens, then picked up a fire engine and followed it to the scene—standard procedure for getting to a fire without pausing for traffic lights. You're not supposed to follow fire engines, but the firemen were tolerant if they saw a press card in the windshield.

It was a tremendous fire—banks of giant grain elevators in flames. I parked in a field and ran a quarter of a mile to the fire. What to do first?

I spotted two men in overalls, covered with flour. I headed for them. They had been working inside one elevator, and had been blown through the door. They were lucid enough to give me a description of the explosion, and more importantly, the names of the eight or ten men they knew were in the elevators and hadn't escaped.

I ran a half mile to the nearest working phone and called in the story.

An hour later I was with some firemen near their engine along the railroad tracks. We were about two hundred feet from the burning structures. A high wall started to collapse.

The firemen shouted, and I joined them in diving under a freight car. The wall crashed down in front of us. A few bricks and shards landed near us, but none of us was damaged. A little dirty . . . but whole.

This was an early experience in basic reporting, and taught me a few fundamentals.

Look for the guys covered with flour (or their equivalent in a given situation).

Get to the scene as fast as you can, before investigators button up witnesses and survivors.

Follow the fire engines.

Always have something near to dive under or hide behind or duck into.

Luck has a great deal to do with reportorial success. However, reporters who get to work early seem to have more luck.

Run, don't walk.

Don't ask stupid questions. A few months later at another bad fire at the Brach candy factory on the West Side, two firemen were blown from the roof and were killed.

I asked the crusty old chief, Anthony J. Mullaney, "Did the fall kill them, chief?"

Mullaney looked at me. "No, son. It was the sudden stop."

His heart was breaking, but he was one tough fireman.

I was working rewrite at the *News*. There are busy times on rewrite, and not so busy. When spot news stories aren't breaking, city editors throw obituaries and club notes and overnight junk to rewrite persons, who hate it.

It was an unbusy time, and I was exchanging humorous anecdotes, quips, and banter with my rewrite neighbor. We were pulled up short by rewriteman Bob Faherty, a dour and brilliant contributor to the *News*'s reputation for quality writing.

"Don't laugh," Faherty growled. "Laughter attracts work."

This became a guiding principle in forty-four years of newspaper work.

Boy reporter goes to Union Station to meet train carrying Harold Ickes, Secretary of the Interior and full-time curmudgeon.

On Writing Columns

The two most common stereotypes about newsrooms, nourished by TV and movies, are erroneous.

One is the scene of noise and confusion when a big story breaks. I knew individuals who got excited under pressure, but they were rare and unwanted. Coverage of a major news story is time for calm professionalism.

Second is the idea that newspaper people are callous and indifferent to suffering. Men and women who cover tragedies are as shocked and saddened as are the readers and viewers—probably more so, because they see real blood and real tears. The good reporter subordinates his or her personal emotions so reporting can be objective. But the emotion is there.

I don't know whether it indicates callousness or self-control, but I can recall only one time when emotion forced me to stop talking while I was phoning in a story. It was at the October 1972 Illinois Central wreck south of the Loop, and I was trying to describe the carnage of scores of mangled bodies. I choked up and couldn't talk for a minute.

A good newspaper is a friend of the family, almost a part of the family. That's what the *Chicago Daily News* was for a century. A good newspaper has character and a distinct personality. It does far more than convey information. It helps set the moral tone for a community.

Victor Lawson, the early publisher, was so straightlaced that he paid his employees on Mondays, rather than Fridays, so they wouldn't go out and spend their paychecks on the weekends. He believed Sunday was the day for the Lord, and not commerce, so he didn't publish on Sundays. That proved the eventual undoing for the *News*, because the Sunday editions are the major sources of profit. John Knight sold the *Daily News* when he failed to buy the *American* and the *American*'s Sunday franchise.

I've always felt the *News* was the victim of mismanagement and not of the difficulty of marketing an afternoon paper.

A general column is basically a reporter with opinions. Syd Harris told me the editor gives us the right to be wrong—and hopes we don't exercise that right too often.

There are nightlife columns and political columns and social columns and chitchat columns and think columns and advice columns and national affairs columns and cutesy-writing columns.

The trouble with most columnists is they lose touch with the people for whom they're writing. If the column is successful, their incomes rise. They are feted and dined and flattered and coddled and get special privileges and life becomes soft. Some are booby-trapped into writing to please other writers or people in the newspaper business.

Some begin to take themselves too seriously. Some allow themselves to become indebted to public relations people who are solicitous about their well-being and provide favors, gifts, perks, luxury travel, and unstinted praise. Public relations people perform a useful function, but they are paid to get their clients' points of view before the public, and their interests frequently conflict with those of the journalistic seekers of truth.

I got a generous sample of this when I was a television columnist. When I changed to a general column, I figured that in the long run I'd attract more readers and consequently make more money if I did my own digging for facts instead of accepting handouts, if I kept out of nightclubs and glamorous places and paid my own way and answered only to myself, my newspaper, and most important, to the people who read the column.

To be worth its space a column should be interesting to read, it should inform, it should stimulate thought, and it should accomplish some good for the community.

A columnist can get dizzy trying to pick out subject matter. It is tempting to try to be significant, to try to get over a viewpoint particularly dear to you. I wrote about our wars and the threat of nuclear bombs and about crooks in government, but invariably a few paragraphs on the best ways to get ketchup out of a narrow-necked bottle generated more response than a column on how the state was losing millions to sales tax gyps.

I ended up not trying to guess what readers wanted, but writing every day about what interested me most that day. Some days it was bingo and some days it was the hydrogen bomb.

An immutable rule of column writing is that the quality of the product is in direct ratio to the amount of work put into it. As columnists age they get less inclined to get out on the street and more inclined to sit in their offices and pontificate.

If I were sponsoring a competition for columnists, I'd reverse the method of judging. I'd give the prize for the least bad columns. Anybody can write a great column or story when he feels good and has great material. The test comes when you haven't any material, or you feel lousy, or you have personal problems.

In my competition the judges would watch an entrant's columns for a year, and pick out the three worst. These would be the entries, and the columnist whose three worst were the least bad would win the $1,000.

Yes, Virginia, There Is a Hapless Maroon

A hapless Maroon was a member of a University of Chicago major sports team during the last five years of Chicago's membership in the Big Ten. I don't think one sports story in a hundred in those five years failed to identify the Chicago teams as "the hapless Maroons."

The hapless Maroons became happy Maroons when they got out of the Big Ten and began playing for fun.

Some journalistic clichés seem indestructible. "Yes, Virginia, there is . . ." is the hoariest of all, favored particularly by sportswriters, who perform incredible convolutions to avoid telling the score in the first three paragraphs. These same hacks have also worn out "You've come a long way, baby."

What does a city do after a heavy snowstorm. It "digs out." All fires have been "spectacular" since Mrs. O'Leary's cow. What does a snowstorm do to traffic? It "snarls traffic." What does it do to an airport? "Socks it in." What does it do to the streets? "Turns them into parking lots." What happens inside those cars? "Tempers flare."

If convicted on all counts, what does the defendant face? "Forty-five years in prison and a $200,000 fine." What does the defendant actually get after being convicted on all counts? Four years in Lexington, eligible for parole in eighteen months.

Some day I hope to see a story about an unspectacular fire, or an uncomprehensive survey. What's the difference between a survey and a comprehensive survey? Is there any way to get an accident victim to a hospital but rush? Are all truces uneasy, all bargaining sessions marathon, all robberies either daring or daylight, or both, all Arab nations oil-rich, all changes sweeping, all debates spirited, all yachts luxurious, all conclusions foregone?

If we always refer to Cuba as Communist Cuba, why not Democratic Canada?

New moves are inevitably dramatic, links are inextricable, strife is internecine, needs are spotlighted, heritages are proud, tours are whirlwind, secrets are open, and capacities are official.

Forty-five years ago I sat in a Chicago newsroom and tried to figure out a second-day lead to a crime story that didn't begin, "Police today were searching for. . . ." It was futile, because to this day the all-purpose, all-time favorite second-day lead on crime stories still is, "Police today were searching for. . . ."

How do we legitimize the arrival of winter year after year? The photo editor sends a photographer out to get a picture of a girl writing "Snow" on her auto windshield after a dusting of snow. Or maybe the photo editor doesn't make that specific assignment. Maybe he says, "Go out and get a snow picture." The photographer is powerless before the reflexive pull toward a girl and a car windshield.

How did movie critics function before they discovered the word *genre*? How did the movies function without genre? Movie criticism is the easiest writing in newspapering, and much too often it serves primarily as a vehicle for the writer's verbal preening.

I show my age by my dislike for the practice of referring to women by their last names alone. I don't do it in personal conversation, and I never did it in my columns. The first time I ever saw the salutation *Ms.* was in my column. I answered all my mail, and it was a problem when a woman would sign her letter, let's say, Carol Craft. How did I respond? Dear Craft? Dear Carol? Dear Miss Craft? Dear Mrs. Craft? The first two were offensive and one of the second two was wrong.

My correspondence was very informal, and my solution for a time was to either type or write Mrs. *and* Miss, one on top of the other. It was sloppy but not inaccurate. Finally I decided to make up my own salutation for female correspondents of unknown marital status: Dear Ms. I have no idea whether I was the first to use it.

Jack Mabley's chair.

The Green Chair

The Green Chair is an armless oak swivel chair with the date 6-'29 on the underside. I latched onto it sometime after I went to work at the *Chicago Daily News* in 1938. I liked it because it fit me, I like a swivel, and I don't like office chairs with arms.

Marshall Field purchased the *Daily News* in 1960 and built a new newsroom for the *Daily News* in the *Sun-Times* building. We were instructed that the room was completely furnished and decorated, and when we moved in we were to bring only personal possessions which could be stored properly (and invisibly) in our desks.

A move from our tradition-rich newsroom at 400 West Madison Street was traumatic at best. The staff was concerned that we would be swallowed up by Field and would play second fiddle to the *Sun-times*. The fear was justified.

I was reluctant to sacrifice my chair for several reasons—sentimental, emotional, and posturepedic. Getting the chair into the new newsroom became a challenge. I, and my friends, spent hours figuring how to get the chair out of the old newsroom, past the guards at the *News* and the guards at the *Sun-Times*.

We considered hoisting it out of the window, bribery, and disguise. I finally opted for bluffery.

We moved on New Year's Day in 1961. My wife and I drove down to the *Daily News* building and went up to my desk, took out the contents, piled them on the green chair, which has good rollers, and rolled the chair and contents to the elevator and into the hall and the guard station.

The strategy was to forge ahead authoritatively, not look guilty or furtive, and trust that the guards' attention would focus on the cargo on the chair (legitimate) and not on the chair itself (contraband). The chair, in the guards' eyes, would be a dolly to carry the cargo.

It worked at both buildings. We piled the chair and the papers into my station wagon, parked in front of the *Sun-Times* building, pulled out the chair, piled the papers and books and files on it, rolled it into the lobby and past the guard and up to my desk.

Phase 1 was successful. Phase 2 was to retain the chair. I placed it at my desk by a window overlooking the Chicago River in the back of the newsroom. Obviously on the first night the building staff would confiscate the chair and replace it with a new one in keeping with the motif of the newsroom—a bland shade called *desert sand*. Everything was desert sand—the walls, desks, chairs, ash trays, everything. It was a decorator's delight and a newsman's nightmare. We had strict orders that nothing was to be tacked, pasted, or otherwise applied to any wall. Every night before we left, our desks were to be clear.

I bought a heavy chain and strong lock and chained the chair to my desk when I left. The rattling of the chains and the commotion was an irritation to the management, but other than some unfriendly stares, there was no resistance to the chair.

The chair was a rallying point for much of the staff . . . the one remaining symbol of our past at the *Daily News*. I think Art Snider, the science editor, managed to get an ugly coat rack into the room, but I don't remember the circumstances.

After Marshall Field III bought the Chicago Daily News, *he made a tour of the newsroom with editor Stuffy Walters, introducing Field to the troops. Everybody acknowledged the introduction with obsequious remarks, and I decided to break the monotony.*

"Are you the guy to see about getting a decent typewriter?" I asked Field. He laughed.

The next day Field and Stuffy walked into the newsroom with a new typewriter for me. Good gimmick—and I got a machine that worked.

Eleven days after our arrival Marshall Field returned to the city. His staff provided him with a chart of the newsroom with a picture of each occupant of each desk. Field visited the newsroom and began working his way back toward my desk.

I stood up respectfully when he arrived, and unfortunately revealed the non-conforming chair. I had had several good meetings with Field, and one lunch, and liked him and felt we were friends. He didn't even look at me.

"Jack," Field asked. "What do you see in that chair?"

Maybe I thought he'd welcome, or at least understand, a small sign of individuality in the middle of all that desert sand. I don't remember my reply. I was thinking that if he had to ask the question he'd never understand the answer. He looked at the chair as if it was a carrier of disease.

Thirty minutes later the managing editor came to my desk carrying a furniture catalog.

"Jack," he said, "I want you to pick any chair in this catalog. The old one has to go."

Shortly afterward a man in overalls came and wheeled my chair out of the newsroom. An unnatural silence came over the newsroom as my friends watched the chair go. Our defeat was unpleasant and ominous.

Ten minutes later the wall was desecrated for the first time with a sheet of long copy paper, at the top of which was typed:

"Jan. 11, 1961. BRING BACK MABLEY'S GREEN CHAIR!!"

The signatures were Terry Turner, Robert G. Schultz, Buck Walmsley, Harry Schaudt, Pat Dalton, Janet Cartwright, Don Henehan, A. Snider, Dave Meade, Harry Swegle, Dick Stout, Ed Baumann, Paul Gapp, Lucia Lewis, Gruenberg, Adrienne Danlon, Alberta Friedlander, Jeanette Sarkesien, Shirlee De Santi, Eileen Kelliher, Nancy McKinney, C. Sherman, Tony Weitzel, Nick Shuman, Bill Furlong, Ed Rooney, Isabel DuBois, Joyce Vavrosky, Kathleen Noe, and Jay McMullen.

Three weeks later I resigned and went to work for the Tribune Company. I wrote Field and asked if I might have my green chair. He graciously had it fished out of the warehouse and sent over.

I used it for some twenty more years in the different offices I occupied in Tribune Tower. It invariably clashed distressingly with the decor of whatever cubicle I occupied, but the *Trib* bosses were tolerant. "We have to put up with a little eccentricity," they acknowledged.

Hazards of a Reporter

I was in danger occasionally during my years on the street, but I was never hurt or damaged. One reason was that I assigned all the dirty jobs on the column to my assistants. Like going to nudist camps, determining if you could live for a week on food salvaged from restaurant garbage cans, staking out hoodlums, infiltrating radical groups.

These assignments resulted in only one instance of violence. We were running an investigation of lawlessness on Chicago's Near North Side. Our stories on prostitution and violence resulted in a few raids. Then we focused on the safety of citizens walking on North Side streets.

Kenan Heise was doing the dirty work for me on the street, and I arranged for what I thought was the best possible protection. Kenan was accompanied by an undercover sheriff's policeman named Bill Kelly. Bill was a personal friend, and I thought he was the toughest and most fearless man I'd ever known. Before becoming a policeman he was a carny wrestler. That is, he traveled with carnivals and took on all comers in no-holds-barred wrestling matches.

At half past twelve in the morning of a July 4, Kelly left his badge and gun in his car and he and Kenan set out walking east in the 350 block of Schiller Street. Kenan tells what happened:

"In the dark, under the elevated tracks, we suddenly saw four men . . . they seemed to be in their twenties . . . blocking the walk. I didn't think too much of it, and stepped off the curb to go around them.

"Suddenly a huge arm had a hammer lock around my neck. It happened without warning. My first thought was they were horsing around. Then my glasses flew off, and my thought, rather absurdly, was: 'What do I do next?'

"A second one jumped me, and I was on the ground, with the two of them pounding me. Bill was taking on the other two and I guess he was landing a few punches.

"He started pulling the two off me and he yelled, 'Run!' This thought had occurred to me, but inasmuch as I was flat on my back, I couldn't do anything about it.

"Bill ran . . . I knew it was to his car to get his gun. The two he was fighting tossed two bricks at him. One caught his arm and put a huge gash in it. He figured then he needed his gun.

"I didn't get away. I got to the middle of the street when all four hit me. One of them ripped the pocket off my pants. I managed to get between two parked cars. They kept after me. One threw a punch but hit the arm of another who must have had a knife. I felt a sting on my neck, and later found a long, but shallow gash on my neck.

"Now they had me down on the sidewalk. One guy kept yelling, 'Hit 'im in the belly, hit 'im in the belly!' I could feel my trousers being ripped. One of them shouted, 'Get his wallet!'

"I shouted, 'You already got my wallet!' They kept on ripping the legs of my trousers. Then after a few more kicks they started running away. One stopped, turned, and threw a brick that hit me squarely on the elbow.

"I picked myself up and looked around. Tourists from Old Town were walking toward me. There were two or three men and two or three women. I looked quite beat up and was prowling around the pavement for my glasses.

"The tourists were solicitous. One said, 'You need a cigarette.' I agreed. They wanted to give me a ride home. Then Kelly got back with his gun in his hand. We didn't have much chance of finding the guys, but we went looking.

"It was strange that my feeling at that moment was one of amusement. It really was shock, and I literally felt no pain. It wasn't until I got home and inventoried my injuries that I began to comprehend what happened. Then I began to hurt."

Kenan's injuries were painful but superficial. Had the knife gone a fraction of an inch deeper in his neck the injury could have been serious or fatal.

I hate to capitalize on someone's misfortune, but it made a good story.

The Man in the White Raincoat

The first murder I covered was of little consequence to anyone but the victim and the murderer. The police didn't do much persuading to get a confession, but when the killer was ready to talk, there was nobody in the Warren Avenue police station who could type.

The sergeant asked if I would give him a hand. So I typed out the man's confession as he told it to the police. There was no lawyer present, and I think if the man had demanded his rights he would have got a whack on the head.

When Suzanne Degnan was kidnapped and murdered, I was the first reporter to get to the Degnan house on Sheridan Road. One cop guarded the house. I asked if the ground-floor bedroom was the one from which she had been kidnapped. He said it was. I asked if it was OK if I crawled through the window and looked around. He said go ahead, which I did.

After looking around I backed out of the window and landed feet first in the soft ground under the window. Months later I learned that a set of footprints under the window was the major clue to the kidnapper. This is the first time I have had the nerve to reveal that those footprints were mine. (The fact that my home was on the same block as the Degnans' would have made me an ideal suspect.)

After the Grimes sisters were murdered, the sheriff decided that a drifter named Bennie Bedwell was the killer. Bennie was arrested and taken on a tour of the scene of the crime so photographers could get a few thousand more pictures of everyone involved in the matter. This was followed by the discovery that Bennie Bedwell had nothing to do with killing the Grimes sisters. He was enjoying the spotlight as much as the sheriff.

Criminal investigations today are conducted with a reasonable degree of propriety. But before medical examiners replaced coroners, they were more media events than anything else. The discovery of the body signaled the race by the coroner and photographers. The coroner always wore a white raincoat to the scene of the crime. Why? So he would stand out in the pictures.

After the victim and surroundings were milked, the coroner called an inquest. The coroner subpoenaed witnesses, survivors, suspects, and anybody else he thought might liven the proceedings.

Photographers and reporters had free run of the inquest room. The coroner or deputy coroner knew what the press wanted, and gave it to them. It was a set formula, with the dramatic highlight usually the testimony of the most coherent, prettiest, and weepiest relative of the victim.

After every possible emotion was wrung from the cast, the coroner's jury retired to reach a verdict. This jury was composed of six men who didn't have much else to do, so made a career of being on juries. They got a few dollars per case. After due deliberation they would return their verdict: "Death by gunshot wound by person or persons unknown." It didn't require all this foolishness to establish what everybody already knew, but the press and the coroner had to be served.

When the police found a suspect, the next event was to take the suspect to the scene of the crime for what was known as "a reenactment." There was a lot of pushing and shoving and maneuvering for position before the cameras. This was before TV cameras took control of media events. I shudder at the idea of TV being added to this circus.

Reform began before television arrived. In the sixties the Democratic machine responded to public disgust at the spectacles and named a physician who didn't own a white raincoat to be coroner. He was Dr. Andrew Toman, who advocated that the office he occupied be abolished.

I think the change became a reality when Richard Speck was arrested for the murder of eight student nurses. Seven days after Speck's arrest he had not been photographed by any press photographer, no reporter had been near him, there had been no reenactment of the crime, and the coroner's inquest was postponed indefinitely.

Speck was convicted after an investigation, prosecution, and sentencing with no reversible error.

Mismanaging the News

Three stories about efforts to manage the news, and why they failed.

Robert Welch was getting his John Birch Society rolling in 1960. Welch was irrational, but he owned a big candy company, was a member in good standing of the National Association of Manufacturers, and had persuaded several prominent members of the NAM to be on the board of his Birch Society.

He was organizing in the Chicago area, establishing local chapters, holding meetings. Welch's brand of conservatism made today's far right look like pinkos. Welch wrote a book which was available only to his inner circle, in which he called President Eisenhower "a conscious, dedicated agent of the Communist conspiracy. There is only one possible word to describe his purposes and his actions. That word is treason."

John Foster Dulles and General George Marshall were similarly labeled.

One Chicago businessman who accepted an invitation to an organization meeting heard these allegations in disbelief and shock and anger. He knew one of the *Chicago Tribune*'s senior reporters, told him about the Birch movement, and invited the reporter to attend a meeting.

The reporter did this, on his own. He shared the shock and surprise. He prepared a thoroughly documented report for the *Tribune*, and asked to write the story.

The *Tribune* rejected the material. I don't know why. Maybe they didn't believe it. Colonel McCormick's right-wing political philosophies still dominated the *Tribune*'s editorial stance, and that might have been a factor.

Whatever, the reporter wanted the Birchers and Welch exposed. Through a mutual friend all of his notes and material were given to me. Including a copy of Welch's book, *The Politician*, which spelled out his incredible accusations.

Welch might have been dismissed as just another right-wing nut except for the presence of influential establishment businessmen on his board.

My stories appeared in the *Chicago Daily News* on the first two days of the Republican National Convention which was being held in Chicago. They caused considerable impact. Welch was furious. He said I had no right to have his book. But I had it, I reproduced the part about Eisenhower, and Welch could not deny his allegation.

The story was picked up nationwide. Because no other paper had a copy of *The Politician* I received calls from papers throughout the country which were investigating the Birch movement in their cities. I gave them access to all of my material. One of them, I believe, won a Pulitzer Prize for exposing the Birch society.

Investigative reporting always was my first love. Sometimes you could work your head off for months and the payoff would be one story in the back of the paper. And then you might sit at your desk and somebody would come by and drop in your lap all the material for an exposé of national significance.

• • •

After a Latino committed suicide because he was so heavily in debt to credit sharks, Mayor Daley appointed a consumers' bureau to clean up the credit sales racket. He put John King, a feisty, honest lawyer in charge. He also gave him a tough cop for muscle, and a state accountant for figuring.

This little task force started visiting auto dealers, and discovered that not only were a lot of them gypping poor people on credit sales, many were cheating on their state sales tax payments. These dealers kept two sets of books, one for themselves, a second set for the state. The real accounts might show a sales tax obligation of $45,000 a month. The phony books would show a couple of hundred dollars owed. King's approach when his group walked into a dealer's office was less than subtle. He'd ask to see the books. The manager would produce the phony books. The cop would pull out his gun and snarl, "Now give us the &%$&?%@# real books!" It worked every time.

King and company built a case and handed the information to the *Daily News*. The *News* printed the story with an eight-column headline on page one. For one edition. I was at the *American*, and we were thoroughly scooped. Except when the *News*'s second edition came out, the story had vanished. There was no reference to it anywhere in the paper.

Inasmuch as this story involved crimes which cheated the state of at least $40 million a year and were to put several people in prison, we were puzzled. Then somebody pointed out that the worst cheaters in the *Daily News* story were major advertisers in the *News*.

King and his troops were angry. They came across Michigan Avenue and handed me all the material. The next day we carried a front page story, with a lot more information, and we rode the story for months, ending up with new state laws making the dealers' gouge impossible.

What kind of bribes were needed to steal $40 million a year from the state? Ridiculously little ones. An auto dealer told me how it worked.

"The only state people I saw were the guys who came around every month or two to look at our books. Field inspectors I think they're called. They'd walk into the showroom and say they wanted to look at the records of our sales tax payment for the past three months.

"I'd get the auditor and he'd lay the books on the table. The two state men would glance at them and say 'OK.' They'd get up to leave and I'd take fifteen or twenty dollars out of my wallet for each of them and say 'Go buy yourself some cigars.'

"This wasn't a bribe. It was chicken feed."

The episode took about ten minutes. The inspectors could make four or five stops an hour. Projecting that into a forty hour week, and only ten dollars per stop, a crooked inspector's annual income would be $80,000, tax-free, with two weeks off for vacation.

• • •

Boxing was very big on television in the fifties, with many championship fights on prime time. Boxing was controlled by the International Boxing Club. The mafia also had a hand in the sport. There's always been a lot of corruption in boxing. I was writing sports at the *Daily News*, and went on a fishing expedition—fishing for fixes. A colleague and I located an old heavyweight fighter named Harry Thomas, who told us that he once took a dive for $6,000 in a fight with Max Schmeling which was a buildup for Schmeling's return match with Joe Louis. The story had current relevance because the man who gave him the $6,000 in a room in the Drake hotel was also the virtual czar of boxing in its television renaissance.

We got one eyewitness, gathered other corroborating evidence, and I handed in a story. The editors gave it to our lawyers who sent back a list of ten points to answer. I answered them. The lawyers gave me ten more questions. I now was getting the message that the paper was afraid to run the story. They seemed relieved when I suggested we stop playing games because they were not going to run it.

I called T George Harris, then head of *Time*'s Chicago bureau. *Time* went into action. A high-priced lawyer flew in from New York. Thomas passed a lie test. Every piece of evidence was checked. *Time* said "Let's go with it."

The story appeared in one of the early issues of *Sports Illustrated* under my byline.

Now the sweetest payoff. The *Detroit Free Press*, a sister paper of the *Chicago Daily News*, picked up the story from *Sports Illustrated* and ran it prominently on page one. My editors in Chicago got a copy of the *Free Press* and asked me to rewrite the *Free Press* story, crediting my story in *Sports Illustrated*. So in the end my story appeared in the *News* and I was ahead $1,500 and exposure in a national magazine.

• • •

Here's one where I suppressed a story, and it never did see print. We were getting a lot of rumbles at the *American* about unsanitary conditions in restaurants. I assigned Mike McGovern, a very aggressive, street-wise reporter, to see what he could find. The first phase was getting the Board of Health to give us a health inspector who went around with Mike making unscheduled and unannounced spot inspections of kitchens.

They found filth everywhere. It turned my stomach to read his memos. Mice, mice droppings, cockroaches, bugs of every kind, grease buildup, filthy dishwater, food handlers fresh off Skid Row. In some twenty restaurant kitchens they visited, I think there were two which had no violations, which were as sanitary as an average housewife's kitchen. The surprise was not in finding the dirt, but finding it in prestigious restaurants.

Mike took a job as a banquet waiter in one of the big hotels. Detail: one of the waiters dropped a tray of rolls on the floor while setting up a banquet. He picked them up, and finding three of them soiled, wiped them off on his pants. Detail: If you send a dish back to the kitchen because it is too cold or too hot or too something, it will come back to your table with a new ingredient—spit.

I had all of Mike's material. It was devastating. It also would do grave damage to the restaurant business in Chicago, because the good restaurants would be hurt as well as the offending ones. I called the head of the Restaurant Association and told him what I had. I said it would be terribly damaging, and he agreed. I said I'd make a deal. I'd sit on the story if he would take aggressive action to clean up the kitchens. He acted quickly and effectively. He sent letters to all the members warning of their vulnerability. He wrote a new sanitation code, or renewed an old one, and sent it to all members. He had placards printed for posting in the kitchens.

I didn't print the story, but warned we'd be checking in the future.

Where were my editors through all this? They never would have stood for suppressing the story, so I didn't tell them anything more than, "Oh, that didn't work out."

Was this bad journalism? Let someone else judge. It happened.

I had twenty or so assistants through the years. They contributed beyond measure to the column. None were better than these four, who came to my Retirement Thing at the Tribune: *Mike Powers, John Gorman, Kenan Heise, and Dick Atcheson. While my first assistant, Walter Jacobson, has earned more money than any of them, all have gone on to success, mostly in journalism.*

The Retirement Thing was, at my request, open house in my office at noon on a workday at the Trib, *with 600 of Moe's corned beef sandwiches cut in half, soft drinks, and a lot of goodies made by my wife. A lot of good friends stopped by.*

How to Stay Out of Jail

This should be of special interest to journalism students: some ideas on how to conduct investigations.

I was subpoenaed dozens of times in criminal trials, civil trials, by grand juries, by legislative investigating commissions, state athletic commissions, liquor commissions, and a few others I've probably forgotten. I never considered the police or courts or any branch of law enforcement to be my antagonists, with the exception of J. Edgar Hoover, who regarded me as a menace to society. However, his Chicago agents didn't suffer this delusion, and I worked closely with them many times.

The protection of news sources troubles many in journalism, the courts, and in education. The practical application of judicial principle and freedom of expression conflict at times. Protection of news sources is a sensitive issue. A TV columnist named Marie Torre became well known when she refused to tell the court a source and spent ten days in jail sleeping, eating, and reading the complete works of S. J. Perelman.

On the problem of being subpoenaed to bring your notes and relevant material, a smart investigative reporter won't have any notes, or will have misplaced them. If he or she is asked to rely on memory, the memory can become very foggy. Ethical? I'm not sure. Done all the time? You bet.

Several times I acquired tape recordings of conversations which, when printed, resulted in prominent people going to prison. A legislative commission and a grand jury repeatedly demanded to know how I got these tapes. In one case I got an anonymous letter with a key to a locker in the Greyhound bus depot, which contained the tapes.

It was suggested that I was in cahoots with the person or persons who planted the illegal bugs which produced these tapes. This was never proven.

It's appropriate to tell the mechanics of one operation. Dick Cain, a top sheriff's police officer, planted a bug on the phone of the man in charge of finding a person to direct the Crime Investigation Commission.

Cain had a copy of the tape delivered to our reception desk by an anonymous messenger, with an anonymous letter accompanying it. I was subpoenaed by the grand jury and told to bring the tape and the letter and any notes I had. I ignored the subpoena for this reason. Cain had acquired (stolen?) stationery from the state's attorney's office—plain paper, but with an identifying watermark. The prosecutor decided he didn't need my testimony.

Suppose I had been asked under oath if I knew the source of the tapes. What would I have answered? I don't know. The point is that such a dilemma was avoided by proper preparation.

Cain later laughed that there were so many taps on the phone that he had trouble finding a place for his. Cain later was killed by syndicate hit men.

I was in charge of covering the street activities before and during the 1968 Democratic Convention in Chicago. I hired a young man who had just graduated from Cornell College, and told him to join the radical movement, using his own name and never lying. The radical Students for a Democratic Society rebuffed his effort to join them, but he did join the Movement, that is, Abbie Hoffman and his group, which was the planning agency for the convention demonstrations.

I told the FBI I had a man in the Movement so they wouldn't start a subversive file on him. I also kept daily records of his and my work, and I also spoke daily with the FBI, trading information. I think I gave a lot more than I got. After the rioting the government indicted the Chicago Seven. I offered the testimony and notes of our coverage to both the government and the defense. We had a lot of facts very pertinent to the case, we were objective, and we were willing to provide this information to either side. It turned out that my assistant testified for the government and I testified for the Chicago Seven. In my mind it didn't matter which side called us. We were at the service of the court.

Also, for what it's worth, I did all this without consulting our lawyers. Most times if you ask a lawyer if you can do something a little risky he or she will say no. So I didn't ask.

Joe Woods of the Better Government Association and I conducted an investigation which resulted in a major story which ultimately sent some high state officials to prison. We broke the story at 9:00 A.M. on a weekday, and at 9:10 A.M. Joe and I got in my car and drove to Springfield, where we handed all of the evidence supporting our story to the state's attorney. We both testified before the grand jury. It was an ideal example of cooperation between a civic organization, the press, and the judicial system.

The system works well when competent and ethical journalists are dealing with honest and capable law enforcement people. It's when the people in government and the law are corrupt that ethical problems arise. When is lying justified? When is a faulty memory justified?

I got another Greyhound locker full of tapes containing weeks of conversation among currency exchange lobbyists in a Springfield hotel room. It gave facts, figures, and names involved in wholesale bribery in the legislature. An outraged legislature appointed a special committee to investigate the charges.

This committee subpoenaed me half-a-dozen times over two years. Trying to find more details of the bribery? Not on your life. They were banging on me to find who put the bug in the hotel room. I didn't put it there. I told them it was true that I reserved the room next to the lobbyists' room, but what the head of the Better Government Association, who asked me to make the reservation, did with the room was his business.

The special committee made a lot of noise and denounced me and my unnamed collaborators, but that was all. They never did get around to looking into the bribery.

My Kind of Town

The Friendliest City in the United States

I recently interviewed a young man who moved here from the South because he felt Chicago held the greatest opportunities. "I can't get over how friendly everybody is," he said. "When I was first in the Loop I had a map, and every time I stopped and looked at it people came up to me and asked if they could help. And I mean every time."

Chicago has a lot of tangibles going for it—the lake, the space, the transportation hub, the mass transit, the buildings. But the city's greatest asset is its friendliness.

It's difficult to measure this intangible on a scale involving six million people (I'm including the suburbs). Individual experiences alter cases. One rude waiter makes a city seem like the pits. A cheerful attendant at the airport can make it seem ideal.

A visitor from Wales had some negative experiences, and wrote back to the *Tribune* that Chicagoans had long faces and were grouchy.

A lady from Carson City, Nevada, was changing planes at

O'Hare. She picked up the *Trib*, read the Welsh visitor's complaint, and sat down and wrote me.

"Please excuse the stationery, but I'm at the airport, and this is all I have with me," wrote Linda Ryan. "If I delay I'm afraid I won't write.

"I agree with the Welsh lady entirely. In all of Britain, not just Wales, people smile and call out greetings to strangers, and I love it.

"The people there will go to any amount of inconvenience to help others or to answer questions. On several occasions I have had people stop and offer assistance just because I looked perplexed.

"However, I want to point out another side. It's ironic that I read your column just about ten minutes after writing a note to the manager of the Carson Pirie Scott coffee shop at O'Hare, telling him/her how enjoyable it was to have a friendly and efficient waitress.

"In my opinion Chicago is the friendliest city in the country. I agree it's a far cry from the friendliness and safety in Wales, but I believe it exceeds any other city and most towns, at least those I have visited.

"If your Welsh friend had moved to the West, she probably never would have recovered from the cultural shock. I love Nevada, but the treatment people (customers) receive in Reno and Las Vegas is deplorable.

"California is even worse. Rude and hateful service is quite normal. Restaurant employees, cab drivers, bus drivers, everyone who seems to have public contact (especially San Francisco hotel workers) treat people as though everyone is a tourist and all tourists are dispensable.

"This is a rather convoluted letter, because I'm in a hurry, but I want you to know that as long as I live in the United States, Chicago will be my favorite place. It may not be perfect, but it's far better than the cities in the West and the few I know in the East. I wish I could live here."

Probably the best-read columns I did at Chicago Today *were the neighborhood walks. I spent part of a day walking in a Chicago neighborhood talking with the people and writing what I saw and heard. The pieces were simplicity itself, and very popular. The interviewees here in Rogers Park are Theresa Cervantes, age seven, and her puppy.*

Cocktail Party for the Press

I had twenty-four or twenty-five assistants with my general column. But I didn't call them assistants, and I hated the term *legman*. They were associates, because they provided much of the material for some eight thousand daily columns. The highlight of one summer's columns was a report of a visit to a nudist camp by Walter Jacobson. At the *Tribune* I was sometimes known as Mike Powers's rewrite man, Mike being my associate for five years. Kenan Heise introduced to me the poor poor of Chicago.

Dick Atcheson could write rings around me. I sent Dick to interview Hugh Hefner and Hefner hired him away from me at double his pay. Dick had a very successful career as a magazine and book writer.

I hated press conferences and cocktail parties and similar organized assaults on the press. They were bad enough before the TV cameras dominated them. I received an invitation to an "Informal Cocktail Party for the Press" at a place called Kismet. Dick thought he might like to go. His report:

"It's a cocktail lounge on a street called Tooker Place. It was quite cold inside, and a number of workmen were running around in overalls when we walked in.

"There were no lights. One powerful flashlight lit the corridor.

"It was also quite cold. My companion and I groped to the end of the corridor, dodging ladders and loose wires.

"There was a lady there wrapped in a mink coat. She greeted us, 'We seem to be having a teeny weeny bit of trouble with the lights,' she said through chattering teeth, 'and we are *trying* to get the heat on. The workmen wouldn't make connections today because this is Veterans' Day or something.'

"On her advice, we kept our coats on and moved into the crowded darkness where a lot of people could be felt and heard, if not seen, huddling together for warmth around a bar.

"The bartender in an overcoat mixed us a pair of Rob Roys. He said there were tables in the rear.

"He failed to tell us there were two steps down near the bar. We missed the steps and barely kept from going flat on our faces.

"Once seated, our principal entertainment was watching unsuspecting young ladies plunge over the steps.

"My companion, male, asked about the sensuous dancing girls mentioned on the invitation. Finally we spotted some exotic harem girls, who seemed to be wearing Oriental sequins and gauzy harem pants under the street coats they kept pulled about them.

"An orchestra started playing in the gloom about four drinks later, but their fingers apparently were so cold the music was rather out of tune.

"Meanwhile, workmen were padding through the place, hammering here, tacking there. Surges of guests moved from somewhere to somewhere.

"Finally, we figured we'd seen enough Oriental delights. We left and went out to get some coffee."

Ding

An old Chicago tradition is the ding. It's a poor relation of the sting. Dinging isn't confined to Chicago, but that's where I'm familiar with it.

You're late, and there's a line at the ticket window. You tap impatiently as the line edges forward. Finally you reach the wicket.

"One ticket to Memphis?" smiles the clerk. "Yes sir. That will be $33.06."

You give her forty dollars. She drops the silver change in your hand and leafs out the singles. "That's thirty three oh six seven eight nine forty. Thank you and have a nice trip." The clerk keeps two dollars.

Dinging was introduced to America by gypsies at the high cashiers' stands at carnivals.

It is also called shortchanging, and it is far more prevalent than most people think. It doesn't make the crime statistics because victims seldom report it to the police. If they did it's almost impossible to prove. If you're dinged and count your change the skilled dinger will have the single or five or ten dollar bill he or she kept, hand it you, and apologize for being careless.

I took a short ding survey in the Loop and went first to a parking garage. After five minutes I saw a young man hand the cashier a twenty-dollar bill. As he walked away I approached him. "Did you count your change?" I asked. He looked in his hand. He had change from ten dollars.

A cashier who had been selling tickets (honestly) for fifteen years said, "Nine out of ten people don't even look at their change. What gets you is, most people are so trusting. They feel anyone who has the responsibility of dealing with money must be honest. It is an unspoken and unconscious trust.

"If they only knew."

A hotel doorman smiled: "Everybody does it—cab drivers, bartenders, waitresses, cashiers. A good dinger can make $50 a day."

I watched one lady come charging back to a Loop cashier waving a handful of change.

"Oh, I'm sorry," the cashier said. "You know, I handle a lot of customers. Are you sure I didn't give you the right change? Well, if you say so. You look honest."

Restaurants have a high turnover of personnel and a real policing problem. Said an owner:

"You have to be careful with a waiter who does his own banking. He'll make out two checks—one for the correct amount, and another with a dollar or two added on. He gives you the inflated check, takes your money, and gives the correct check to the cashier. He pockets the difference.

Credit cards help but aren't foolproof. One waitress in an expensive club was fired when she was found kiting the tip. If a customer wrote five-dollar tip on the bill and she didn't think it was enough, she would write the figure one in front of the five.

Dinging is mostly small potatoes, but it does add up. It's tax-free. One Chicago cashier told a friend he picks up $10,000 to $12,000 a year dinging. He buys a new car each year and has put two children through college on ding scholarships, so to speak.

Sid's Junction

Sid's Junction was the last of Chicago's Skid Row saloons. It was urban renewed out of existence.

The owners, Sid Block and Maury Wasserman, sat disconsolately on stools in their empty 142-foot bar, eyeing a couple of junk dealers pawing over fixtures.

"You know," Wasserman mused. "We were making money right to the last when the city bought us out. We had six, seven thousand men on Skid Row at its peak. It didn't take these guys much to live on. They paid $43.50 a month for a cage in the hotels. They didn't eat much and they didn't change clothes. I wouldn't know some of 'em if they changed clothes.

"It was known across the country if you can't find work in Chicago, forget it, mister, there's no work anywhere. The gandy dancer was a hard worker and a hard drinker.

"Most of them had no family ties and if they did they couldn't care less. The flop houses, the hotel cages were their homes. The bar was their athletic club, their country club, their home away from a long-forgotten home.

"Two police sergeants and four patrolmen came in here one afternoon and said, 'You're closed.' I said, 'What about the customers?' They said, 'They can finish their drinks.' "

Skid Row was a journalistic staple for years because the bums in the gutters were so photogenic. Suburbanites using the North Western commuter line shuddered at the derelicts sitting on the curbs or passed out in doorways.

Those were the transients, the dregs. The regulars were in the flop houses and saloons.

Wasserman: "We never had a robbery here. We were never held up, and we didn't have any trouble with moochers."

Sid's Junction's regulars worked hard when they worked, pounding rail spikes, repairing roadbeds, clearing tracks in the blizzards. The peculiarities of the railroad pay system, plus their modest financial needs, allowed most of the men to work six months, and then lay off six months with what they called "rockin' chair money."

"They're not as drunk as you'd think," Wasserman said. "Most people have the wrong impression. Most of what these guys have in common is they just couldn't shoulder family responsibilities."

Sid and Maury kept a jar for donations for the retarded. Over the years Sid's customers gave thousands for the Forgotten Children's Fund. Contributions to the fund from places which served liquor were in inverse proportion to the exclusivity of the establishment.

Cats

The 5600 block of North Kerbs Avenue in Chicago has relatively new, expensive, and beautifully maintained homes and yards. Officers from the city health and building departments knocked on the door of Miss J., a retired school teacher.

"Do you keep 186 cats in this house?" they asked Miss J.

"Oh, no!" was the answer. "It can't be more than 100. Yes . . . somewhere between 50 and 100."

Miss J. was a pleasant, intelligent lady. The grounds of her home were immaculate. Her living room was spotless. Her problem was that she couldn't say no to a cat. It is not uncommon. Animal control officers have removed as many as 150 cats from a home. Thirty to forty is common.

These homes with multiple cats have one thing in common besides the animals. It is the smell, an overwhelming, pungent ammonia-type fume that can't be contained by the four walls, and is the usual reason for calls to the police by neighbors.

Miss J. made what she called "a recreation room for my cats" in her basement. Glass partitions divided the basement into three rooms. Cats lolled in and on top of open cages. Cats were draped on every step and on top of stepladders. A cat was curled on the fireplace mantle.

There were 52 visible cats—small, large, long-furred, short-haired, tiger cats, Siamese cats, alley cats. How did she get all these cats?

"I don't know," Miss J. answered. "I just got them over the years."

The city officers gave her a week to get rid of all but four or five cats. She tearfully accepted the inevitable.

Animal Control Officers Hal Ruther and L. C. Watson visited an apartment in Edgewater in which lived a Miss M. and 35 cats, with the usual stench. Miss M. was allowed to retain two.

"I love each and every one of these cats," Miss M. wailed. "They're my whole life. I had a hundred cats and moved to three different apartments with them."

She spent about fifty dollars a week to feed her animals. They didn't get cat food. She cooked chicken and hamburger and vegetables with rice.

"Much more than I spend to feed myself," she said. "Look at how skinny I am." Indeed she was. Also her legs and arms were covered with sores that Ruther speculated were from flea bites and scratches.

Miss M. offered to sing several songs she wrote about cats, and said she was trying to sell a cat story to Disney. She called each cat by name—Spotty, Mouse, Shadow. . . .

There was cat fur everywhere, and cats on the floor, on tables, chairs, bookcases. It looked like a Booth cartoon.

Two vans took 33 cats to the animal pound, where it was found most of the animals had distemper, as well as ear mites and fleas.

"This was an easy one," Ruther shrugged. "The woman was cooperative and the house wasn't filled with excrement and dead animals, which is often the case."

As they left the house, some neighborhood children told them there were 25 dogs in a house down the street.

It's not unusual for people to love their dogs or cats more than they love their children. If they are childless a pet may get more affection than would a child.

It's easy to love a pet. They are relatively undemanding, appreciate a good meal and a warm bed, are good listeners, don't talk back, and don't care whether their owners wear Gucci shoes or sneakers, or are white, black, or green, thin or fat, hairy or bald.

However, they bring a lot of dirt into the house. Some make loud noises. They all produce waste that smells and has to be disposed of.

There are more cat collectors than dog collectors. I asked Jay Shaffer of the Anti-Cruelty Society why.

"We look upon cat people not with disdain, but with regret," Shaffer answered. "They usually are nice people, but lonely people. We consider a cat person anyone who has more than four or five.

"We've had cases where women would rent houses just to keep their cats. Their landlords would tell them they couldn't keep them in an apartment, so the women would rent some old house, put the cats in, and then go visit and feed them every evening."

How do they get that way?

"Well, a person starts off with a cat or two, or four or five. A cat in the house attracts other cats. The cat person sees the cat sitting there looking at her, big-eyed and begging, and she can't say no to a cat."

The Bartender's Side

John Gorman, my associate for several years at the Tribune, *tended bar in his spare time before he got married. He tended bar around the world to help finance his travels. In Chicago he liked to observe people. I asked him for the bartender's viewpoint.*

Most of the girls in the singles bars, or meat markets, are good-looking. The best-looking ones take the attitude: "OK, Buster, I'll give you thirty seconds of my time, but you'd better make it good."

If Buster's line isn't good enough, she just says she doesn't want to talk with him any more. The Beautiful People.

Each bar has its hard core of regulars who insist on knowing the names of the doormen, floormen, and bartenders. To show they belong. Many of these regulars are fresh from Nebraska, or from a suburban divorce, and need a home base. The bar is home base.

Anybody who snaps his fingers or bangs the bar with his glass to get my attention gets ignored. They are very irritating.

Also the guy who shouts his order like a drill instructor. Also the girl who whispers her order so low that I have to lean over the bar to hear her. Also the nickel tipper.

Other irritants are the coy girl who wants a free drink. We're told to give the lookers freebies now and then because they decorate the place and attract males who pay cash.

You can spot the suburbanites the minute they walk in the door. Saturday is their night. Usually middle-aged couples, thirty-five to forty-five, come in after theater or dinner. He's usually a little loaded, wants to sing and dance and get into whatever is happening in New Town.

What is happening Saturday night is nothing. Anybody in a singles bar Saturday night failed to score on Friday night, so they drink more and feel terrible.

Rush Street is phonier, more expensive, and more regimented than Old Town or New Town. Nothing's changed since I first worked there nine years ago. Games are ritual. The secretary becomes a flight attendant, nurses become doctors, grad students are management trainees, middle management trainees become executives. Each pretender maintains his facade. Truth is uninteresting, therefore offensive.

Married men come in to see if they still have that old touch—see if the old line still works. Most of the girls can spot them a mile off. They don't score, and they become offensive.

Girls expect the hopeful suitor to buy the drinks. A lot of them drink up all night, then walk out leaving the fish with a big tab and not even a phone number. And he thought each drink was one step closer to her bed.

Being from Chicago is important on Rush Street. In New Town you rate higher if you're from somewhere else. Denver is good. Back from Europe is terrific. A tan in winter means you ski and may be interesting, too.

Coming into the New Town pubs stoned on grass is funky fashionable. On Rush Street it is poor taste. New Town drinkers get drunker than in the other sections. Jeans go on Broadway. Tipping is almost unheard of there.

A plus behind the bar is that women feel free and easy to talk with you. I'm a friend on one side of the bar but a wolf on the other side. Without my apron, I'm the same guy, but ritual is ritual.

Women don't seem to feel propositioned when the bartender starts a conversation with them.

The job has the ideal escape from boredom. If some guy bores me, I can walk away without being offensive. Duty calls.

In Old Town the bars attract an older, freakier, more straightforward crowd. The emphasis is less on how you look than on what you have to say. Friday nights it's the old meat market, but other nights Old Town places are more like Chicago neighborhood bars—talk, cards, darts, a drink after the show.

Thursday night a guy ordered two one-dollar drinks, and handed me five dollars and one dollar. Each time this happens it's tempting to pocket the extra four dollars. I didn't and I told the man of his error. He said, "Oh."

Garbage

The days after Thanksgiving, Christmas, and Easter are good days for people who get their food from garbage cans. Specialty food stores throw out their unsold esoteric holiday foods. The gray people with long overcoats and shopping bags hanging from their arms pad down alleys, lift garbage can covers, and smile. Artichokes tonight.

Here's what two men who shopped regularly in alleys behind food markets and expensive restaurants took home for dinner over a period of weeks:

- Eight one-pound bags of shelled walnuts.
- As many as three dozen eggs at one time. They were thrown out when one egg broke and dripped on the others.
- Half a case of apples in good condition.
- Artichokes and avocados, slightly bruised.
- Bushels of outside stalks of celery.
- Six lemons.
- A bag of slightly frostbitten onions.
- Fifty loaves of day-old bread.
- Endless bottles of jelly and syrup, slightly sticky. They were thrown out when one bottle broke and dripped on the others.

• Flour, dried eggs, boxed items which were discarded when a knife accidentally cut or bruised them.

Karl Meyer was a social activist, in the sense that when he found hungry men, he fed them. He truly believed in fundamental Christian values, and practiced them not through agencies, but under his own roof, and on the streets. He was an expert on alley shopping, as were many of his guests. Their community effort provided much of the food on the Meyer table.

"A lot of people depend on that food," he told us. "When they come to the end of their relief checks, and if they are diligent, they can live on it.

"I suppose there are 100 people I know of who do their food shopping in alleys. At least a hundred.

"The best time is Saturday nights and before and after holidays when they have all the special food and can't keep it. But any time during the day is good. They throw it out all day long.

"I'd appreciate if you wouldn't print names and addresses of these places because they might read it and the managements might say this has got to stop. Or the stores might start putting it in a special place instead of the garbage can, but then this could become respectable and everybody would go there. Only the really destitute will lift a garbage can lid."

The poor could be well fed with the food that is thrown away every day, at no cost other than moving it from discarder to the consumer. Prodigious amounts of fruits and vegetables are thrown away when they get a little old or bruised.

My wife was shopping at our neighborhood supermarket and saw a clerk taking armloads of bread and heading toward an incinerator. She asked the manager why day-old bread was burned. He said it was cheaper than sending it back downtown for recycling or whatever. She asked if she could take it. He said he saw no problem.

For the next four or five years, three mornings a week on the way to work I loaded my car with day-old bread from the store and delivered it to Erie Neighborhood House, where they gave it to the poor. I averaged several hundred loaves each trip. The car trunk, the back seat, and the front seat were piled to the roof with cartons of bread.

And that was just the discarded bread from one store.

My bread service ended when the store's head office found out about it. Pick your reasons. Liability. Everybody will want to get in on it. Bad PR to throw away good bread.

I have no doubt that tens of thousands of loaves of day-old bread are going into incinerators or dumpsters today and every day.

Many needy people could be clothed if another nasty little social custom was redirected. Many churches and charitable institutions have shops where they sell used clothing, furniture, and other items that are donated. Many of the donors ask for detailed receipts so they can take deductions on their income taxes for charitable gifts.

Some of the gifts are sold, at bargain prices. Many are thrown out. This same wife was at a resale shop and saw them tossing bundles of clothing into a dumpster. She asked why. No room in the store, they said. She asked if she could take the stuff. Go ahead, they said.

Since then we've picked up hundreds of big plastic bags containing thousands of suits, dresses, pairs of shoes, sweaters, coats, jackets, shirts, almost all in good condition and clean. From K-Mart and Field's, Ralph Lauren and Laura Ashley. They were distributed at Erie and other places where people lacked decent clothes.

And this was just one resale shop.

The shops had a crisis in December of 1986 when thousands of people emptied their closets and trunks to make "charitable donations" to the resale shops before the December 31 expiration of favorable tax laws. These people got their deductions, and most of their stuff was thrown out.

Don't Say the Word *Beatles*!

When the Beatles surfaced in England, I made some fun of them in the column. A reader had written me: "What is your opinion of the Beatles?" This was the answer:

"I think they're funny. They keep telling interviewers they can't sing. They're laughing at music, they're laughing at the kids, they're laughing at the world, and even at themselves."

This wasn't too offensive to their fans, because the National

Association for the Advancement of Beatle People made me a member, No 122. Among the NAABP members I was not regarded as one of their most ardent enthusiasts for Beatle music, but I hadn't studied it carefully. Every time I heard them perform all I could hear was screaming.

When the Beatles made their first American tour, the Chicago promoter Frank Fried asked me to introduce the Beatles at their concert at the Amphitheatre.

I accepted because it was a unique opportunity to report on a major social, or sociological, event. I anticipated, correctly, that I'd get no more attention than a pillar at the side of the stage.

The Amphitheatre was jammed with about ten thousand teenagers, mostly girls, and three thousand or so parents. The promoters warned that when I was introducing the opening acts or anything else before the Beatles appeared, I was not to say the word *Beatles* because it would set off hysteria. "We don't want them to get any more excited than they are," I was told.

After the second act, the place became relatively quiet, and I got cute. "I have been instructed not to mention a certain seven-letter word or everybody will start screaming," I said.

Everybody started screaming. Well, not the parents. But the young ladies kept up a deafening, piercing scream that rang in my ears for hours.

After the final preliminary act, they knew the Beatles were next, and the screaming intensified. My assignment was to go to the mike at the front of the stage and introduce the Beatles. I did just that, except that I didn't say a word. I mouthed the introduction. Nobody was paying the slightest attention to me anyway.

When the Beatles came on stage I took a position at the rear. I was being a reporter. A girl near me leaned over the rail of her box and started shouting, "John. John! *John. John!!!!* John? *John!!!!!!*" Her face alternately reflected agony and ecstasy. She kept calling for thirty minutes without missing a beat. I'd been chatting with her before the show, and she was a nice, clean, normal-looking girl of fifteen or so.

Nearby a girl in red leaned out of the balcony so that the rail hit her at about her hip bones. She spent the entire concert with her torso at a ninety-degree angle over the rail, screaming *"Ringo!!!!!!"*

Girls sat transfixed with tears streaming down their cheeks. Others leaped skyward, arms outflung, loosing piercing screams.

Girls buried their heads in one another's shoulders. One would look up at the Beatles and both would scream and shake in apparent agony. They fell to the floor and writhed.

It was an incredible scene, an emotional jag almost beyond belief. And it wasn't just a few emotion-charged youngsters, or show-offs, or exhibitionists. All but a tiny minority of the youngsters were caught up in the delirium.

I was warned to take cotton for my ears, and I thought this was a gag. It wasn't. I wanted to get some instructions from the manager of the show. I put my mouth as close as I could to his ear without touching him and shouted as loud as I could. He just shook his head. He couldn't hear me.

The people who traveled with the Beatles show said this crowd was one of the best behaved on the tour. They looked and dressed and acted like any group of nice young teenagers out for a good time.

They were courteous and responsive to the opening acts, and didn't resist the abnormal amount of regulation imposed on them by Frain ushers, policemen, and firemen.

It was only during the thirty minutes of the Beatles' performance that their behavior became, collectively, phenomenal. There had never been anything in the U.S. entertainment world to that time remotely resembling it. The wildest demonstrations for Frank Sinatra of earlier generations paled into tea party dimensions compared with the frenzy of the Beatle pandemonium. It was thirty minutes of raging mass dementia.

Through it all, the four young men were the most composed people in the Amphitheater. They were unruffled by debris and jelly beans showering on and around them. They performed their act, smiling wryly.

In Beatles concerts in other cities scores of youngsters had been carried out on stretchers. Chicago was prepared, though. A hundred Chicago firemen walked the aisles with small bottles of ammonia and wads of cotton.

When a young lady would seem to pass out or become trancelike or fall to the floor, a fireman gave her a hefty sniff of ammonia. This was done hundreds of times. In every case it alleviated the need for stretchers.

Andy Frain armed his men with flashlights, and when a girl stood on her chair or tried to force her way into the aisle, a flash went into her face. It was effective. Relative order was maintained.

The climax was surprising. The four young men ran off the stage through a door in the rear. The performance was unquestionably over, and as if someone had turned a switch, the screams stopped, and a normal crowd situation prevailed. Most of the people got up and started toward their homes.

Several bodies were found under the seats. They were carried to the first-aid room where all revived, albeit with some hysteria.

Half an hour after the show with the huge auditorium nearly empty, a girl was spotted in a corner of the balcony. She was doubled over in her seat, crying uncontrollably. Four policemen tried to comfort her, and then they had to half-carry her to the first aid room.

An old fireman watched as she disappeared through the door. "There goes the last of the Mohicans," he growled. "Didn't want to go home. She wanted to stick around for the late late show."

He didn't understand.

It was difficult for parents, myself included, to comprehend the hold the Beatles had on young people. The *Daily News* ran a headline, "BEATLEMANIA—GOOD OR BAD?," and asked readers to write answers.

The replies didn't settle a thing. The kids adored them; the parents wondered at it. Most of the stories written by adults about the Beatles and their effect on teens were arch or condescending or deadeningly academic.

I infuriated three young ladies in my household by writing that the Beatles wouldn't even be remembered in twenty-five years. It took me about two years to understand and appreciate their music. After the concert I talked with a young lady, Judy Stambler, then seventeen, of Highland Park.

"I think it's definitely music," said Judy in trying to explain the Beatles to me. "It has a good beat, you can dance to it, and you can follow some of their songs.

"But I think their appeal is other than music. In this crappy world, they are something that's just fun. There's one good, happy thing left."

That was in 1964.

Urban Legends

Surely you've heard about the cobra in the clothing section. Or the rapist with the hook hand. Or the kidnapping of grandmother's body.

These are urban legends, or fairy tales.

A girl went into a fast-food place and bought a take-out dinner. When she got home she opened the box, bit into a piece, and found to her horror she had taken a bite of a deep-fried rat.

It never happened, though it was repeated thousands of times. It always happened to a friend or a friend of a friend. Scholars in an academic discipline called *folklore* have interviewed thousands of people trying to pin down this and other urban legends. They have yet to find a legitimate origin of the widely circulated legends.

They'd be funny if they weren't so costly. Usually the rumors name a specific store or fast-food place, and these companies have had to spend millions to counteract the rumors. One of the most vicious and most expensive involved the "man-in-the-moon" trademark on Procter & Gamble products. A rumor went across the country that this symbol somehow involved witchery. It didn't and doesn't.

Business suffers when these rumors involve stores or specific products. A bubble gum company in the East had to take out full-page ads to put down a rumor that there were spider eggs in their gum. The company hired investigators to try to discover the origin of the rumor.

Sometimes denial of a rumor only accelerates its circulation.

The stolen grandmother legend comes in various forms, the most common being about a young couple vacationing in Mexico with one's grandmother.

The grandmother dies in Mexico. Fearing complications getting her body back to the States, the couple puts the body in the trunk of their car. They clear customs and after a few miles stop for coffee. When they come out of the restaurant, the car (with the body) has been stolen.

A professor of folklore at Indiana University said, "Everybody swears up and down they know the couple it happened to. But when you go to the people they name, they refer you to someone else. It's an endless chain. It always is."

The baby-sitter story has countless versions, usually embellished with each telling and retelling. The main one involves a baby-sitter getting threatening phone calls. She asks the operator to trace the calls. The operator tells the baby-sitter to get out of the house in a hurry—the call is being made from an extension phone. The spinners of this fairy tale overlook the fact that it is impossible to make this kind of call.

Students were frightened when a rumor swept campuses that a famous psychic predicted twenty-five girls would be slain on campuses by an ax murderer. The psychic denied the prediction, but that did little to alleviate the fear for months.

Larry Danielson, an English professor at the University of Illinois and a student of folklore, told us he heard the fried rat rumor "three or four years ago, and just the other night at a dinner party, a faculty wife brought it up."

He also heard three or four versions of a story about a man injured in an explosion while smoking near his wife's hair spray. On the way to the hospital he fell out of the stretcher and broke a leg.

Rumors generally are "grotesque stories," Danielson said. "They're usually within the realm of possibility and involve grotesque incidents, often with bodily mutilation."

Many of the grisly rumors seem to appeal to adolescents, he said, "because they're going through such dramatic physical and psychological changes. They have a lot of anxiety about physical malformations and death."

There's the poisonous spider in the clothing from Singapore. The cult leaders hypnotizing children at the supermarket. The teenage girl who reappears every year at the scene of the crash that took her life.

Rumors for every purse and purpose. Legendary bunkum.

City Hall and Other Urban Peculiarities

Mayors from Kennelly, Martin, to Washington, Harold

Mayor Daley presides over the St. Patrick's Day parade, but halfway across the city one of his friends lies dead. She is the mother of a Chicago policeman and everyone has been to the wake to pay their respects—the firemen, the Holy Name, the chaplains of the department.

"Doesn't she look grand!" one of the mourners asks, gazing down at the dead woman. She is laid out in a fine new dress, her worn rosary is twined in her prayerful hands and she seems at peace. On her dress, glinting in the soft light, is pinned a large badge, printed in green with the legend "DALEY IN '75."

Eugene Kennedy, a Maryknoll priest, writer, and self-appointed Daley watcher, told that story.

I enjoyed Daley for his great laugh. Often it was more a giggle than a laugh, but it came from inside and never was forced. It was spontaneous and mirthful and to me revealed the real Daley more than his serious public facade, or the infamous picture at the Democratic Convention when his face was twisted with rage as Senator Abe Ribicoff described the police riots.

Daley had many sides. His power was unquestioned. His personal honesty was universally accepted. His tolerance of knaves and connivers in subordinate jobs was undeniable. He rationalized that you couldn't run a giant city and a powerful political machine with a bunch of do-gooders. Yet he was a major factor in bringing Paul Douglas and Adlai Stevenson into public office.

Kennedy said, "He's the center of a very complex political structure and he is the source of its energy. He's the man in charge, and it's something to see. You can really sense that these huge squadrons of blue-eyed Irish and brown-eyed Italians draw energy from him.

"I felt the energy. Did you ever stand close to an electric power station and feel the hum? I think that's part of how I felt. He doesn't have the graces of a media candidate, but we've been media-candidated to death. That's why Daley can live on South Lowe Avenue. He doesn't need the trappings."

I saw that quality in Daley in public situations, but I never felt it in our occasional one-on-one meetings. I recall one time in particular when we were waiting together for the start of an annual reunion of his high school, DeLaSalle. Daley was quiet, introspective, and gentle. No electricity. I simply liked him.

Running Chicago and the Democratic machine was likened, not too originally, to having a tiger by the tail. Daley was different. He rode the tiger. A little better than hanging onto the tail but equally hazardous. Lose your hold and the tiger will turn and eat you.

Almost every time a mayor makes a decison he (or she) makes enemies. Daley made hundreds of decisons every week. No one agreed with all or almost all of his decisions. But most people accepted that his decisons were based on what was best for the city, and not necessarily best for Richard J. Daley.

A vain or venal man would have abused the immense power Daley enjoyed. Daley liked the power, and he had no idea of giving it up. But he honestly believed that good government was good politics.

Daley's personal life was private, but well known. His tenderness toward his wife was evident. He made a jillion banquets, but seldom ate because he tried to get home every evening during dinner hour.

I asked his son Rich if he had learned some political maxims or philosophies from his father which would help him in politics.

Rich spoke as softly and thoughtfully as his father. "My father

City Hall and Other Urban Peculiarities

Mayor Daley wasn't close to any newspaperman. In fact he wasn't close to anybody outside his own family. When this picture was taken, I was mayor of suburban Glenview and was working with Daley to set up an organization of suburban mayors to cooperate with Chicago on common problems.

said to stay away from pettiness, from defamatory statements, from mud-slinging.

"He said there are no enemies out there, only opponents. Nobody loses in an election. Some win, some don't win. But there aren't losers."

His voice raised. "Your political life, your personal life, your whole life is *ruined* if you start thinking in terms of enemies out there."

Before Mayor Daley

Mayor Daley's place in American political history is secure. But does anyone remember his predecessor, Martin J. Kennelly?

Kennelly was a businessman who was tapped by the Kelly-Nash-Arvey machine to be mayor as a reform candidate. He served eight years until 1955, when the machine dumped him because he was too square and Daley was ready to take over. Kennelly never accepted the inevitable, and spent the last six years of his life in bitter isolation. He was criticized as a naive, plodding journeyman.

Daley extended a friendly hand, but Kennelly wouldn't go near City Hall after he left the office.

Daley got credit for a lot of things that Kennelly did.

Kennelly inaugurated great public works and slum clearance projects. The expressways, the water filtration plants, the city and park district garages, street lighting, sewers, the Chicago Skyway, the assembly of land for O'Hare airport and other projects started or went forward with Kennelly's leadership.

He foresaw the possibility of autos strangling the city and put center strips in the expressways for rapid transit, and he built huge parking garages in the Loop. He took politics out of the schools, revived civil service, and instituted a central purchasing office. Traffic deaths were reduced.

Kennelly knew his accomplishments, and was understandably resentful and miserable at his treatment.

Mike Bilandic

When Daley died Mike Bilandic was the right man in the right place at the right time. He was straight, not very charismatic, was close to Daley, and was the logical compromise choice to be interim mayor when the wolves couldn't decide among themselves who would be the new boss.

The interim mayor did a decent job, mended some fences, and decided he'd like to be more than a fill-in mayor. He ran for the Democratic nomination. His opposition was Jane Byrne, who had run the city's consumer bureau for Daley, and who was considered flaky for thinking she could take on the mighty Democratic machine. She had little visible backing, but she had a lot of chutzpah and a keen instinct for getting in front of television cameras when the red light was on.

Her cause was almost hopeless until the famous snowstorm, which paralyzed Chicago and, seemingly, Bilandic. There was so much snow that no human or political or governmental machine could have cleared the streets satisfactorily. Bilandic's mistake was allowing the operators of the elevated trains to adjust their schedules so that the South Side trains passed all the stations in the black districts without stopping.

This literally created the scene of elevated trains speeding past el platforms at Thirty-Fifth Street and Forty-Seventh Street and other stops while thousands of angry and frustrated blacks shook their fists at the cars. Bilandic was the scapegoat. Byrne rushed TV commercials showing her standing in the snow with the common folks, also called voters.

Mike made one other mistake that I think cost him the votes that would have carried him through the very close election. He had, and has, a lovely wife, Heather. Mike's campaign advisers had a TV commercial made which showed Heather Bilandic as an aristocrat from the highest level of Chicago society, which she was. It was a stiff and stuffy high-fashion commercial which might have played in Lake Forest, but bombed in Chicago.

Eliminate the snowstorm, or the Heather commercial, and Bilandic might still be mayor. Instead he is a judge, and seems more cheerful than any mayor I've known.

Madame Mayor

I've never met Jane Byrne. I didn't write much about her when she was mayor because she had such enormous media coverage I didn't think my contribution would add anything.

She regards television as her best precinct worker because it goes into every living room. So as mayor and as a candidate she was constantly on television. As mayor she had almost daily (and Sunday) press conferences. She showed up at fires and parades and dedications and accidents, shortly after the TV cameras arrived. She gave network interviews and local interviews and went on all the talk shows and face-the-press groups. She watched the ten o'clock news faithfully and sometimes phoned in a rebuttal to criticism while the program was still on the air.

I was sitting at my kitchen table one evening when she called to criticize that day's column, in which I said the tricks and antics of the St. Patrick's Day parade were amusing.

"These tricks weren't funny," Mayor Byrne told me. "Do you know one of the things they were thinking of doing? They were going to drive an Oldsmobile into the water and then pull it up, with a Kennedy sign on it. Chappaquiddick. That isn't funny."

I commented that they didn't do it.

She said Richie Daley had been out to get her since the day she was elected.

"All that booing at the parade," Mrs. Byrne said. "Richie wouldn't put the Eleventh Ward into the parade, but their people were strung out along the line of march, leading the booing."

She said the media are unfair in their criticism of her and she didn't think that day's column was fair.

Fortunately she hadn't read the next day's column, which was worse.

Harold

Washington was elected and reelected because his opposition has always been more than one white person, or a Republican. Most of his energy in his first four-year term was spent fighting off the opposition, which held almost equal power in the City Council.

Whether Washington will be a competent mayor will be determined in his second term. He has almost as much power and control as Daley had. He vowed he'll be in office longer than Daley. He might if he'll stop smoking and cut down on his intake of food.

The media, and especially television, distort the picture of city government. They concentrate on personality conflicts and council wars and disputes over where to put a new stadium. The nuts-and-bolts business of making the city work are virtually invisible to the press.

Every day thousands of city workers make sure that pure water comes out of millions of faucets, that building regulations are observed, that health care is available to all, that the world's busiest airport keeps functioning, that streets are cleared of snow and debris, that garbage is collected and burned or buried, that criminals are apprehended and uncontrolled fires controlled, that traffic keeps moving, and that laws are passed or revised.

These chores will be done with a reasonable degree of competency no matter who is in the fifth-floor office at City Hall.

There is no indication they have suffered with Washington in command.

As the new Boss he has the same basic problem that Daley had and didn't handle too well. That is to keep his troops honest and working, to avoid putting crooks into influential offices where they can shake down contractors and property owners and line their pockets with some sleazy scheme or another.

Chicago was called the city that works when Daley ran it, and it seems to be working pretty well under Washington, considering the obstacles facing any big northern city.

Campaign Idiocy

Stealing hundreds of thousands of votes, as the Democratic machine did in Chicago a generation and two back, was not a laughing matter. But some of the less extreme tactics in Chicago politics were so bizarre they have to be classified as humor—grim, ludicrous, unintentional, intentional.

A pioneer in political shenanigans was the immortal Chicago sewer rodder, Thomas D. Garry, Chicago's Voice from the Sewers, who set off a stampede for Franklin D. Roosevelt in the Chicago Stadium in 1940 by rigging up an extra microphone in the public address system and blaring through the giant hall: "We want Roosevelt!"

I had to admire the tactics of Ed Hanrahan, an outwardly staid and reasonable politician, who took on the Democratic machine candidate for state's attorney, Ray Berg. Swede vs. Irishman. (Daley always matched unalikes—Pole vs. Lithuanian, German vs. Irish, black vs. white, Catholic vs. Protestant, Jew vs. gentile. *Never, never Irish vs. Irish or black vs. black.*)

Hanrahan naturally was excluded from a big dinner rally of twelve hundred precinct captains at the Sherman Hotel. Hanrahan's troops got into the ballroom early and placed fortune cookies at all twelve hundred places. When the Daley loyalists opened their cookies out popped the message: "Hanrahan's the Man."

Chicago's mayor determines the pecking order in the annual St. Patrick's Day parade. Daley put Berg at the head of the parade, and Hanrahan was assigned a place behind some horses. Hanrahan was undaunted. As he walked past the reviewing stand Hanrahan turned toward Daley and doffed his hat.

A pigeon fell out. It was supposed to fly away, but it had been asphyxiated on Hanrahan's head, and it fell dead on the pavement.

Hanrahan had the last laugh. He beat Berg in the election.

When Jane Byrne was mayor the backers of Ted Kennedy and Jimmy Carter jockeyed for front-row space in the parade. Byrne loftily dismissed Carter because "he's English."

John Hoellen, who I think is German, was a political masochist. For years he was the only Republican in the City Council. He took a lot of abuse, but he was tough, and a needler, and probably had a lot more fun than his tormenters. John was an honest alderman and never had to worry about getting caught.

He volunteered for the hopeless assignment of Republican candidate for mayor against Daley. On St. Patrick's Day he showed up at City Hall carrying two large, live, ugly-looking snakes. He never did explain the symbolism, if that's what he intended, but he got a lot of press, which was what he wanted.

Tennessee Williams's brother, Dakin, always seemed to be running for some public office in Illinois. The highlight of his political career was a fund-raiser in 1975. It was held at a McDonald's on the North Side. He asked his supporters to pay $1.50 for a Big Mac and a Coke. A throng of four turned out, contributing a total of $6.00. Williams's net profit was $1.80, which wasn't enough to cover the tip when he left McDonald's for dinner at Maxim's.

There Goes the Judge

It is surprising that so many Chicago judges are serving prison terms for accepting bribes. Surprising not that they sold decisions, but that they've finally been caught. The number of jailed judges may catch, or even surpass, the number of jailed aldermen.

I watched hundreds of Chicago judges in action, and inaction. A small number obviously were on the take, and/or drunk, and/or incompetent machine hacks. Most of the judges, though, were honest and capable and brought a very useful characteristic to the non-civil cases. They had the street smarts. Most of them had worked their way up in the party ranks, from precinct worker on. The common man got a fair shake in the court rooms of the non-corrupt judiciary. In domestic relations court, Solomon supplied more law than Chief Justice Holmes.

One of my early encounters with the Chicago judiciary came in police court on the South Side. I was fresh out of journalism school, working for the City News Bureau. When the judge spotted me taking notes, he asked me to come up to the bench. He pointed to a chair at his side and asked me to sit there.

His clerk resumed the call—disorderly conduct, assaults, domestic quarrels, gamblers, shoplifters—the usual call in Municipal (pronounced *m-yoony-sippel*) Court. I quickly became aware that the honorable judge was bombed out of his skull, and needed a lot of help dispensing justice. After hearing each case and mumbling at the litigants he would lean over to me and whisper, "Whash should I do with this guy?"

I had studied "Press, Courts, and the Law" at Illinois, and had a minor in political science. But they hadn't prepared me for a situation like this. Inasmuch as I tend to be sorry for everybody who comes to court, that morning the judge set a new record of telling defendants, "Get outta here and don't do it again."

I'm not naming this or other judges because their children and nieces and nephews and grandchildren are still around, many practicing law, some on the bench, and it isn't fair to them to sully the family name for the shortcomings of the patriarchs.

One of the chores of the wagon cops at the Des Plaines Street station was to make a nightly sweep of Skid Row, collect the drunks out of the gutter and others who were incapable of finding their way home, and to house them in the Des Plaines lockup overnight.

The first order of business when court opened at nine o'clock was to parade this bleary-eyed mess of humanity up to the court for the dispensation of justice. One Saturday morning a particularly mean judge was presiding. He was vicious enough when he felt good, but I think he was badly hung over this morning and was mad at having to work on Saturday.

The bailiffs opened the lockup door and out stumbled seventeen of the saddest looking men imaginable. They stood in a line in front of the court. The judge glared. He looked at the arrest sheets. He looked up and in what I can best describe as a loud grunt asked the defendants: "How many of you want to stay out of jail raise your hands?" He said it so fast it sounded like "Howmanwanstay-jail razor hands?"

The sodden defendants had no idea what the judge said. One decided to raise his hand. The honorable judge growled to the bailiff, "That one goes home. Thirty days for the rest. Next case."

The bewildered sixteen were led off to jail wondering what they'd done wrong.

The presiding judge in traffic court is an important position, because the only contact most citizens have with the police and the court system involves traffic violations. Unfortunately, traffic court for generations was less than a model of what the judicial system should be.

One judge drew unwanted attention to himself when he turned loose an ex-convict who was arrested by a traffic policeman for drunk driving, speeding, and running a stop sign and two red lights. The judge accepted the word of the burglar over the policeman's.

We decided to spend a couple of days watching this judge dispense justice. Here are some exact quotes from the judge to defendants:

"If I could, I'd waive all these fines for three minutes in a room with you and your wife. When I got done with you, she'd wish for the fines. I'd punch your head in. If you don't think I'd do it, you got the wrong man."

"You are a man of humble beginnings and humble intelligence, I can tell that."

To the wife of a defendant: "Do you have a club at home? Or do you have a large frying pan? If you'll use it on your husband, I'll guarantee a discharge."

"You work for Railway Express? Do you know that with one phone call I could have you fired?"

"What concerns me primarily in these cases is the attitude of the defendant."

"If you have another accident, I'll make you wish you were back in Mississippi."

To an Italian: "I'm an Italian by adoption. My best man was Italian. That's why I can't understand why you would want to be abusive to the police. I don't understand where your family comes from, but they must come from the lowest part of the boot. If you break our agreement, you'll pray to the Almighty for another crucifixion. If I have to take it out in your blood, I'll take it. There'll be another crucifixion. I'll crucify you. Are you giving me your oath as an Italian that you'll sell your car?"

"You know what I'd like to do with you? I'd like to get you in a room with a flight of twenty stairs and then I'd knock you down them. Then they'd say I'm cannibalistic."

"I'm not a preacher and never have been noted as being one."

"I'm not interested in the details. Let's get down to the attitude."

These quotes appeared in my column which was on the streets at 9:20 A.M. By one o'clock this judge had been transferred out of traffic court and into an innocuous civil court.

Don't Believe the Crowd Estimates

A close relative of mine was working for the Interstate Commerce Commission in Washington, and one of his assignments on occasion was to go to the White House lawn and cheer the Reagans when they took off in a helicopter. Which—for me—answered a nagging question: "Who are those people?"

At a papal mass in Grant Park in Chicago in 1979, estimates of the size of the crowd ranged up to 350,000.

At every big outdoor event the crowd numbers are wildly exaggerated, usually in multiples of 50,000 or 100,000. A political rally or protest march believes it is downgraded without outlandish superlatives.

Usually it's safe to divide the crowd figure estimate by five or ten. The estimates of the crowd at the papal mass followed the usual hyperbole. The *Tribune* asked some crowd experts to evaluate the numbers. They ranged from 65,000 to 350,000. The commander of the First District police said, "Whoever made those estimates is absolutely crazy. There were 1,750,000 people at the mass." The mayor's press secretary estimated 800,000.

Some analysts count heads, some figure the number of bodies that fit in a given space. The *New York Times* put a helicopter over a Washington rally, took a photo, and literally counted heads. They found some 37,000 bodies in a crowd that had been estimated at from 100,000 to 250,000.

Mayor Daley was a master at assembling and manipulating crowds at political rallies. Well, he should have been able to control them—most were city workers ordered to attend. Specified police captains were assigned to keep the peace and estimate the crowds at

Loop events, and they dutifully picked a number out of the air and multiplied by ten. "How big's the crowd today, captain?" "I'd say 300,000."

Rallies were and are staged happenings with two purposes. One is to charge the batteries of the workers, to generate enthusiasm and excitement, to make them want to go out and work work work for the candidate. This is a valid goal and usually is effective.

The other and now major purpose is to create a happening for television. For this part of the rally the workers are not passive participants, but are essential elements of the cast.

The formula makes it necessary for the candidate to say something to be cheered. The things he says are distributed beforehand to reporters and commentators, a few excerpts are printed, and the talking head appears on the evening news. Reagan, of course, has refined this to perfection, if perfection is defined as getting yourself elected without saying much.

Ted Kennedy came to Chicago to speak at a rally for George McGovern, running against Nixon in 1972. A platform was set up at State and Madison streets, traffic was rerouted, and the crowd filled the streets and sidewalks for nearly a block in three directions.

The *New York News* story estimated the crowd at 150,000. The First District police commander said there were 80,000 to 100,000 people at the rally. The *New York Times* put the crowd at 40,000. The *Chicago Tribune* quoted estimates from 20,000 up.

I was an editor at the *Tribune*'s afternoon paper, the *American*. I asked our photographers to go to the roofs of surrounding buildings and get pictures of the entire crowd.

We enlarged the pictures, and we counted the people, putting a little *X* on each head.

There were 2,242 people facing the speaker's platform. In addition, shoppers and workers on their noon break came and went, squeezing through the crowd. A generous estimate was that their numbers equaled those attending the rally. So at the outside, 4,484 people were on the scene.

A couple of blocks from State and Madison was the big plaza of the Civic Center that has a Picasso and a fountain and room for a couple of hundred thousand people without tying up traffic. But Daley put his crowd at State and Madison, where 4,000 people look like 40,000. At the Civic Center 40,000 people look like 4,000.

Putting big crowds into the streets instead of on a plaza naturally tied up the Loop. Buses had to be rerouted, cabbies were caught in the jam and cussed out those obscene politicians. "The Loop's all tied up with the Kennedy rally," he'd growl to his fare. "Wow, they must have a mob there!"

The *Los Angeles Times* correspondent says to the *New York Times* correspondent, "Looks like Daley's done it again. What's the crowd estimate?"

"A hundred thousand."

The basic standard was a hundred thousand or multiples for Democrats (and still is), fifty thousand for Republicans, half-a-million for Eisenhower and MacArthur, a million for the Pope, and two million for the astronauts.

When I was on rewrite some of us used to fill our unassigned time trying to figure out how many bodies it would take to line one block of State Street, shoulder to shoulder. Then we would estimate the people watching a parade were standing six deep on both sides of the street. Then we would count the number of blocks of the parade.

I'm sorry I didn't keep the exact estimate, but I think we figured that we were off by 1,900,000 in estimating the crowd that welcomed the first astronauts. It was physically impossible to get so many bodies into the space available to watch them be driven by.

To Your Good Health

Live to Be 102

Ninety-nine percent of us are born healthy. We suffer premature death and disability because of personal misbehavior and environmental conditions.

Dr. John H. Knowles, a prominent physician who headed the Rockefeller Foundation, said, "It is easier to sell deodorants, pantyhose, and automobiles than it is health."

Preventive medicine is just beginning to gain recognition in America. Even so, probably more money will be spent next year advertising Alka Seltzer than will be spent nationwide on preventive medicine.

When I was pushing a preventive medicine program at a hospital where I volunteer, some doctor friends were offended. "We practice preventive medicine," one told me heatedly.

In a sense. He gives physical exams, and recommends that a patient quit smoking, eat less, and get more exercise. But he, like most physicians, never studied nutrition, and has little patience with nutritionists.

Dr. Knowles was blunt. But anyone who bosses a foundation that gives away millions of dollars does attract attention.

"Most individuals do not worry about their health until they lose it," he said. "Asceticism is reserved for the hair-shirted clerics and constipated cranks, and every time one of them dies at the age of fifty, the hedonist smiles, inhales deeply, and takes another drink."

Science eliminated most of the diseases which decimated populations in past years. Now the great killers are diseases that thrive on individual unhealthy living habits.

The individual has control over health habits.

- Three meals a day at regular times, no snacking.
- Breakfast every day.
- Moderate exercise two or three times a week.
- Adequate sleep (seven or eight hours a night).
- No smoking.
- Moderate weight.
- No alcohol, or only in moderation.

A 45-year-old man who practices three or fewer of these habits has a remaining life expectancy of 21.6 years. The man who follows six or seven of these habits has a life expectancy of 33.1 years. And he's going to feel a lot better in those years.

Walking

"Of all exercises, walking is best." —*Thomas Jefferson*

Jefferson and his friends *had* to walk a lot. Today we go to great lengths to avoid walking. Just watch men and women maneuver their vehicles in shopping center lots, and how long and far they'll drive to park twenty feet closer to the store.

Wives drive husbands five blocks to the commuter station. Suburbanites buy second cars to avoid walking, kids are carted ten blocks to school in yellow buses. Their parents and grandparents gained good health by walking.

More than half the muscles in the body go to work when you're walking. Back muscles, legs and feet and hip muscles are used, abdominal muscles support weight, diaphragm and rib muscles are expanded because of deeper breathing, neck muscles hold the head erect.

Dr. Paul Dudley White, the famed heart specialist, recommended a minimum of one hour a day, seven days a week. "Besides being good exercise, walking is good psychologically," said Dr. White. "The best tranquilizer is physical and muscular fatigue. You don't need to take hypnotics or tranquilizers. You can combat stress by taking a walk."

Walking is a good reducer. At a quick pace—four to five miles an hour, you burn five to six calories a minute. If you maintain a normal diet and begin walking an hour a day, you will burn off three pounds a month, thirty-six pounds in a year.

One happy aspect of walking is you can lead a sloppy, fat-filled sedentary life and then recapture vigorous health by regular walking.

Dr. White never cared much for sports and often scoffed at exercisers. But in his late fifties he began to tire easily. "I decided to take some exercise daily, and was astonished how quickly it offset my fatigue," he said. "This kindled my curiosity and I began studying data on the physiological effects of exercise. Soon I awakened to the fact that exercise plays a far greater role in preventing illness and deterioration than most physicians realize."

One reason women outlive men is they walk so much tending their houses, husbands, children, and now in the eighties, their jobs. At home their big problem is that walking takes them to the refrigerator and cookie jar.

You Are What You Eat

Physicians are at their best when confronted with serious, diagnosable problems. They prefer cases that challenge all their skills and experience and instincts.

The 70 or 80 percent of patients with assorted aches and pains and stomach distress and sore backs and joints and complaints and wheezing and sneezing and headaches provide essential income, but are unchallenging and bothersome. Most will cure themselves anyway.

The change in the medical industry got momentum in the early eighties when business and industry finally realized the enormous cost of health care, and used their financial leverage to demand reform. The federal government joined with Medicare changes, and the medical industry was, or is being, revolutionized.

Excess treatment, excess testing, and excess hospitalization are coming under control. The most effective way to bring this about is for the government or insurer to pay a set sum for specific health care, so that the provider—physician or hospital—makes more money by keeping its patients healthy and out of the hospital. The main instrument of this system is the Health Maintenance Organization, or HMO.

Preventive medicine is coming into its own. One component is not doing bad things. Another is doing good things. A third is recognition of the healing powers of the body without any outside intervention. Voltaire said the successful doctor is the one who keeps his patients sufficiently amused while Nature effects a cure.

Nutrition is both a positive and a negative. Stop eating junk and start eating the good stuff. Everybody knows the difference. (If it tastes good, it's bad for you. If it tastes bad, it's good for you. A feeble joke, but it is the nutritional guide for a lot of people.)

Billions are spent to persuade Americans to consume more sugar, smoke more tobacco, drink more alcohol, and eat and drink more junk food. Billions more are spent on pills and syrups and assorted nostrums to counteract the effects of the junk.

But common sense has some power, and an increasing number of people are giving up smoking. The cigarette industry tries desperately to recruit new smokers to replace the 350,000 a year who die from smoking-related ailments, and the million a year who quit.

Hospitals and schools are beginning to meet their responsibilities in health education and wellness programs. Even some medical schools have started nutritional classes for the future doctors. Health clubs have joined singles bars as places to meet new friends.

Competition

I played every sport except water polo as a kid. In my adult years until I was forty-five, I played competitive softball, touch football, basketball, golf, and volleyball. At forty-five I dropped those sports and began serious tennis.

I prefer competition with my exercise. Competition stimulates the mind and spirit. It builds character, and teaches you how to lose. This is important. If you learn how to cope with losing in a game, you can better handle it in life, where there's lots of losing.

I'd rather lose a close, well-played contest than win a one-sided rout. Sports have helped me deal with adversity. They have taught me not to give up when things look bad.

The muscles and tissues and blood vessels and heart and brain are made to be used, and they thrive on use.

Without sufficient use, they shrivel and get clogged and the fat piles up and the mind dulls and all the systems in the body become susceptible to germs.

The beauty of exercise is that it is cheap and available. It is one of the best forms of preventive medicine.

Sugar Blues

I was born with a sweet tooth that got out of control at times. I ballooned to 190 in high school. College and a good wife trimmed 10 pounds of that. I came back from World War II at 165. A postwar eating jag added 15 pounds in a month. More home cooking and eating all night in the newsroom on the midnight shift produced a disgusting 205 pounds. Some discipline brought it back to 190.

I never did use any diet as such. To reduce I just ate less, usually less candy, cakes, cookies, pies, and ice cream. In the seventies a new element was introduced—fear. It was produced by increasing evidence that sugar is a major factor in heart disease. It was incentive enough to cause me to sharply reduce my sugar intake. As a result I settled down to a consistent 170 pounds, give or take a few, and that has remained my weight.

I mention my ups and downs to establish my credentials as a certified weight problem.

The fear of too much sugar was provided by John Yudkin, M.D., Ph.D., a prominent British nutritionist, in his book, *Sweet and Dangerous.*

Dr. Yudkin's documentation boiled down to the striking correlation of sugar intake and coronary heart disease.

In a study of fifteen countries, the coronary death rate was 60 per 100,000 people for those who ate 20 pounds of sugar a year, and rose to 300 for people who consumed 120 pounds a year.

More than two pounds a week seems like a lot of sugar for one person. But that's roughly the amount consumed by the average Irishman, Dutchman, Australian, or Englishman. The average American each year consumes between 102 pounds—the sugar industry's figure—and 120 pounds—Yudkin's estimate. Some eat less, some much more . . . as much as three pounds a week.

Sugar comes straight, spooned over cereal and into coffee and on grapefruit, and processed, in candy, cakes, pies, pastries, puddings, colas, fruit drinks, ice cream.

Yudkin studied sixty-five male patients with myocardial infarction or peripheral arterial disease, and fifty-eight other men without any heart disease. He found the men with heart disease ate an average of 140 pounds of sugar a year. The sugar intake of the other men was 80 pounds a year.

African tribes, such as the Masai and Sumburu, eat little sugar and have virtually no heart disease. Yemenite Jews had little heart trouble until they moved to Israel and sugar was introduced in their diets.

The evidence is lengthy and persuasive. Coronary heart disease was rarely known—or diagnosed as such—a hundred years ago. Now it is one of the principal causes of death.

The sugar industry, understandably, isn't very keen for Yudkin, or for Roger Williams's *Nutrition Against Disease,* which also blames sugar for many ills. In 1987 a new study refuted much of Yudkin's and Williams's claims, making it a little more comfortable for people who can't control their yen for sweets.

It may be wishful thinking to put down those coronary disease statistics. If you are afflicted with the sugar problem you might try my remedy, fear. Both of these books are available in libraries.

Listen to the Doctor

"It's the public, not the doctors, who increase health costs," a doctor friend asserted to me.

Leonard Berlin, M.D., is a noted radiologist, and a member of the faculty of the University of Illinois School of Medicine. We both have served many years on the board, and terms as chairman, of a suburban hospital.

"It's the public that demands the latest and finest diagnostic and therapeutic measures," Dr. Berlin said.

"People increase costs by running to their doctors for every real and imagined ache, pain, and finger splinter. It's the public that demands that surgeons replace their painful hips and knees, and resculpture their noses, chins, faces, and breasts. It is the public that demands total body x-rays after auto accidents so they can file more effective personal injury lawsuits.

"It's the public that continues to indulge in cigarette smoking in spite of the millions of dollars spent attempting to inform everyone of the connection between smoking and lung cancer. It's the public that continues to consume huge quantities of alcohol despite the fact that the dangers of alcoholism are well publicized.

"It's the public that seems to require pills of all kinds to sleep, to stay awake, to get tranquilized, to get stimulated, to be able to cope with normal everyday stresses, to derive the usual pleasures of life.

"Doctors are criticized for not concentrating on preventive measures. But doctors do what they are trained to do and believe in: they treat. Since the beginning of medical history, physicians have always been considered as healers and comforters, not as preventers.

"If the success of medical care is measured by increasing the life span, then the greatest medical advances in the last hundred years have probably been the development of sanitation measures, the invention of immunizations, and the discovery of antibiotics. None of these came from practicing doctors.

"You accept the premise that preventive measures can significantly diminish illness. I question it.

"We are finding more and more that diseases are genetically related, which means that perhaps they are less within our control than we have previously thought.

"Jogging has been espoused as a means to prevent heart disease. Jogging makes people feel good, but I don't think anyone has shown that it increases longevity.

"Perhaps the preventive medicine we need to practice is the kind of our parents and grandparents. They didn't know about the effects of saturated and unsaturated fats, carbohydrates and proteins, but they did know that a balanced diet was good and that any food in excess was bad.

"Our government has given us plenty of very expensive medical tools. Government funds have been provided to build, expand, and supply our hospitals and the most expensive equipment in the world.

"Insurance companies have assured their utilization by limiting reimbursement for in-hospital services only. Politicians have sold the public on the notion that health care is a right, which means that most citizens now demand the ultimate in health care, regardless of cost.

"And if the doctors and hospitals don't provide it, they get sued.

"In the 'old days,' medical care was rationed because individuals had limited financial resources to pay for it. Today government and insurance pay for everything.

"Unlimited funds, coupled with the people's insatiable appetite for the finest medical care possible, have brought us to this age of incredible health expenditures.

"Eventually people will have to be convinced to limit their use of medical facilities. Only then will the cost go down. Perhaps if everyone had to pay a greater share of his hospital and doctors' bills, there would be less utilization.

"Reforms are needed, all right. I don't really know what form these reforms should take, or how they should be implemented. But I do know it would be pointless to direct them to the doctors.

"They should start—and end—with Mr. and Mrs. John Q. Public."

Smoke

I doubt if there's a smoker over eighteen who isn't sick to death of the barrage of statistics and horror stories about smoking, so I'll not belabor it further. In fact, I'll try to be of service.

This is an unorthodox and inexpensive approach to making smoking undesirable. No need for will power, no fright, no mass hypnosis, no lecturing.

You'll need a horse.

Make friends with a mounted cop, or visit a riding stable.

Extract a hair from a horse's tail.

Cut the hair into cigarette-length parts. Insert the hair into each cigarette. Light the cigarette. Puff. I am assured by people who have tried this that you will instantly lose your desire to smoke. The lady named Gert who told me about this didn't say if it was necessary to repeat the procedure whenever the urge to light up returned, or whether there is danger of running out of horses.

The anti-smoking people need another Lucy Page Gaston, the Chicago lady who was the organizer and fireball of the Anti-Cigarette League of America early in this century.

A Chicago man who used to see Lucy in action in and around her office in the old U.S. Express building at 58 West Washington related:

"She was the kind of a lady who, if you had a cigarette in your mouth when she got on an elevator, would pull it out of your mouth and stamp on it. I saw her do it once to a young man. He was embarrassed. She was an old lady and nobody would hit her."

This Carry Nation of the smokes stormed across the nation with her crusade, and was responsible for the Illinois legislature passing a law forbidding the sale of cigarettes in the state, which they neglected to enforce.

Lucy visited high schools to scare kids out of smoking.

She thought cigarette paper was as evil as the tobacco.

"If I put a saucer of milk with a cigarette paper in it on the floor," she would solemnly inform the students, "and a kitten came and drank the milk, the kitten would drop dead before it could reach that door."

She never demonstrated her theory, but she stimulated an intense curiosity among a number of her teenage cat owners. An untold number of Chicago cats were given unscheduled saucers of milk, and there is no record that they did anything but lap up the milk around the paper, lick their noses, and stroll steadily out the door.

Kenesaw Mountain Landis was a noted federal judge who became the first commissioner of baseball in 1920 after the Chicago White Sox scandal. One day Lucy Page Gaston charged into Judge Landis's chambers as he puffed on a cigarette. She unloosed a verbal barrage.

Judge Landis took a contemplative puff, looked Miss Gaston in the eye, and with the manner he used in charging a jury, asked:

"Have you ever smoked a cigarette, Miss Gaston?

"No? Well, then, you've never sat out in an open boat, on a pitch-black night, when it was so dark you could see nothing but the comforting glow of your cigarette before you.

"You've never tramped through the woods until you got so tired you could tramp no farther, and then leaned back against a mossy log and inhaled the sweet fragrance of a good cigarette.

"You've never been in a situation where a cigarette gave you more comfort than you could get from ten times its weight in gold. You've never known what a real friend a little paper and tobacco cylinder like this can be.

"Miss Gaston, don't you think a man would be a pretty cheap dog to desert a friend like that?"

Miss Gaston died at sixty-four of cancer of the throat.

Kenesaw Mountain Landis died at seventy-eight of a heart ailment.

The Forgotten Children

Forgotten Children... and Adults

The neighbors thought the old man lived alone. But when he died, they went through the house and heard the noise in the attic. They went up and found a human being.

Hairy, filthy, crawling on his hands and knees, eyes like gray marbles. They carried him out of the house, placed him upright in the backseat of a car, and drove him to the Alton State Hospital.

At Holly Center, a building housing mentally retarded adults, they cleaned him up and started the long, arduous process of reclaiming this human soul.

I asked Peggy Barr, the Holly administrator, if they measured his IQ.

"No," she answered. "There was nothing to measure. He was zero. No response. He was still crawling. To get him off the floor we tied him to a chair. He couldn't feed himself. Apparently he had been eating off the floor from a pan, like a dog. We had to start toilet training him.

"He was fifty-one years old, we found. We don't know how long he'd been in that attic. Maybe all his life. He'd never had any medical or dental attention. The doctors marveled that he survived at all.

"When we got him there was just no response. He couldn't distinguish between a table and a person. They were just objects that he could dimly see."

The therapists at Holly had one thing in their favor. There was no place to go but up with this man. They named him John, and it quickly became John-John.

Dr. Joseph Gruber, a bearded bear of a man, was the superintendent of this unusual institution.

John did not become a patient, nor a resident. He became a "client." Gruber wouldn't even tell me John's name until he phoned John's new residence and asked his permission.

"He has a right to privacy and we're going to protect it," Gruber boomed. "We have an advocacy system here. When a client arrives he's immediately assigned a primary therapist . . . a person who'll explain his rights, always listen, get anything he needs, and make sure he never, never gets lost in a back ward. We don't have any back wards here.

"We have clients because our mission is to perform a service for everyone who comes here. That and to get them out and into society as fast as we reasonably can."

The first tasks with John after cleaning him up and trying to get him to overcome his fear of water were to get him toilet trained, eating with a spoon, and walking. Helen Lakes and Wilma McAninch told how they taught him to walk.

"Each of us would take one arm and we'd walk into the dining room. He'd get better a little bit each day. Then we'd walk him up and down the corridor for fifteen minutes twice a day.

"At first he was frightened of everything. He was like a big baby. Gradually there was progress in everything. He stopped putting his hands in the food and started using a spoon.

"It was hard to get a response from him. Apparently his toys in the attic had been a coat hanger and a spoon. We'd hit them together, to see if he'd respond, and he did. Not immediately. But he'd hear the sound, and in a moment look around.

"He learned to recognize his name. Then he was walking by himself. Our greatest day came when he got up and very slowly, very tentatively, walked over to the window, pulled back the curtain, and looked out. We felt like cheering."

On the wall at Holly Center was a poster: "If a man does not keep pace with his companions, perhaps it is because he hears a different drummer. Let him step to the music he hears, however measured or far away."

John spent two years at Holly, then moved to the state institution at Anna, where, as noted, he gave permission to have his story told.

A Version of Hell

Nothing in my work meant more to me than my involvement with the mentally retarded, and their families, and the men and women devoting their lives to helping them. I helped raise money and gifts for the retarded in state institutions, lobbied for legislation to help them, and have done volunteer work since leaving the *Tribune*.

In 1960 the state institutions at Dixon and Lincoln had five thousand mentally retarded in each. I was familiar with the horrors of both institutions, but one day when I was touring Dixon I balked when my guide approached cottage B-13. "Go ahead without me," I said. "I've had it. I can't take B-13."

The building was home for 160 retarded female residents. I won't try to describe it. But I can report how the institution itself described B-13.

"It was bedlam, a snakepit. There was no other honest way to describe it.

"Behind its locked doors, the stench was heavy. Feces at times littered the terrazzo floor. Many of the patients wandered naked about the dayroom.

"Others sat in corners, rocking endlessly or burying their heads between their knees. They struck, bit, scratched, and shoved one another. They yelled and wailed."

Nobody hated the conditions more than did Margaret Kammes, the chief nurse, and her assistant, Pauline Rapp. Theirs was largely a holding action.

They were helped by two or three attendants—called psychiatric aides—on each shift. Also helping were twenty-four residents who were mildly retarded. It was a form of slave labor. Without these twenty-four it would have been physically impossible to keep the cottage functioning.

The residents were fed, bathed when time allowed, watched for serious illness or injury, and generally kept alive. Taking care of these basic needs eliminated any attention to grooming, individual kindnesses, or therapy. It was a dismal, hopeless place.

That was a typical scene in Dixon and Lincoln, though there probably were none worse than B-13, and some were better.

In 1960 a new administration took over in Springfield, and Governor Kerner initiated a sweeping reform of Illinois's care for the mentally retarded. A large bond issue was passed. Fifteen new institutions were built, and most were models of good institutional care. However, a move to deinstitutionalize the mentally retarded and get them into normal living situations gained strength in the eighties, and the trend today is toward keeping only the most severely retarded in institutions.

A year after I balked at going into B-13, I returned. The working patients had been eliminated. Each shift had a supervising nurse and fourteen aides. There also were a practical nurse, two janitors, and a clothing clerk.

The smell was gone. A new ventilation system helped. Individual attention had resulted in effective toilet training.

A twenty-two-year-old girl said to me, "I go show. See cowboys. I color. Comb hair. Brush teeth." A year earlier she seldom spoke a word.

Residents had their teeth brushed and hair combed, and were given baths when needed. Injuries from scuffling and falls were cut in half. Destruction of furniture and clothing was reduced. The residents left the building for occupational therapy, Saturday movies, Monday afternoon dances.

Lora

Chaplain Gerald Oosterveen of Dixon Developmental Center told about Lora, twenty years old.

"We buried another of our residents," Reverend Oosterveen related. "By 'we' I mean the funeral director and his assistant, seven members of our grounds crew who had dug the grave and were waiting for me to finish the ceremony so they could close it again, six nursing aides from the cottage where Lora lived, a social worker, and me, the chaplain.

"Lora lived the last five years of her life at Dixon. Here she died, worn out early by a birth defect which had left her tragically misshapen and mentally retarded.

"She could smile and frequently did, but that was all she was able to do. The words of Job came to mind: 'Like a slave I have been allotted months of emptiness, and nights of misery have been apportioned to me.'

"But a slave, at least, was considered someone's valuable possession.

"No one claimed Lora."

Chaplain Oosterveen knew that somewhere were a mother and a father. Lora had spent her first fifteen years at home, cared for by her family.

"It must have been a titanic task that filled their days and interrupted their nights," said the chaplain. "I marveled that they had shouldered that burden so long. Somewhere, I knew, were brothers and sisters who once did their part to make Lora's life less painful.

"Somewhere there was perhaps even a church which had counted her as a member. Somewhere . . . they were all somewhere. But no one was here to spend a few minutes with us beside this open grave."

For ten days after Lora's death the Dixon staff exhausted every possible means of contacting the family. Finally and reluctantly the decision was made to go ahead with the burial.

"Perhaps the family didn't want to know," Chaplain Oosterveen reflected. "You see, since Lora left her home five years ago there was no direct contact with the family. They never sent a card or responded to letters.

"Birthdays came, but never a present. Christmases, and not one sign of love from home. All during those five frustrating and futile years our social workers kept trying to trace the family. It was as if, to the family, Lora was dead five years before she died.

"Is it possible that the constant care for a child or sister can draw all love from a person's heart? Is it possible that after running for so many years, the well of inner strength can finally be dry?

"Parents of the retarded are sometimes told that God must love them very much to entrust to them a child who will require much special care. Only exceptional parents, so the saying goes, receive exceptional children.

"That sounds pious, compassionate, and logical, but usually only to those whose own children are healthy and of normal intelligence. In reality, there are no exceptional parents who, unlike 'normal' parents, have a great reservoir of wisdom, courage, and unfilled time waiting to be utilized.

"No one is ever prepared for the entrance of a retarded person in their family, nor does anyone really expect it will happen to them. When the tragedy comes, it can be devastating."

Rarely have I seen a more compassionate or understanding description of the retarded. I understood when I learned that Chaplain Oosterveen was the father of a retarded child.

The Pottery Instructor

There are inspiring stories to balance the story of Lora. One of my favorites at Dixon was Joey Urbani who arrived there in infancy, a twisted, misshapen vegetable-like being. Heroic patience and dedication by the staff brought Joey to boyhood as a bright, eager child. With no use of either arm, he used his feet the way others use their hands. The last time I saw him he was in his twenties and giving pottery lessons to college students. He used his feet to shape the clay.

The Chin-Up Club

The finest social organization I ever saw was the Chin-Up Club, a do-good organization started by some girls in Dixon. Aggie Binkowski was the first president, and other founders included Edna May Brown, Mary Maris, Mary Ujka, and Catherine Longa.

The purpose of the club was "to help people less fortunate than ourselves." Their big problem was finding people less fortunate than themselves. Aggie was paralyzed from the throat down. Edna May was blind, the two Marys had cerebral palsy, and Catherine had scissor paralysis.

They were also classified by the state of Illinois as mentally retarded, and lived in Cottage B-11 at Dixon. Aggie was no more retarded than I was. Mary later wrote a book. Aggie was dumped into Dixon in 1937, when she was ten, after her mother died. She remembered the judge in Chicago saying, "Aggie, I wish you a lot of luck. From now on it's up to you how you'll survive in an institution."

The Chin-Up Club wasn't some device dreamed up by a therapist at Dixon: "Okay, girls, let's have a club, and we'll call it Chin-Up."

For one thing, no therapist ever got near that jam-packed hellhole that was B-11.

No, the girls sat around in their wheelchairs and lay propped in their beds and decided they had to make something of their lives, such as they were. Chin-Up had sixty-five members. Fifteen were able to move around.

That left fifty worse off than the 15. They gave the less fortunate love and friendship, a rare commodity then at Dixon. They wheeled to the commissary to buy treats. Those who could write, wrote. They begged visiting parents for pictures or trinkets to brighten the walls of one of the dreariest rooms in the state of Illinois.

President Binkowski stated: "We strive to be honest and obedient, to dress and eat properly, and to keep ourselves clean and neat." This was a major challenge at Dixon. B-11 was a little better than B-13, but not much.

The surviving Chin-Up members were scattered around the state as Dixon was reduced and finally converted into a prison. I get a Christmas card from Mary Ujka every year.

I visited Aggie in a nursing home in Mount Carmel, Illinois, ten years after our first meeting. She was painting by holding a brush in her mouth. She recalled the bad days at Dixon.

"Oh, it was rough," Aggie said. "But I made up my mind in spite of my affliction I was going to get ahead. Dixon was like home, but I had to prove I was human like everybody else.

"It's better here. I paint three times a week for ninety minutes each time. Is it hard? Not really. I enjoy it. I have to have someone take the brush from my mouth and dip it in the paint, and give me back the brush.

"It can take me two months to do a picture, but if there's not too much in it, I can do one in two or three weeks. I exhibited at the Mount Carmel Art Show last year. I've sold seventy-five water colors. I get $25, $35, maybe $50 if I'm lucky.

"My dream is to be self-sufficient. I don't want to stay in a nursing home all my life. Others can make it outside. . . . I have a very good friend . . . he and I are very close. He was a patient here once. Now he's on his own. We're very good friends. Maybe some day. . . ."

Aggie never made it out. To her dying day I never heard a word of complaint or self-pity from her.

Danny

There was Lora, and there was Danny. Chaplain Oosterveen wrote about Danny's mother. The editor of the *Tribune* thought enough of it to run it across the top of the front page on Mother's Day.

> She has been coming to this place
> for thirty years
> on the bus
> every first and third Tuesday
> to visit her child.
>
> That's seven hundred twenty visits,
> one hundred fifty thousand miles,
> eight thousand hours, at least.
> What an enormous investment
> of time and money.
>
> But mothers don't keep track
> of hours or miles or dollars.
> What can compare with
> a mother's love?
>
> Danny can't talk.
> In thirty years
> he has never called her
> "mother." Never will.
> He knows her, a little,
> and responds to her love.
>
> So she's been coming to this place
> for thirty years,
> on the bus
> every first and third Tuesday,
> with two weeks of loved stored up
> for a child who never calls her
> "mother."
>
> And she worries over
> who will visit him
> when she is dead.
>
> What can compare with
> a mother's pain?
>
> Perhaps she would hurt less
> if she loved less.
>
> But she's his mother.
> God bless mothers like her
> not just on Mother's Day.

Shorts

CHICKEN PLAYS PIANO

One of the highlights in my travels came at the state fair at Salem, Oregon. On the midway there was a glass box on a pedestal. Inside was one medium-sized chicken, a toy piano, a tube from the ceiling, and an electric light bulb.

"Hear the Chicken Play the Piano. 10 cents," read a sign.

Never having heard a chicken play a piano, I was entranced. A couple of farm lads sat on a nearby fence eyeing the city visitors with amusement.

I reached in my pocket for a dime. The chicken hopped in anticipation. I didn't know chickens enjoyed music that much.

I put in the dime. The bulb lit. The chicken went to the toy piano and pecked at the keys for some twenty seconds. The light went out, and out of the tube dropped one lousy grain of feed, which the chicken gobbled up.

When Liberace was getting started he played the Palmer House, but he took second billing to his piano, advertised as worth $25,000. All in all, I enjoyed the chicken more.

HAVE YOU PLAYED JOLIET?

In the glorious days of stage shows at the big movie houses, they used to try out the acts in Joliet before sending them to Chicago.

Joliet audiences were tough. When the Chicago Theatre in the Loop was being renovated, they found a sign backstage: "If You Think You're Good Go To Joliet."

BONE GAP? MUDDY? PERKS?

Quiz: What do the following have in common:

Enterprise, Energy, Unity, Blood, Black, Block, Birds, Harvard, Yale, Princeton, Maud, Edgar, Archie, Calvin, Horace, Mortimer, Muddy, Bone Gap, Perks, Inclose, Rising Sun, and Golden Gate?

They're towns in Illinois that I went through or near on one trip downstate.

A PRETTY GIRL IS LIKE THE COPS ARE HERE

Chicago really was a wide-open city a generation ago, and the newspapers got a lot of mileage out of exposing vice—gambling, prostitution, whatnot.

Once, to quiet criticism, a Chicago Avenue police captain began making personal inspections of joints accused of generating prostitution. The captain's car would pull up in front of a joint. He stopped the motor. He got out. He stood on the sidewalk. He pulled out his pipe, slowly filled it with tobacco, tamped it, lit it, puffed a few times, and strolled into the saloon.

As he walked in the music being played invariably was "A Pretty Girl Is Like a Melody." It was the signal for the belly dancers, B girls, and prostitutes to head out the back door. The captain reported truthfully to the press and his superiors that he had personally inspected the places and observed perfect decorum.

He also got sick of hearing "A Pretty Girl Is Like a Melody."

HOW'S THAT AGAIN???????

I supervised a Consumer Bureau at the *American*, and tried to help people who were victimized by fast-talking and unscrupulous salesmen. One time we hid a tape recorder and asked a salesman: "How does this plan work?" This is his reply. Keep in mind that the words came fast with no pauses.

"On the sales we're talking about the percentage is where the limitation comes in you recall my stating to you, in other words, the limited amount is what the contract calls for actually to the nearest one hundred dollars in other words sixteen hundred dollars. In other words this is an addition because what I told you if you recall in other words I was just putting this down for your protection see not for mine I wanted you to understand that you will also receive a 5 percent commission, now this has no limitations in other words we will be thrilled, happy, exuberant to pay the five thousand dollars in a year's time just to get us enough sales I mean that goes without saying I mean we would be awfully stupid not to want that and not to pay you for it see so the reason I put this down here so that you know that this is over and above this."

WHOOPS . . . WRONG WEEK

The doorbell rang about half-past-six one night while we were lying around in our old clothes. I opened the door to find the smiling faces of a couple we knew, dressed to the nines. He looked at me and sort of gurgled, "Ah . . . isn't this the night of the party?"

They were a week early. Later they said they went out for dinner and had a fine time.

CHRISTMAS IN AUGUST

The folks on a cul-de-sac in our town put Christmas lights on their houses every year. The guy in the last house to get them up had to pop for dinner for everyone else.

One man who had to buy dinners vowed, "You'll never catch me again." The following August he drove his daughter to college. When he got back, every house on the street had Christmas tree lights up.

SNACK TIME

My wife's grandfather on a Wisconsin farm was an incurable taster. Every evening when he got home from work he had to stick a spoon or his finger or something into whatever was cooking or being stirred in the kitchen. One night grandma was cooking up potato peels and garbage for pig slop. He tasted it.

HIT AND HOME RUN

The car of one of my neighbors was parked in a shopping center lot in the village. Another car, pulling out, sideswiped it, and kept going. A witness took the license number. My neighbor reported the damage to the police, who traced the license of the hit-and-run car to my neighbor's house. His wife was the hit-and-runner.

SPEAKING OF NATURAL FOOD . . .

When my children's grandma was a bride, she baked bread at home. One day the dough didn't rise, so she took it out in the backyard and buried it so her husband wouldn't know about her failure. When he got home from work he found a large mound in the backyard. The hot sun had baked the bread.

OUR BIG PARTY

My wife and I aren't much on celebrations, but we decided to do our twenty-fifth up big. Six months before the event, we talked of having many friends and relatives for a large party. Two months before the big event we hadn't done much, so we decided to hold it down to family.

Two weeks before the event we still hadn't done much so we figured let's just keep it small—the kids, a big dinner, that's enough.

A week before the event we decided we'd just go out by ourselves to a nice restaurant. Two days before the event she stumbled over our dog and broke her toe. We celebrated our twenty-fifth watching TV.

We're making big plans for our fiftieth.

GODSPEED, CAPTAIN

A captain in a suburban police force retired. Most of the officers were glad to see him go. However, it was decided to follow the usual custom and take up a collection for a gift for the retiree. His secretary started it with six dollars in an envelope which was left at the desk so all three shifts could contribute.

When the secretary counted the receipts the next day, the total in the envelope was five dollars. One dollar was gone.

WHO WAS HITLER?

I asked reporter Mark Miller to buttonhole forty-five or fifty people at a suburban shopping center and see if they were as ignorant as some sociologist said they were.

Thirty-one of forty-five identified Nazis with World War II. Five of the remaining fourteen said Nazis were communists. Here's a conversation with a teenager:

"What does the word *Nazi* mean to you?" "I don't know anything about Chicago."

"Who is Adolf Hitler?" "I've heard of him, but I don't really know who he is."

A woman of forty: "I used to think Nazi meant un-American, but I don't know any more."

A man of seventy-two was the only one who answered all questions knowledgeably.

Forty-four of the forty-five correctly identified Archie Bunker.

THE ODDS AGAINST REAGAN

Reagan defied a couple of statistical probabilities which might have made a lesser man hesitate before running for presidency.

Every president elected every twentieth year since Harrison in 1840 died in office.

If that's not enough, five vice presidents whose names ended in *e* served under presidents who died in office, or whose successors died in office. Mondale served under a president who survived in office.

One more, but this is a positive, at least for Reagan. Twenty-two of fifty presidential elections have been won by candidates whose last names ended in *n*.

Some people spend a lot of time figuring out these things.

The Good Old Days

A New House for $6,500

We bought a brand-new four-room house for $6,500 when I got back from World War II. There were a lot of shortages because of the war, and our new house had a coal furnace, like in other houses I'd lived in.

Most houses until a few decades ago had chains on the living room or dining room wall. They led to the basement. One went to the draft on the furnace and the other to the damper.

You pulled up the draft chain to increase the fire, and pulled the damper to slow it down.

I was a lousy fire tender. Each night I'd bank the fire, and time after time I'd get up in the morning and the house was ice cold. What a miserable way to start the day, shaking ashes, cleaning out the fire box, laying a new fire, and hoping it would catch.

It was a great emancipation when we got automatic heat. All we have to do today is jiggle the thermostat. If you tended a coal furnace you really appreciate automatic heat.

There are other chores connected with coal heat, of course. Coal had to be delivered, by the ton. You needed a coal bin in the basement to store it. Coal generates ashes, and the ashes had to be hauled out to the alley to be picked up, or spread on the driveway, or used to fill low spots in the then-unpaved alley. One of my early business enterprises was hauling ashes for a nickel a bushel.

Iceboxes. All this stuff sounds primitive to young people today, but it didn't seem so bad at the time. The automatic refrigerator liberated us from the icebox, with which young people are familiar as trendy (and expensive) antiques. The icebox contained ice in the top compartment and food below.

Ice was delivered. The ice man gave you a card a foot or so square, with the numbers 25, 50, 75, and 100. If you wanted him to deliver 50 pounds of ice, you put the card in the window with the 50 showing.

Most iceboxes had drip pans. Ice melted, and the water had to be carried out. If you neglected to empty the drip pan regularly it overflowed on the kitchen floor. If you let it get too full you spilled it all over the floor while carrying it out. Oh, life wasn't simple.

It was a domestic sin to leave the icebox door open any longer than necessary.

Hot water? It wasn't something you got by just turning the tap. Some folks had automatic gas water heaters, as almost all homes do today. But a lot of us got hot water by going into the basement and building a wood fire in a special hot water heater. Only after it heated up could you turn on the tap and get hot water.

The automatic washing machine was another emancipator, followed by the automatic dryer. I think somewhere in the junk in our basement we still have an old washboard, and I know we have an old copper boiler, used by Fran's mother to wash. It was an exciting day in her household when her first washing machine was delivered, and a very bad day when her arm got caught in the wringer. That wasn't an uncommon household accident.

Washing usually was done on Monday, and you knew it was Monday because clothes were hanging out to dry on clotheslines in almost every back yard. Is there any fresher, cleaner smell than newly washed sheets and clothing after they've dried outdoors?

I can remember vacuum cleaners from my youngest days, but it's interesting that a lot of carpet and floor cleaning was done with a carpet sweeper and/or broom, and both of those devices have survived very well into the eighties. I suspect they'll be just as useful fifty years from now.

Formica is a lovely invention, but oilcloth had more character. We covered the kitchen tables with oilcloth, which was adaptable and washable and durable everywhere except at the corners.

Vitamins weren't on the scene, at least not in tablet form. You got that kind of stuff from lettuce and spinach and broccoli. Zippers were uninvented. We had buttons, snaps, and hooks. They never jammed.

Men's trousers buttoned in the front, and I can't resist recounting a vulgar custom of my boyhood. I don't know how widespread was this game, but it was a constant threat to the unwary boys in my neighborhood. It was simplicity itself. With a deft swipe of your hand you grabbed the edge of your victim's fly and yanked.

If one button came open, it was a single. Two buttons was a two-base hit, or double. Three buttons was a triple. But every boy's goal was a home run—four buttons pulled open.

Can't do that kind of stuff with a zipper.

Time was approximate. We not only didn't have quartz watches, there were no electric clocks. Clocks had to be wound, and they gained and lost time, depending on individual idiosyncracies. Interestingly enough, in this age of electric clocks and clock radios and any number of electronic wake-up devices, I still keep two windup alarm clocks in our bedroom and use them when I need a wake-up alarm. When I was supervising a few people at work I got awfully tired of the excuse, ".The power went off and my alarm didn't work." You can count on losing power during the night a couple of times a year.

Evaporated milk was sold in cans. People usually punched a couple of small holes in one end to get the milk out. So when the milk was gone, there remained a can with both ends relatively intact. This may generate a "So what!" from today's reader, but the can became a major source of recreation in our generation.

We placed the cans on the sidewalk and stepped on them, hard. The cans crumpled in the middle and wrapped around our shoes, and off we went, clunkety-clackety down the street until we or our parents got tired of the racket.

Not having Little League or any organized recreation, we were pretty much on our own to be creative when we weren't playing softball or soccer or football on the corner lot. I think most city kids at one time or another built a scooter using an old roller skate for wheels. You attached the skate wheels to either end of a two-by-four. To that you nailed a wooden apple box. That was it. You could add nice touches like a tin can with a candle to serve as a headlight, and maybe paint of some kind.

One sport that needed no equipment was spitting for distance, technique, and accuracy. No tobacco juice was involved, just plain, natural juices. The most dazzling techniques were the "rolled tongue" and the "tooth gap." The distance competition was held in high winds, and by aiming high and catching a gust of wind some spitballs landed six or seven feet away.

On hot summer days the spitting contests were embellished with tar. We chewed it. I'm not sure why. Because it was there, I suppose. Tar got soft and chewy on street patches and around roofers, and what is a city kid to do when he encounters such a commodity? Throw it, step in it, or put it in his mouth. Some unsung pioneer started chewing it, and a new junk food was born. We never swallowed it, of course. It was wonderful for spitting competition, and we also thought it whitened our teeth. I doubt if our parents would have agreed if they'd found out.

Around the ages of, oh, roughly seven through twelve, every Saturday afternoon was spent in the local show, where the main attraction was the Saturday serial, usually cowboys and Indians stuff. Once I came home from a Jack Hoxie western and was immediately pushed into the garage and told to get rid of my clothes. It seems the theater had been stink-bombed, and I had sat in it. In a crowd of several hundred small boys the smell of a stink bomb is almost indistinguishable from the smell of old sneakers and similar juvenile scents. I had sniffed nothing out of line.

We collected cigar bands and tin foil. We hitched onto the backs of ice wagons to get a hunk of ice to suck. We marveled at the milkman's horse, which always stopped at the right houses without being told.

We never saw a pregnant woman. They stayed in their houses. Three kids was a big family.

Spending money was raised by such chores as hauling out the ashes and by finding glass milk bottles which could be redeemed for a nickel. This nickel was good for a generous supply of penny candy—Mary Janes, green leaves, licorice whips, and the ghastly reddish liquid that came in wax containers and tasted like poison. The wax made for good chewing.

A sign of maturity was attaching metal caps and cleats on your shoes, so that two boys walking down a school hall sounded like a regiment of horses galloping on terra-cotta.

Shine Your Own Shoes

Twenty years ago the 5 percent inflation rate was considered scandalous—practically out of control.

Since then it's been a roller-coaster ride for inflation, interest rates, good times, and bad times. I can't begin to guess what will prevail between my writing this and your reading it, but the chances of a spell of hard times are fairly strong.

In '69 I wrote a column of tips on how to beat inflation. Ten years later the wife of a reporter who had saved the column sent it to me. Almost everything was still applicable. Now a decade later, most of it still makes sense. If things aren't tough at the moment, just hang on to it. Here's the 1969 advice:

- Go to the movies before the price changes.
- Shine your own shoes.
- Fly coach.
- Take advantage of the library instead of buying books. (Except this one.)
- Do your own house decorating.
- Buy black and white instead of color TV.
- Buy gas where it's 32.9 cents instead of 37.9.
- Get a mutt instead of a pedigreed dog. Or get a kitten for nothing.
- Grow food in your yard or a vacant lot.
- Buy everything on the Bohemian Easy Payment Plan—100 percent down, nothing more to pay.
- Young parents, work out a reciprocal baby-sitting deal with friends. Older parents, sell your kids on the advantages of attending a state university.
- Pick apples in orchards in the fall.
- Cut whole milk with powdered milk.
- Buy a hair-cutting outfit.
- Play tennis instead of golf.
- Carry your lunch to work.

- Make a compost heap instead of buying bagged fertilizer.
- Buy used cars instead of new cars. Sixes instead of eights.
- Reduce. It lowers food bills and will save doctor bills.
- Buy furniture in February and August, white soft goods in January, Christmas wrapping paper, candles, cards, and decorations the week after Christmas.
- Buy unpainted furniture and paint it.
- Use want ads and garage sales.
- Hang on to clothes enough years so they become fashionable again.
- When you save a buck, don't start figuring how you'll spend it for something else.
- Stop smoking.
- Stay in tourist homes on the road.
- Buy day-old baked goods and bread (like the Sara Lee factory near my home, where if they get too many raisins in the coffee cake, they sell it cheap).
- Use coin-operated dry cleaning machines.
- Buy good clothes and take care of them.
- Buy cheap watches and throw them away when they give out.
- Sit in the bleachers.

Bleacher seats were sixty cents when I wrote that. What are they now . . . four dollars?

I'm well aware that if many people adopted all these economies the whole American economic system would come tumbling down.

If everybody started paying with cash instead of plastic, we'd plunge into a catastrophic banking crisis.

Worry not. We who were raised in the Depression, or were starting out in working life then, are phasing out and are being replaced by spenders and borrowers who can't seem to comprehend the cost of 18 percent carrying charges.

I hope they make it. But heaven help them if we do get into another depression. They won't know what to do.

That's what I wrote twenty years ago, unedited. Except for the tourist homes and price of gas, everything is pretty much applicable today. For what it's worth, I followed most of those tips to some degree, except that we have German shepherds and a color TV, and I go to the barber shop.

Rationing

On Thanksgiving Day, 1942, we'd been in World War II for nearly a year. The nation was one week away from the start of gasoline rationing. Chicago ration boards advised that the new coffee ration stamp was in the sugar ration book and would be needed "to purchase the first pound of coffee for each person over fifteen years old."

It's hard for younger people to visualize needing government-issued ration stamps to buy a pair of shoes, or a pound of butter, or a tire, or a pound of sugar, or coffee.

You didn't need coupons to buy a car. They weren't being manufactured.

The restrictions on our personal lives imposed by the war effort are unthinkable today. So were they unthinkable a year before we got into World War II. It was surprising how well we adapted.

I couldn't get gasoline, so I bought a used bike. Housewives found new ways to stretch coffee and sugar. A jury of our neighbors on draft boards determined which men were eligible to go to war.

Much of life went on as usual. The demand for turkeys pushed up the price to 52 cents a pound. The War Production Board ordered a halt to production of whipping cream.

Six-room ranch houses in Arlington Heights and Barrington were selling for $11,000. Carson's advertised white shirts at three for $5.25. Milk deliveries to homes were cut to three a week to save tires, and the dairies sought a one-half cent-a-quart increase to sixteen cents.

Cable Piano Company was selling *The Nutcracker Suite* on three twelve-inch LP records for $1.99. Of course, before you bought any phonograph record you took it into the little booth in the store and played it to make sure you liked it.

Russia was our military ally. The Douglas Oil refinery in California was being dismantled for shipment to Russia.

In Orchestra Hall, Charlie Chaplin told an audience, "Nobody is shocked by the word *communism* any more. They've been our friends since 1917."

Lieutenant-General Dwight Eisenhower sent a wire from North Africa to General Motors: "On this Thanksgiving Day let us thank God for labor and management which has given us the weapons to conduct our campaigns."

The response of General Motors, Chrysler, Ford, Packard, International Harvester, and all major industrialists was near miraculous. Assembly lines were converted from trucks to tanks in a few weeks. And a government war contract for making howitzer parts was let to a Chicago machinist who made the parts in his basement with friends.

The War Production Board ordered that men's pajamas be shortened three inches, and that cuffs, sashes, collars, and ornamental braids be eliminated. I was the ultimate pajama patriot. I didn't wear any.

We often wondered if these orders were just for show or if they really made a useful saving in fabric or other material. Lucky Strike cigarettes had to stop using green ink on their package because the green was needed for war material. The cigarette company immediately launched an ad campaign: "Lucky Strike Green Has Gone to War!"

President Roosevelt showed how to use old coffee grounds to give a cup of coffee "real flavor."

The siege of Stalingrad was in its ninetieth day. The Germans, caught without winter equipment, were wearing wicker wrapping for shoes. They were dying at the rate of three thousand a day outside Stalingrad.

On Alley Picking and Other Fun Things

"No more pencils, no more books, no more teacher's dirty looks." On the last day of school we'd troop down the street after the last class, gleefully chanting that chorus. We'd hit at the air, kick cans, throw things.

There was so much to be done. Alley picking. Playing ball. Playing marbles. Building apple crate scooters. Going swimming, digging caves. These were major activities. There also were hundreds of minor diversions. If there was a body of water within walking distance, you went fishing. This involved scrounging a bamboo rod, usually from someone who had a rug delivered. The hardware store had a cheap fishing line for fifteen or twenty cents, and a little bag of hooks for a dime.

We probably spent more time looking for worms than fishing. Everybody dug for worms, either in your backyard or a vacant lot. We'd squat around a little patch of ground, poking and probing.

"There's one!" "Where?" "There! His tail just went in the hole."

Dig dig dig. "Wow, is this a fat one! Stick him in the can." Finding a fat worm was just about as rewarding as finding an empty milk bottle in the alley that you could get a nickel for at the store.

Preparations for summer camp didn't change much from when I went to when I sent my own children. Two pairs of pajamas, warm socks, a canteen, sleeping bag, and don't bring more than ten dollars spending money because you won't need it.

Over the years the woods after dark are just as scary and the noises that come out of them are just as spooky. A mosquito bite itches the same today, and feet get just as tired after a ten-mile hike.

Most summers included a motor trip to relatives in another state or to a state park somewhere. Motoring was more of an adventure. Three hundred miles was a good day's mileage, because the main highways were two lanes wide and went right through the center of every city, town, and hamlet along the way. I especially hated Pittsburgh before they built the Pennsylvania turnpike. You lost an hour winding through those Pittsburgh streets, barely able to see the buildings through the smoke from the steel mills.

And how well we came to know Gary, Indiana, coming back to the city after a weekend in Michigan.

Accommodations at night were more fun, partly because they were so cheap. Tourist homes and cabins were the place to stay. Today's sleek motels are efficient and impersonal, but when you holed up for the night in the old tourist homes or cabins you usually left the next day as personal friends of the owners. Three bucks a night bought a room, and five or six dollars a tourist cabin. Bed and breakfast places today are a refinement of the old tourist rooms, but at a considerably stiffer tariff.

If there was any change from one generation to the next in kids in the car howling, jumping, twisting, screaming, fighting, and wanting to go, it escaped me. Station wagons were invented to give the kids more room to get into mischief, and to add dogs, cats, gerbils, and other live, squirmy things to the cargo.

GM—72 to 7⅝

"What was the Depression *really* like, Dad?" my fifth grader asked. She was studying the Depression in school.

"We ate a lot of tapioca pudding for dessert," I told her. "We wore shoes until there was a hole in the sole, and then we put in cardboard to cover the hole, and avoided puddles.

"Men who had been millionaires sold apples to get enough money to eat. I was lucky when I got out of high school. I got a job for fifteen dollars a week. The hours were 8 A.M. to midnight Monday through Friday, 8 A.M. to 5 P.M. Saturdays, and 9 A.M. to 1 P.M. on Sundays."

I offered more, but that satisfied her.

There's much more. The people who suffered most from the Depression were those least responsible for it. Men wanted work, and would work long and hard hours. But there were no jobs.

The panic on the stock market in 1929 started this economic disaster. There followed a vicious cycle of falling sales, which led to lower corporate income, followed by attempts to restore that income by cutting salaries and laying off employees.

This increased unemployment, which reduced sales, which increased losses of business, which led to more wage-cutting and discharging of employees.

How far did the market sink? Here are some quotations from 1929 to 1932. General Motors common was at 72 in 1929, and sank to 7⅝. Radio Corporation common peaked at 101 and sank to 2½. United States Steel, a bellwether of the stock market, hit 261 in 1929 and 21¼ at the depth of the panic.

I was a teenager through most of the Depression and I never went hungry or lacked for shelter. My family was quite poor before the Depression. A memory that sticks is sitting on the front porch of our (rented) flat the morning all the banks in the nation were ordered closed. I read and saw and heard the panic reaction, and the fear that people wouldn't ever get their money from the bank. This fear was absent in our house because we didn't have anything in any bank.

If people didn't have a cash supply on hand they were in big trouble. They couldn't go to the bank to draw money, and nobody would cash their checks.

Many banks never reopened, and depositors got back only part of their money. Bankers became vacuum cleaner salesmen.

As the Depression progressed, my friends and I certainly were conscious of an extreme shortage of money and jobs, but we thought that was normalcy.

A depression teaches you to make do, and because almost everybody was in the same boat, you didn't feel too self-conscious with homemade Christmas toys.

A bean bag could be made with beans, some cloth and a needle and thread, and a board with a hole cut in it, plus a little paint.

Some cup hooks and rubber canning jar rings made a good ring toss game.

Clothing was patched and repatched, but necktie sales stood up through the Depression. Bright new ties were a cheap way to spruce up an old wardrobe.

Families doubled up in houses and flats, and pooled their resources. You could ride Chicago streetcars for seven cents, and the buses for a dime. Gasoline sales competition was intense, and I can remember filling up for 10 cents a gallon.

More people walked. It was hard on shoes, but shoes cost less and lasted longer. Women knitted and sewed and patched, and people grew their own food. Chicken and ice cream were delicacies we didn't have too often.

The government created jobs with the WPA, PWA, and CCC—Works Progress Administration, Public Works Administration, and Civilian Conservation Corps. These were work projects for men and youths, and consisted mainly of work with picks and shovels. In the late thirties, though, I remember a federal theater project for men and women in the arts, and a very professional adaptation of Gilbert and Sullivan called *Hot Mikado*, which I enjoyed more than the original.

There were many ways for families to tighten their belts and make do. Many families picked greens in vacant lots and in the country. A huge soup bone, which today might cost dollars, was yours for the asking from the butcher.

You could go to the bakery and get day-old bread for five cents a loaf instead of the seven it cost fresh. Soap could be made by saving cooking fat and adding lye or something. Little roll-your-own cigarette-making machines came into use in the Depression.

Upstairs rooms were closed when not in use, and registers were shut to save heat. Cooking was done on top of the stove because the oven used too much gas. When you did use the oven, you put in roasts and cake and potatoes and everything to use the heat.

These economies were so firmly ingrained in a lot of young people that they're still practicing them today, to the puzzlement of their children and grandchildren.

As bad as things were, imagine how much worse they would have been if we'd had plastic credit cards. Six percent interest on any debt was called usury—"excessive or illegally high." There wasn't too much buying on credit, probably because not many merchants would risk giving credit.

Newspapers cost two cents. In 1932 *Chicago Tribune* Silvernail cafeterias advertised a roast duck special with mashed potatoes—fifteen cents. At Harvard Cleaners, forty-four cents would clean a suit, $2.50 would clean six.

Governor Leslie of Indiana called the National Guard to quell striking miners near Terre Haute. They walked out when their old contract providing $6.10 a day expired. They refused management's offer of $4.00 a day.

Halsey Stuart & Company advertised "12 Sound $1,000 bonds" at $520 each.

In the want ads a fast, hard-working laundress was offered employment at $2.50 a day. Restaurants and hotels were half-empty. Hilton wooed permanent guests with rents below costs. Whole floors were closed to save heat. Phones were removed from rooms to save fifteen cents a month. An "efficiency expert" went through the *Daily News* and removed every light bulb in the toilets except one.

Fathers with nothing to do gave the museums a big play on free days. Big family picnics were held in public parks, and families generally were a lot closer than they are today. And bigger, as older parents and unemployed brothers and sisters and aunts and uncles and cousins in desperation sought help.

It was cheap to make fudge at home, and have taffy pulls. Jigsaw puzzles that were cheap or could be rented provided home entertainment for evenings on end.

If a family had a dog, no matter how broke they were the dog stayed and shared in the table scraps. I don't think the canned and dry dog foods we have today were available in the thirties.

Youngsters grubbed for money finding old milk bottles and redeeming them for a nickel. They (we) mowed lawns, ran errands, emptied ashes, shoveled snow.

It wasn't impossible for a teenage girl to find work. Here's one want ad from 1932, under "Help Wanted, Female": "Maid, white, young, healthy, $3." That's three dollars a week. And included all the housework, cooking, cleaning, and caring for the kids.

Baked Bean Sandwiches and Bread Pudding

Here are some stories of the Depression from friends of the column. First is a visit with Grace and Bill Gorman and Marion and Jimmie Rowland, Chicago North-Siders.

"For my lunch at school I packed baked bean sandwiches," recalled Grace Gorman. "We were big on bread pudding, too. No one would ever throw out stale bread because you could make bread pudding for dessert. Lots of stews, too."

"I drove a truck six days a week, 7 A.M. to 6 P.M., for $42 a week," said Jimmie Rowland. "My helper worked the same hours for $15. I was lucky. I had a job. Guys in factories were getting 25 cents an hour."

Bill Gorman: "As late as '39 things were tough. I was making $22 a week at Horder's. But we'd go to the store and buy all our groceries, including meat, for $5. Our rent was $37.50."

"When we ironed, we put the iron on the stove, waited for it to warm up and then ironed until it got cold," offered Mrs. Rowland.

"The bane of my existence was rayon stockings," said Mrs. Gorman. "I had to wear them to high school. Before the Depression stockings were silk. The rayon stockings were coarse and folded over your knees. And then you'd spend two hours a night sewing up runs. You never threw away stockings.

"I remember my brother getting his hair cut at home. All the boys would get these short haircuts and the girls their Buster Browns. You hear jokes about bowl haircuts. They really were just that. Mom or dad put a bowl on the boy's head and cut all the hair that stuck out."

Bill Gorman: "People say those were the good old days, but I don't know that I'd ever want to go back to them. We complain about high prices now. But look what we have—cars, televisions, eat out all the time."

Grace Gorman: "Yes, but I don't know that we're any happier

now than we were then. I think it was a good experience for us, even though it wasn't one you'd wish for yourself. Everyone was more concerned about everyone else. You appreciated what you had."

Marion Rowland: "People weren't afraid of each other. You'd talk to strangers without being afraid."

Grace Gorman: "If you ran out of money, the grocer would stake you till payday. And you'd be there bright and early payday to pay him back."

Marion Rowland: "It was rough on our parents. They all had such high hopes for us. It wasn't as tough for us because we felt a sense of unity. We were all in it together."

Here's another account from a South Sider:

"We had to apply for welfare. My mother was long overdue for surgery, and my grandmother was too old to work. I was twelve or fourteen. My father and grandfather were dead.

"They allowed us $14 a month apiece. We got a supplement of dried milk, peas, cured meats, eggs, and dried fruits. We picked this up at various depots and got them home the best way we could. Coaster wagons were the usual conveyance.

"We weren't allowed telephones or electric lights. We burned lamps. We cooked on an old coal and wood-burning range. It heated the house, food, and water.

"We were allowed coal, but this we had to get home, too, any way we could. This in a family of one sick woman, one old woman, and one teenage girl.

"If you could pin down your caseworker, she or he might give you a supplement for clothing, but this was considered a luxury, so you waited a very long time.

"The fuel allotment never lasted. We had to give away part of it to get it hauled to the house. I lost time from school. No shoes. We went to bed early some nights to save fuel. We also went to bed early because of hunger.

"My only luxury was a small dog, and he suffered right along with us."

Here is the scene in a stockbroker's office described by a survivor:

"I saw them sold out, dozens of them, scores of them. I watched their faces when the customers' men gave them the news. I saw men's hair literally turn white. I saw a woman faint dead away; they carried her out cold. I heard a middle-aged doctor say, 'There goes my son's college education.'

"Terrible sights. Terrible sounds. Sitting there hour after hour watching my own investments shrink and shrivel, my heart ached for the poor people around me."

Adversity does build character . . . if there isn't too much adversity. In many ways we were toughened, and certainly we learned to appreciate today's riches. But it was a tragic, mean time, and the suffering far outweighed the little good that came from it.

The Good Years?

Suppose you could choose any period of the world's history in which to live—without naming particular conditions (long life, a dukedom, wealth, power). What would be your choice?

I've indulged in a lot of nostalgia in print. It's our nature to filter out the negatives and look back on previous generations as relaxed and gracious and loving and altogether much more attractive than the present.

After I had paid tribute to the Victorian way of life in McKinley's time, Ernie Tucker, the *American*'s erudite city editor, said, "Maybe," and offered some contrary evidence.

- Yellow fever killed 13,000 in an Alabama epidemic.
- Cholera killed thousands in a New York epidemic.
- In spite of the fact that smallpox vaccine was a century old, hundreds of thousands of Americans bore badly pitted faces and other thousands died.
- Of fifteen girls who were close friends of Ernie's aunt (born 1872), eleven were dead of tuberculosis before the age of 30.
- Breast cancer was called "decay of breast" and insured death within six months.
- Morality of public officials was a joke. Senators were openly bought and sold by railroads, iron and coal barons. Morality of newspapers was a joke.
- Life was gracious and easy for perhaps 10 percent of the population. The rest worked twelve to sixteen hours a day under indescribable conditions, from Pennsylvania coal towns to New York sweatshops. Domestic servants were slaves.
- Carry Nation, the Temperance Cadets, and "Father Dear Father

Come Home with Me Now" are funny now. They weren't then. Drunkenness was all but universal.

• Prostitutes thronged the streets of every city in spite of vaunted Victorian morality. V.D. was at a dizzy pinnacle. White slavery was common. So was dope addiction; junkies bought morphine openly.

• The nation's cultural tastes were abysmal. Outside New York there was nothing except Chautauquas, Uncle Tom and Toby shows, and county fairs. Elsie Dinsmore and Little Lord Fauntleroy were widely regarded as the epitome of literary pretension.

• Half of the adult females went through life in a state of gentle muzziness induced by nostrums for feminine difficulties, all of which had roughly the same effect as a martini. Babies were loaded with paregoric to keep them from crying. Quacks and medicine men made millions. There was no control whatever over the quality of foodstuffs.

• True, life was more relaxed and slower, but this is not necessarily a virtue. It also was sharply divided into (a) work and (b) sleep. Leisure was minimal. A lot of it was devoted to being bored.

• We decry the sentimentality and preoccupation with death of the Victorian era. They had to be that way; infant and child deaths were horribly common, and there is no indication that our grandfathers felt it any less than we would. They lived in constant terror of kids' diseases which are hardly more than words to us.

OK, which is better? The Victorian era, or the nuclear age?

Beyond the City Limits

The Suburban Curse

"The dream cottage in the country has turned into a nightmare of mortgage payments, two-car maintenance, time payments, family counseling, and a peptic ulcer on the way."

This garbage was in a TV series titled "Is Suburbia Really Worth It?" Most writers live either in the city or far out in the country. Many of them—particularly TV and movie writers—compound their insularity by living in New York or Los Angeles.

Most writers seem to resent the suburbs.

More of their nonsense: A suburban transformation "could be indexed by a set of quaint symbols—the ranch house, lawn, barbecue, and two-car garage; modern and 'functionally designed' churches, schools, and shopping center.

". . . Massive long-distance commuting, transient residency, awkwardly joining an intense obsession with the repair and appearance of the home, hysterical neighboring and joining, the kaffee-klatsch as an institution, not to mention lack of privacy and an attending intolerance of the offbeat."

Suburbanites don't write that kind of muck about the city.

In *Sportworld. An American Dreamland*, Robert Lipsyte saw "a million Little Leaguers standing for hours while a criminally obese 'coach' drills the joy of sport out of their souls, makes them self-conscious and fearful, teaches them technique over movement, emphasizes dedication, sacrifice and obedience instead of accomplishment and fun."

Where do these guys dream up this nonsense? Does Lipsyte see one fat coach and decide they're all criminally obese? The man who coached my Little Leaguer was an athletic neighbor who grew up in Mayor Daley's Chicago neighborhood and moved to our suburb. He loved the kids, taught them the fun of the game, and taught them sportsmanship.

More people live in the suburbs than live in Chicago. We might as well learn to coexist.

But the sociologists and essayists will keep right on sniping at the suburbs with their tiresome and ignorant clichés about the picture-window culture and the cocktail parties and sterile lives and all their usual rubbish.

You can find almost anything you look for in the Chicago suburbs and in the city among the three or four million people living in each. I grew up in the city and have spent my adult life living in the suburbs and working in the city. I like both.

When I commuted by train I enjoyed the walk at either end of the trip, and the reading during the trip. When I drove I avoided the rush hour and had an easy thirty-minute drive. What's wrong with a ranch house? I wouldn't trade mine for any other. Lawns? If you like the exercise of mowing, as my wife and I do, you can get a place with a lawn. If you don't like mowing, don't buy a lawn.

I never heard my "neighboring" called hysterical. We cherish our friends from our neighborhoods. Transients? Every year or two somebody on the block would get transferred and we'd hold a terribly suburbanish going-away block party. No booze more often than not.

I was sorry my kids didn't have the advantage of the diversity of friends, economic and ethnic, that I had while growing up in the city. But the compensation was excellent schools, great parks, and a well-used library four blocks from our house.

The worst part of living in our suburb was, and is, environmental. Specifically, the constant, unwelcome, annoying, pollutant against which we are helpless—low-flying, fume-spewing, ear-splitting jet planes flying low over our homes into the city of Chicago.

In the Boondocks

I had some of the best times and met some of the most interesting friends when I got out of Chicago and into the country. I was attracted to North Manchester, Indiana, by an ad in their newspaper. It read:

> How NOT to Fight Inflation. Real Estate. Raise your Sales Commission Rate to 6% or 7%. A real Exercise in Greed and a real Ripoff.
>
> "As REAL ESTATE Values are already much inflated, we feel ENOUGH IS enough. We pledge that our real estate commission rate will NOT be raised from only 3%.

Eldon M. Wright's stationery for his law and real estate business proclaimed: "North Manchester—the Crown Jewel of Hoosierdom and the World's Finest Place to Live, Work, Play, and Become Wise."

North Manchester is the only town I ever encountered that claimed you could get wise living there.

Eldon M. Wright's office at 116 East Main Street resembled a miniature Hyatt Regency lobby done in 1950's decor. I sat in one easy chair and he sat in another that squeaked every time he moved. I said I thought 3 percent commission on selling a house was indeed wise.

A man walked in. "Major," said Eldon M. Wright, "I want you to meet this man from the *Tribune* in Chicago."

"Oh, I listen to WBBM all the time," said Jim Burton. "Isn't that right, Eldon? Never have the radio on anything else."

"Why?" I asked.

"Mayor Byrne and all her money thing. Paying her husband and daughter . . . that kind of stuff. It's entertaining . . . really entertaining."

Wayne Garman strolled in, sat down in another easy chair, picked up a copy of the *Tribune* and turned to the stock tables.

"Wayne ran the two movie houses," Eldon M. Wright explained. "Leases ran out and they closed."

"Never lost money on 'em," Wayne Garman commented as he scanned the stock tables.

I asked why they bought the Chicago paper instead of papers closer to North Manchester.

"It has the best stock tables," said Garman. It seems I was present at a regular morning assembly in which Wright and

Dan Walker was elected governor of Illinois in 1973 on a gimmick: he walked the length of the state. His opponent was Dick Ogilvie, the incumbent who had assured his own defeat when he saved the state from financial disaster by instituting a state income tax. I walked a few miles with Walker near Sterling, Illinois.

Garman and Major Burton and other local investors discussed investment results and opportunities.

They mentioned the Dreyfus and Oppenheimer money funds with favor, as well as a Kansas City brokerage which provided instant deals by phone.

Now, what about wisdom?

"Well," offered Eldon M. Wright, "it's *prima facie* evidence we're smart because we choose to live in North Manchester.

"Jim here is a retired Air Force major who's lived all over the United States and the world, and he came back here to live. I've been around the world a time or two, and I'm leaving for China Sunday, but it's always best to get back home."

North Manchester removed its parking meters when a shopping center opened on the outskirts. There was little crime. "In fact," said Eldon M. Wright, who used to be the judge, "there's hardly enough business to justify keeping a court.

"A motto in town is 'Never a boom or a bust.' We know there's a recession, but it's not too bad. Wabash has a General Tire plant and they're hit harder. We have four or five little factories that make coils and stuff for the auto industry, and they're still going.

"In this town, over $200 a month for rent is considered excessive—terrible. They'll complain about $200 a month and then go out and pay $500 a month for a car. People have priorities, but rent isn't one of them.

"Houses are rather high for a small town—$60,000 to $80,000 for a good newer house. You can get 'em cheaper—$20,000 for one that needs work."

Our meeting adjourned to the Farm House Restaurant a block away. The presence of a Chicago reporter in town caused momentary panic among some entrepreneurs involved in a proposal to build a huge chicken farm close to town.

Three hundred thousand chickens in one structure produce an enormous amount of chicken manure. The stink is terrible. The last thing they wanted was a Chicago newspaper poking into the great North Manchester chicken smell controversy.

Eldon M. Wright knew that the reporter came only to find wisdom, and he just smiled.

City Man in the Country

Gary Williams used to operate a news agency near Wrigley Field. Then he ran a saloon, Queen's Paradise, at the (then) unfashionable corner of Clark and Ontario streets. In 1975 he and his wife, Brooke, sold their house and business and bought a beat-up old farmhouse on seventy scrubby acres on Blackjack Road six miles out of Galena in western Illinois.

"I might get some cattle, maybe hogs. I'm not sure yet," Gary said in his half-finished living room before a fire in a Franklin stove. "All I know is I've always wanted to be a farmer, and we made the decision, and here we are.

"I have one major problem. I'm neurotic about borrowing. I never borrow," said Gary, a dark, trim, handsome man.

Brooke, who was an English major in college, added, "Gary's been haunting the farm auctions."

They picked up some antiques and planned to make a striking Victorian farmhouse when Gary finished the carpentry, wiring, plumbing, and decorating.

He bought a corn planter for $130, a hay mower for $170, an old pickup truck for $200.

But his prize was a 1948 John Deere tractor for $500. Brooke laughed: "When the clutch went out Gary got a ten dollar part, fixed it himself. Same thing happened to our neighbor's $10,000 tractor, and it cost $200 to take the whole engine out."

Any farmer looking at a city guy with no experience and a thing about borrowing and seventy hilly acres and no stock and a $500 tractor would lay 100 to 1 he'd never make it. I asked how the neighbors were taking it.

Gary shook his head. "They look at us and I know they're thinking, 'I wonder how long they'll last.' But they are marvelous . . . simply wonderful."

Brooke said, "We moved in too late to put in a proper garden, so all summer long the neighbors brought us fresh green beans, tomatoes, melons, potatoes, squash, and on and on.

"The children love school. Last year at Lyons High School our freshman paid eighty-nine dollars in fees. This year we paid twelve dollars. No one uses locks on the lockers because nothing gets stolen. There are no narcs in the washrooms. The lounge is student supervised, and there aren't police at the doors when school's out.

"Our eleven-year-old required medical attention. At the hospital they suggested we go down the block to the office of the three doctors who serve Galena."

"Without an appointment?" I asked.

"We went over, they took us right in, and the receptionist didn't even ask for insurance, bank account numbers, or my mother's maiden name.

"When I stood there with cash in hand, she said, 'Wait till he gets the stitch out. You can pay then if you want.'

"Everyone goes out of his way to be helpful.

"We've discovered what life can really be like. Gary used to work day and night, seven days a week. He never saw the kids, and not much of me. Now he's home. We've discovered things like reading, and the games the kids like—checkers, Authors. Sunday we went hiking and picnicking out in the back.

"Fresh air, no smog, no jets, birds, animals. Peace, quiet, room to run. Stars at night with a better display than the Planetarium."

Did they make it? Five years is a fair measurement, and I drove out for another visit in 1981.

"How's the tractor holding up?" I asked.

"Works perfectly," said Gary. "Just ordinary maintenance is all it needs. I bought another '48 just like it, same price."

"How about your livestock?"

"Thirty-eight head of cattle, and a pig or two for butchering, and a few chickens."

"Tell him how you got the herd," Brooke said. Gary declined, so she told. Every animal in the herd was bought as a three-day-old calf and bottle-fed by Gary.

Brooke was working in town as secretary at an engineering firm whose president moved the company from a Chicago suburb after combing the nation for the most desirable place to live and work. Gary worked about half the time as a carpenter. He had three acres in feed corn and ten acres in hay. "Just enough to feed the herd."

He was clearing wooded land for more pasture. His minimal machinery cut and baled the hay, but Gary manually gathered the seventy-pound bales and stacked them in the barn.

Their freezer was loaded with beef and pork and preserved and frozen beans, peas, broccoli, beets, tomatoes, tomato sauce, apple sauce, pickles, corn, relish, chili sauce, strawberries—all from the garden.

The wood lot provided most of the fuel to heat the handsome remodeled house.

Gary still refused to borrow. "I can't sleep at night if I owe money," he said.

So he avoided the trap that has ruined thousands of farmers. His family was leading a good life . . . not a rich life materialistically, but a good life. They ate well, didn't lock their doors, and took a two-week tour of Europe to visit their son in the Army.

They read the *Tribune* every day and listened to the news on Chicago radio, and found it quite entertaining.

Ladybugs and Praying Mantises

At ten o'clock on a June night near Pocahontas, in southern Illinois, Ruth Korte steered the family station wagon through a huge alfalfa field. Clarence, her husband, sat on the tailgate as the auto bumped through the dirt.

At his side and back were thousands of ladybugs, which he tossed into the alfalfa. If this were daylight, the ladybugs would fly away. At night they immediately start eating weevils.

I visited the Kortes because they farmed 520 acres without using chemicals. Organic farming never has caught on widely. The Kortes used only natural materials to combat weeds, disease, and insects.

Some farmers who depend on chemicals scoff at the Korte method. Clarence started with a borrowed $1,000 and twenty-three years later owned 520 fertile acres, 400 beefalo, and equipment and buildings valued at $2 million.

American farmers spend hundreds of millions a year to spray and dust their land with poisons to combat mites and gypsy moths and grasshoppers, ants, spiders, bollworms, earworms, white grubs, rootworms, chinch bugs, and hundreds of species of lesser bugs. Millions more are spent for chemicals to kill weeds with as many identities as the bugs.

Why don't bugs eat and weeds weaken Korte's corn, soybeans, wheat, and alfalfa?

Ladybugs and praying mantises are one answer. "A praying mantis will get on a plant and he'll stand guard on that plant all season," Korte said as we talked at a picnic bench in the yard of his handsome log house. "They'll eat every insect that comes along."

He said the main ingredient for organic success is a fine balance of the elements in the soil. If the soil is right, the plants will be healthy, and chemicals will be unnecessary.

"You have to apply a product to the soil to balance the elements," Korte said. "Most elements are in the soil, and it's a matter of getting them unleashed. When there's balance, the weed problem goes away.

"When you just feed fertilizer into the soil every year, you get lazy soil. Today's agriculture isn't farming the soil—it's mining the soil."

Korte's main addition to the soil was a humus from New Mexico that he brought in by the truckload.

We got into his station wagon and drove through miles of alfalfa, wheat, beans, and new corn. At the south boundary of the Korte farm a field of wheat adjoined a neighbor's wheat. The neighbor used chemicals. There was no visible difference between the two fields.

Korte had such faith in the balance of nature that he believes that when everything is in harmony a rain cloud could pass over the land and not drop rain if it isn't needed. Such a belief invites skepticism until you look at the miles of lush crops on the Korte farm.

I asked Korte why he stopped using chemical pesticides, sprays, and fertilizer. He wasn't exactly sure. "My father died when I was six," he said. "We had three horses and one mule, and when you walked behind them you could see into the soil . . . see the conditions. That never left me.

"I guess the catalyst for change was when dairy inspectors detected residue in my milk. It was only one part per billion of an insecticide, but that scared me. It's a terrible thing to have to rely on to kill pests and bugs. To kill the bad guys you have to kill the good guys.

"When I was a kid a priest said, 'As you sow, so shall you reap.' I went further—if you sow poison, you'll reap poison. What we were doing was wrong. I knew we could do it the old way."

I wondered why more farmers don't go the organic route.

"Well, I don't want to offend anyone," Korte said. "And I hope none of your relatives teaches in ag schools. But the chemical industry pours millions into those schools for research and consultation. If I could have somebody subsidize teaching the value of organic farming, it would be different."

Korte had little use for grain speculators. "Maybe you remember learning that the Lord got mad at moneylenders in the temple," he smiled. "So he drove them out of the temple. They went to Chicago and started the Board of Trade."

Four large deep freezers and a walk-in cooler provided grains, fruit, vegetables, and meat from their land. They ground their own flour and cornmeal. Honey replaced sugar.

"We have no family doctor," Korte said. "We rarely see a dentist. I had more dental problems before I was twenty-five than our whole family has had since. We can even see a difference in our babies born during our chemical time and since then.

"I am greatly concerned about the proliferation of poisons. Farmers have been conditioned to be scouts to look for new insects. They see something new and run to the phone and the dealer sends them a new chemical."

A major concern of American farmers is the exodus of their young people from the farms. The five Korte boys, eighteen and under, were committed to stay in farming. Three daughters were helping on the farm. The oldest girl lived on a nearby farm. The Kortes need no hired hands.

The best part of writing a general column was the occasional travel. My wife Fran always came with, and I think people were happier to see her than me. She's a very upbeat lady with strong curiosity about everything and everybody. While I'd ask the routine journalistic questions she'd be off talking with anybody who got in her path, and getting more insight into my assignment than I'd get. While a hard-working columnist contemplates a virgin prairie in central Illinois, his wife looks around for somebody to talk to.

The Johnnie Gann Chronicles

One of my favorite newspaper stories was in the *Tri-County Herald*, Daviess County, Missouri. Reporter Mrs. Johnnie Gann reported the following events in Lily Grove, Missouri:

Johnnie Gann bought two cows and two calves from Everett Stith Monday.
Clarence Johnson finished plowing soy beans on Johnnie Gann's farm Tuesday.
Mr. and Mrs. Johnnie Gann started cream at the Lamoni Creamery Company Monday.
Mr. and Mrs. Johnnie Gann visited Mrs. Orpha Kennedy at Kidder Friday.
Johnnie Gann has been cutting and hauling oats and putting them in the barn.
Homer Sutton called, was selling the Watkins products Monday morning.
Mr. and Mrs. Johnnie Gann were in Chillicothe Tuesday afternoon.
Wednesday is the Fourth and people will be going to celebrate somewhere.

Dessert with Jackie O.

I attended only one social event in Washington during my newspaper career. It was memorable.

Because of my newspaper's work with the retarded I was invited to the first international awards dinner of the Joseph P. Kennedy, Jr. Foundation. Dorothy Kilgallen wrote that this would be one of the giant social events of the year "and is probably as close as this republic can get to a command performance."

It meant acquiring a dinner jacket. But I welcomed the chance to see if Burt Lancaster's hair was real and if Judy Garland showed her age. Yes on both counts.

My introduction to Washington society was intimate. Everybody had to line up to get table assignments, and the crush was about as chic as the day after Thanksgiving in the Loop.

I drew Table Sixteen. I was one of the first in the ballroom. The place cards put me between a Mrs. Cushing and Pearl Buck. I quickly tried to remember when I had last read Miss Buck, and figured it was *The Good Earth* thirty years earlier.

Two beautifully dressed women came up to the table as I stood nearby. They read the place cards. One gasped, "We've got to fix this."

The two women shuffled all the cards and vanished. I was now between a Mrs. Mayo and a Dr. Schmidt, and once removed from a Mrs. Smith. One of the card-shuffling ladies turned out to be Mrs. Cushing, who now was as far away from me as the table allowed.

Mrs. Smith walked up, found her place, turned to me and said, "I'm terribly hungry. Are you?" I said I'm an old hand at banquets and had eaten at five o'clock. She turned out to be the President's sister. She wanted to hear all about the retarded kids we helped in the state institutions.

By now all the chairs were occupied. Mrs. Cushing chatted with her chosen companions. A thirty-five-piece orchestra played. Adlai Stevenson was in animated conversation with Lady Bird Johnson. Newton Minow walked by, and Mrs. Mayo at my left informed me the cream of Washington was present.

"That's Judge Bazelon . . . the man with the iron-grey hair," Mrs. Mayo said repeatedly. "We talked with Bobby and Ethel on the way in."

Toward dessert fourteen trumpeters raised their instruments. Adlai patted his remaining hair with both hands, Lady Bird got out her compact and put on lipstick, "Hail to the Chief" blasted out, and the first lady walked in, followed by the President.

Jackie Kennedy wore a simple white gown, with a hairdo that can best be described as carefully organized confusion. She was the most glamorous and one of the most beautiful women I'd ever seen.

The President sat beside his mother. He didn't eat. (He was an old hand at banquets, too.)

Jackie was served a gooey dessert which she ate carefully.

A dozen photographers hovered near. The poor woman couldn't do anything at a place like this without a flash going off. She ate carefully to avoid a picture with her mouth open wide.

After the photographers left, she smoked almost continually, lighting her own cigarettes because Lyndon Johnson was slow on the draw.

The remainder of the evening was like most banquets. I exercised one prerogative denied the President. I sneaked out when Judy Garland began to sing.

A Visit to Sun City

Driving down the residential streets of Sun City at high noon on a September day was spooky. There was no sign of life. Just rows and rows of houses—thousands of them—without a visible human being. No children. No moving cars. No toys on the lawn. No dogs.

Well, it was 105 degrees, and there is a scarcity of mad dogs and Englishmen in this Arizona retirement community.

Somewhere in middle age most of us begin thinking where we want to spend our retirement years. I was on an assignment in Arizona and decided to spend a day at Sun City. Who knows, maybe I'd like to live there some day.

I'd visualized Sun City as a desert oasis with a few thousand old folks doddering around waiting for the inevitable. The vision was wrong. There were more than thirty thousand people in the original section alone which I visited.

There was life in Sun City after noon. In the section to the north, newer residents—mostly in their sixties—were hopping about their busy days, planting cactus in their yards, pedaling to the stores on their three-wheelers, or gliding down the streets in their golf carts.

I watched residents splashing and swimming in one of the mammoth pools. The youngest mermaid may have been in her fifties. I asked a man next to us if he lived in Sun City.

"I'm staying in my brother's house," he said.

"How does he like it here?"

"He loves it, really loves it."

But how about having no young people around?

"Oh, I miss 'em," said our new friend. "I live in Utah on a hill, and the big sport in our neighborhood is to race up the hill on motorcycles with the front wheel in the air. That's what I miss.

"Look, there's no competition here. You can go in the pool if you have crooked legs or a potbelly or spavined knees, and nobody cares, because everybody else has crooked legs. Look at those people. They're contented."

Indeed they were. There's no more healthful sport than swimming, and the people who weren't sunning were swimming easy laps, or floating, or standing in the water talking.

Another vital retirement question: After forty or forty-five years of working, struggling, achieving, being somebody, how do you take a sudden switch to a life the Sun City developers describe as "people living year 'round the way vacationers live for two weeks a year?"

Does a contented existence lie in full-time play, ease, hobbies, sports, travel, recreation, and waiting? In an unnatural community without the laughter and cries of the young?

With no changes in the season? With little rain?

With no challenge?

From observation and conversation, the answer is a positive "yes" from those who chose to end their years in Sun City. Absent from this superficial observation, of course, are those who tried it and moved back home, or those who looked, or took a one-week, reduced-rate sample, and shook their heads "no."

At this stage Sun City had a big hospital, four sprawling medical centers, two newspapers, eighteen restaurants, two lakes, seven golf courses, a flock of churches, a cemetery, and no visible mortuaries. The business was there but I assume the funeral establishments were heavily camouflaged.

If you lived in Sun City the day I visited you'd have had a choice of golf, tennis, swimming, lawn-bowling on the world's first full-sized, synthetic-turfed-lawn bowling green. Also fishing, bowling, table tennis, bridge.

Ladies' gym class met at half past eight, ceramics and knitting at nine; handweavers, art workshop, open sewing from nine to four; canasta club at quarter to one, china painting, ladies' bridge, stag pinochle, and chess at one.

I saw two dogs—a poodle with a red ribbon on its head, and a scroungy old police dog. Both were on leashes.

I was glad to leave, and so was my wife. But maybe we're strange.

Motels

Most motels are clean. Most motels have springy beds, enough towels, hot water, glasses wrapped in wax paper, and paper ribbons saying the toilet seat is sanitized.

Most motels are noisy. Some fortunate humans can sleep through a tornado. Others—I am one—hear every sound in the night. I hear every toilet flush in five rooms in every direction from my bed. I always seem to get a room under Toilet Central, with every flush in the wing roaring through pipes eighteen inches from my pillow.

Noises. Trucks roaring up grades on the Interstate fifty yards from the motel. The guy upstairs doing setting-up exercises in his wooden clogs at 5 A.M. Noisy air conditioners. The dawn buster in the next room who starts his car motor and races it waiting for the Mrs. to get the curlers out of her hair.

The TV sets hitched to the walls in adjoining rooms. The one to the east closes the day with the late late movie and a few hours later the one to the west opens the day with the morning show.

Noises can be interesting when a couple is fighting on the other side of the wall, but incoherent screaming gets monotonous.

Swimming pools are great sleep disrupters. Dripping faucets and running toilets make hypnotic listening at 2 A.M. The worst noise I ever encountered was in Ohio, when the clerk sold us a room which turned out to be directly over the motel's night club. We checked out and found a peaceful, picturesque motel five miles inland at half the price.

Motel smells. The worst is the tobacco stink if you're not a smoker. And many motels have a distinct odor that seems to be a combination of disinfectant and cleaning fluid and whatever other chemicals the housekeepers spray around.

We've had some real surprises checking into motels in strange territory late at night. Once we woke up and found ourselves in a very ethnic resort in the Catskills. We checked into a Days Inn in Fort Lauderdale in the dark and were roused by jets at the International Airport across the street.

Holiday Inns have built a lot of motels around large open spaces they call "fun rooms," or something, which are filled with noisy devices and noisy people and noisy PA systems. Pick your noise—Ping-Pong, videos, electronic games, swimming, jukebox, shuffleboard. In Florida I finally got up at 2 A.M. and asked the desk clerk to please turn off the PA system which was on its eighth or tenth rendition of selections from *My Fair Lady*.

We've tried a few bed and breakfast places and love them. A super place—the White House in Portland, Oregon.

"Take It Off!"

It might help the Supreme Court's effort to define pornography to come along on a visit to a joint in the suburb of Half Day, which once was half-a-day's journey between Chicago and Milwaukee.

"Four dollars, please," says a man in aviator glasses at the door.

Inside, about seventy-five men and a few women sit at small wooden tables. On a stage a woman about twenty-five is bumping and grinding and trying to keep her balance on four-inch platform shoes.

"Take it off!" cries one aroused middle-aged man in a brown plaid sportcoat and orange shirt. He laughs and looks at his buddies for approval.

"Watch those glasses foggin' up, Fred," giggles a man of fifty at another table. The girl gradually removes her clothing but keeps her shoes on. The men, most of whom appear to be visitors to Chicago, punctuate the performance with occasional whistles, cheers, and snorts.

At another table a group of youngish men in business clothes talk among themselves. They keep glancing at the stage, but it seems they don't want the other guys to catch them looking.

A performer named Sonny Skies takes it all off, prances around, then dons a gossamer gown and starts leaping from corner to corner. She looks more like Cloris Leachman than Margot Fonteyn.

She walks off and one hot dog stands up and claps. He is alone in his joy.

The scene has changed little in decades. Same conventioneers, same cracks, same tired broads, the same guy at the door. The main change is that the performing maidens exuded a little more sexuality when the law required them to retain a garment or two.

"Didn't show me nothin' I ain't seen before," yawned a pornography victim with a short haircut as he strolled out.

A Chicago prosecutor remarked, "I think there are enough other problems in America today that pornography is not an issue that outrages a large number of people."

Mostly, it's boring a large number of people.

A Ride in Hitler's Mercedes

In a nation which was goofy over automobiles, and had been deprived of new cars for five years, the arrival in the United States of Adolf Hitler's ceremonial Mercedes Benz after World War II had considerable impact.

A friend, Chris Janus, was looking for ways to raise money for boys' club projects when he heard the Swedish government had Hitler's car. There was a shortage of ball bearings in Sweden. Janus bought $15,000 worth of ball bearings and traded them for the car.

It was shipped to New York, where Janus picked it up to drive back to Illinois. I wrote about the trip for the *Daily News* syndicate. It started with one of the most uncomfortable moments I've had as a reporter. We picked up the car at Radio City, where it had been on exhibit. Chris was to drive it down Broadway with a police motorcycle escort to City Hall, where the mayor would bless it or some such foolishness.

Time to go, and I had no place to ride. "Get in back," Chris motioned. So I sat in the backseat going down Broadway with the top down and the sirens blasting. I felt like an absolute idiot.

The trip to Illinois took several days. There were no expressways then. In Pittsburgh we wanted some motor service, but we couldn't drive into the garage because they felt the car was so heavy it would go through the floor.

Apart from its symbolism, Hitler's car was an astounding piece of mechanism. It was 236 inches long, weighed 7,500 pounds, plus 2,000 pounds of armour, plus another 500 pounds for fuel and coolant.

The engine was a supercharged straight eight, developing 155 horsepower without the supercharger, 230 horsepower with it.

The special phaeton body was comparable to an American seven-passenger touring car. It had two seats in front, two jump seats, and two rear seats, all in rich black leather. The window glass was an inch and a half thick.

The right front seat folded back and a small platform came in place on the floor. Hitler stood on it during parades, grasping a specially installed post with one hand and giving Nazi salutes with the other. On the inside of the right front door was a compartment for a Luger pistol.

A leather-covered sheet of armor cranked up and down behind the front seat. When this armor and all the windows were up, the car was bulletproof except for the top.

When the car was delivered Janus was handed thirteen keys. In addition to thirteen keyholes, the car had forty-five switches, dials, buttons, levers, and meters. But neither Janus nor the Mercedes mechanics could start the car after it was taken off the ship in New York.

The car was ignominiously towed to a Mercedes garage by a vehicle half its size and with no pedigree at all. The mechanics finally found a secret switch behind the dashboard.

Janus sent the Mercedes Benz plant the car's motor number, and they responded that the car had been custom made for the German dictator. Hitler inspected the car while it was being made, and suggested a number of changes. He became quite a nuisance to the engineers and they were glad to see the car go out their door.

It was used principally for state occasions, but Hitler drove several times to Berchtesgaden with Goering, Goebbels, and Eva Braun. Hitler was not overly fond of driving, but the sense of power he got from the Mercedes was said to exhilarate him.

He is believed to have driven the car more than 100 miles an hour once with Goebbels, who was frightened by the speed. Goering, on the other hand, had more confidence in the Führer and encouraged him to drive fast and use the supercharger.

The car attracted crowds wherever we went. Mechanics, clerks, housewives, businessmen, youngsters, truck drivers, war veterans, would stand gazing at it. They seemed to think if we couldn't get Hitler, getting his car was next best.

The trip from New York to Illinois was interesting but relatively uneventful. The only feeling I got while driving the car was nervousness that I might wreck it.

Janus brought along a driver who said he had a good working

knowledge of Mercedes cars. I asked what he would do if the car broke down.

"It won't break down," he answered. "But if it did I've got a book called *Betriebsanleitung für Nergededes Benz Personenwagen.*"

Then he confessed he couldn't read German.

Fortunately the car did not break down.

God's Many Voices

Broadcast pitches for money were small potatoes before the Falwells and Roberts and Swaggarts discovered television's appeal. In 1959 a radio preacher invited listeners to write him, so I did. The letter in return, from the Reverend Bishop M. E. Holmes, read:

"Dear Member and Radio Friend: As I come into your vibration, I am impressed to see you, because there is a condition that surrounds you. This condition causes you and your loved ones to be unsuccessful in all your endeavors.

"As your friend and Spiritual Guide, I want you to bring this letter and $7 for each of the Seven Evils which prevail against you. As a donation, also bring one purse hair comb."

When I failed to show up with my $7 and purse hair comb, Bishop Holmes wrote again:

"I will be flying down to Algiers, Louisiana, for a special oil for all of my very close friends. This special oil will cost $300 per bottle, but all I ask of you is to pay me $10 down. This is the greatest chance you have had this year. All I say is once you have this oil you will thank me for the rest of your life, for this is it.

"As a last request, if you have to borrow this sum of $10 be sure you do this because as your Spiritual Guide I know you can't go wrong. Even if you have to pawn something for the $10 down payment, do that, and you will get out of the rut you are in."

My wife and I, for reasons I haven't tried to analyze, often watch TV evangelists when we're on the road in motel rooms. I was in the shower one day in Florida when my wife called, "Hey, here's a new one. This man says he was cured at home by laying his hands on the TV set."

We've seen countless people swoon backwards into the arms of evangelists' assistants when the preacher laid hands on their foreheads, but this was the first preacher—one Reverend Ernest Angley—who appeared to be healing through the tube.

I rushed out of the shower and prepared to give this healing a shot, and my wife said she'd catch me. Unfortunately, this was a rare moment in my life when there was nothing physically wrong with me except an advanced case of wrinkles. I did not attempt to cure them via TV.

I first became aware of the Reverend Jerry Falwell when a reader sent me a letter from Falwell:

"I am personally very grateful for your Faith Partner Commitment. Because you and other friends answered my plea, Chicken, I now believe we will be able to keep 'The Old Time Gospel Hour' on nearly all our present stations."

The Reverend Falwell's warm, personalized greeting to Chicken went on, promising, among other goodies, a frank talk about homosexuality.

The computer which produced this warm, personal letter to Cobb's Chicken Take Out in Grand Haven, Michigan, had managed to contort the salutation into "Chicken Take O. Cobbs" and "Dear Chicken."

The evangelists' computers weren't very choosy, because I seemed to be on the mailing lists of most of the big money collectors. I never received a letter that didn't threaten some catastrophic consequence if I didn't respond fast with money. They were basically refinements of Bishop Holmes' Forty-seventh Street storefront.

The Reverend Oral Roberts wrote me in 1980 about his now-famous meeting with Jesus—the nine hundred-foot version.

The Reverend Mr. Roberts said he was standing near the construction site of the City of Faith, the gigantic hospital and medical center he was building in Tulsa.

"I felt an overwhelming holy presence all around me," wrote the Reverend Mr. Roberts. "When I opened my eyes, there He stood—some 900 feet tall, looking at me; His eyes—Oh! His eyes! He stood a full 300 feet taller than the 600-foot tall City of Faith. There I was face to face with Jesus Christ, the Son of the Living God.

"I have only seen Jesus once before, but here I was face to face with the King of Kings. He stared at me without saying a word. Oh! I will never forget those eyes! And then, He reached down, put

His hands under the City of Faith, lifted it, and said to me, 'See how easy it is for Me to lift it?'"

Jesus then put the City of Faith back on its foundation and discussed the completion of the building with the Reverend Mr. Roberts, whose problem was a cash shortage to pay the workmen.

Jesus advised the Reverend Mr. Roberts, "Tell your partners to obey what I speak in their hearts, and I will send my angels to stop the devil from stealing their money."

So the Reverend Mr. Roberts wrote us partners to ask for "a Precious Seed to help me pay the bills." Precious Seeds came in denominations of five, ten, and twenty dollars.

Seven years later the Reverend Roberts topped his Jesus sighting with a message straight from God that if the Reverend Roberts didn't raise $8 million, his earthly life would terminate.

There is said to be a core of about 1.4 million American people who respond to this kind of appeal from evangelists who claim they are in direct contact with God. The fact that God seems to be sending contradictory messages to different denominations doesn't bother them. When the Reverend Mr. Roberts was kneeling in his Prayer Tower pleading for his eight million dollars, I suspect that the Reverend Jimmy Swaggart and a few other competitors for the evangelical dollar were praying that the Reverend Roberts would fall short a million or two.

The Springfield Tapes

It's never been officially determined who planted the bug in the Springfield hotel room of the lobbyists for the Chicago currency exchanges. All that remains of that great state scandal is an informative and entertaining text on lobbying and bribery.

Three of the lobbyists were sitting around the room complaining that they couldn't trust the legislators they bribe.

"You see, I wouldn't care if they would take and divide it up the way they should, but they try to cheat each other, and we are the victims," wailed Dave Maslowsky, known as "the grand old man of the currency exchanges."

The problem was that they would give, say, five thousand dollars to the chairman of a key committee with the understanding the chairman would split it with the members. They were complaining that the chairman might keep the money himself because he controlled the votes without buying them.

> MASLOWSKY: Let me give you some background. Sam wants to talk to some of these members and then promises the guy to give him $200. Then he says he gave him $500. What the hell you going to do about that?
> LOBBYIST SAM KAPLAN: Yah . . . he wants a finder's fee. Ha Ha.

Irv Gottlieb, president of the currency exchange association, spoke of an encounter with some Republican legislators who, for the most part, were harder to buy.

> GOTTLIEB: Say Dave, you won't yell at me if I tell you who I was with last night . . . listen to this . . . John Henry Kleine, Clint Youle, Sam Oughton, Hope McCormick, Parkhurst, Mrs. Meany . . .
> MASLOWSKY: All the rubbish.
> GOTTLIEB: I said let's get the hell out of here. How did I get mixed up with all these [obscenities] Republicans . . . the worst kind.
> MASLOWSKY: A good portion of the expenses is Powell and Choate, and I love it when they tell me they'll just leave it to my judgment.

Paul Powell was speaker of the house and later secretary of state, and the most powerful Democrat in the legislature. The conversations indicated Powell was given ten thousand dollars to distribute to some legislators as bribes to vote against a bill that would have helped the currency exchanges' competition.

When Powell died, $8 million in cash was found in shoe boxes in the closet of the hotel room where he lived in Springfield.

The lobbyists were contemptuous of those they couldn't buy.

Gottlieb complained to Maslowsky that they had been asked not to be too visible at a House gala dinner.

> GOTTLIEB: If you don't want to go, fine, but I'm gonna go, and you can go to . . . now wait a minute, I have an

arrangement . . . I have an arrangement to have Katz at our table (Katz was an honest Democratic legislator).

MASLOWSKY: [Obscenity, obscenity] Katz.

GOTTLIEB: Sure, you don't need him this year, you may need him another year.

MASLOWSKY: He won't be here another year. . . . No, it wouldn't be a benefit because the (obscenity) would never do the right thing. . . . He just doesn't think that you people think straight. That's what I find wrong with guys like Mikva. (Representative Abner Mikva now is a judge in the United States Appellate Court in Washington.)

One lobbyist said, "What you may as well get used to is that every time you have a legislative session, you come prepared with about $50,000 . . . and if you haven't got it . . .

Said a second lobbyist: "Forget it."

Maslowsky to Kaplan on golf parties: "Waner says just tell him that . . . uh . . . I should tell him that . . . uh . . . it's all right for him to vote this way and I hope he does and that . . . uh . . . then we owe him $200 worth of tickets for the golf party and of course we know the sonuvabitch will keep it. So prepare yourself to be circumcised and don't . . . say, let's go down and get a bowl of soup."

The Polish members of the House were having a party.

I don't know any newspaperman who was subpoenaed more than I was by grand juries, trial court prosecutors and defense, governing boards, legislative committees, liquor control commissions, athletic commissions, and whatnot.

The top photo is at the Illinois state legislative commission investigating my evidence of large scale bribery in the legislature. Mostly they tried to find out how I got the information.

Below, the Illinois Athletic Commission subpoenaed me after I exposed the fixing of a major heavyweight fight. All I could tell them was what we'd already printed. One fighter took a dive for $6,000. The commissioners clucked their tongues and did nothing. Wendell Smith, a pioneer black Chicago journalist, is at the left, and Joe Rein, associate sports editor of the Daily News, *is at the right.*

GOTTLIEB: Who's bringing the liquor?
MASLOWSKY: I don't know. They're buying their own liquor.
GOTTLIEB: I thought you said we're buying it.
MASLOWSKY: They're buying, we're paying for it.
KAPLAN: Open bar for cocktails at six o'clock. That food'll kill you.

I found these tapes in a locker at the Greyhound bus depot. The legislature spent a couple of years subpoenaing me to try to find who bugged the room. In 1974, nine years after the tapes, the federal government indicted ten current or former legislators and eight other persons on charges of giving or receiving bribes for votes.

The Best State

We Illinoisans grow used to slurs about the Rust Belt and the Sucker State, and we don't really see ourselves as one of the glamorous places on the map.

Yet we have a nice distinction that the other forty-nine may envy. Thirty years ago a prominent naturalist, Donald Culross Peattie surveyed all fifty states, visiting forty-five of them, and wrote an article in the Sunday *New York Times* calling Illinois "the best state of the fifty."

The attractions which generated this opinion still prevail.

"Illinois is the best state because it is so American," Peattie, a Californian, wrote. "It is heartland."

He anticipated protest and ridicule: "What's so good about Illinois?" "Chicago has the worst crime rate in the world!" (Untrue.)

Here is more from his story.

Illinois is beautiful as only a great fertile plain can be beautiful. It has the beauty of plainness that Thoreau would have understood, and which three of its poets gave voice to—Carl Sandburg, Vachel Lindsay, and Edgar Lee Masters.

"Some of the towns are true gems," Peattie said. "I'd pick St. Charles on the Fox River for simple and mellowed beauty. I'd call Galena a positive museum piece.

"I sometimes wish I lived in one of the old towns on the Mississippi, where the gulls make it seem like a seaport."

Peattie loved the old-timeness of Illinois towns, with streets shaded in elms and their yards never fenced against neighbors, while children ran in and out of each other's frame houses.

Illinois is the least touristical of the states, he said, pointing out that we rarely billboard our attractions. "Illinois is just itself, soliciting nobody." (Governor Thompson may latch on to this essay and use it to billboard the state).

Peattie saw the lofty, virgin-white pine groves. He expressed sorrow for the visitor who fails to see Starved Rock with its wild primroses, or Ganymede Spring, "the best, the coldest water I ever tasted" as it comes rushing, crystalline, from the base of a famous bluff, Eagle's Nest.

He loved the Lincoln Country. Peattie never saw a better job of restoration than that of New Salem.

He loved the sounds of frogs and birds in Illinois.

"Camp out on some hillock where swamp and orchard and prairie grass meet, you will hear full more than half of the species of land birds of eastern North America—the wild telegraphy of crows, the 'flick-up wick-up' of flickers, the golden rolling call of orioles, the jingling doorbell of redwings."

Typically Illinoisan, he said, were the canteens set up in railroad stations during the war. No official-sounding organizations or social groups ran them—just mothers whose only aim was to serve the uniformed sons of other parents.

"Corny?" Peattie asked. "If you like. You could call Florence Nightingale corny, or Clara Barton, or Walt Whitman. Illinois *is* corny. It produces the best corn grown in this country, or anywhere in the world."

People

A Talk with Saul Bellow

One of my most satisfying interviews was with Saul Bellow. After the *Tribune* named his *Herzog* Book of the Year my editor told me to talk with Chicago's best known author. Bellow was on the University of Chicago faculty, was known to dislike interviews, and was inaccessible. I phoned his office, and was very surprised when he returned the call.

It turned out he read my column. I can only guess that he thought I caught the flavor of Chicago, and it was useful in his writing about Chicago. Anyway, he said he was coming to the Loop the next day and would stop in. Some of Bellow's observations:

"It's common for a writer to be either lavishly acclaimed or totally ignored. I will say this is a success far beyond anything I ever projected or wanted. And once it's started, there's no way to control it."

Bellow's joy was in the actual writing of his books. He wryly stood aside from the promotional foolishness and social acclaim that normally accompany great literary success.

He was invited to attend the Presidential inaugural ceremonials, but didn't accept. When I asked why, his answer was carefully measured.

"I, ah . . . didn't want to get in the whirl especially. I don't think a writer should get too much involved as a cultural ornament of the administration. It just didn't attract me very much to be in the milieu of power.

"I did it once. I attended a Kennedy dinner in the White House when Malraux was here. I enjoyed that one. I got a taste of glamor.

"But the next day I realized the President had spent the whole evening talking to David Rockefeller about fiscal matters. I didn't get to find out the Presidential views on the future of the novel."

Our conversation was quite comfortable, I think, because we were both city guys, grew up in the center of the city, and considered ourselves streetwise, relatively. He grew up in the Humboldt Park area. I asked if he found the Chicago atmosphere particularly creative.

"Not very. That's one reason I like it here. I don't like the literary atmosphere in the East. Like any kid from the sticks, I had to take on New York, and the avant-garde.

"But after you pit your youthful energies against the place, gotten what satisfaction you can from it, you get tired of cocktail parties and gossip and backbiting and the inbreeding. You find you know no one but publishers and other writers and actors and artists.

"Chicago doesn't have as much real culture as I'd like, but in Chicago you can have a broad range of acquaintances. Here I can go where I like. You know, the American struggle to become a writer disfigures a lot of men. There is no clearly established place in American society for a writer, so he must create one. Sometimes he'll work so hard at this that he forgets how to write."

When Bellow starts a book, is it his intention to please the public, the critics, the book clubs, or himself?

"Well, none of those really. When I set out to write *Herzog* I had a good reputation, but I was used to writing for not too much reward.

"For three years I stayed in that room, running the book around and around in my head as if it were a prayer wheel, making it as good as I could. The most satisfaction I got from *Herzog* was writing it.

"Now I have no clear idea why *Herzog* should be on top of that list. I'm willing to accept any reasonable explanation.

"There is one satisfaction I do experience now . . . getting letters from people who have read it. I get a great many letters, and I think people have been moved by the book. I do have a sense of relevance at having reached so many people deeply.

"Of course in this best-seller business, I think a book acquires momentum when highbrow critics praise it. Many people buy it, and I'm sure a lot of them don't finish the book."

What's next?

"I'm not concerned what I do next. I'm too much of a pro for that. I can always write. I've been at this since I was a young man. Whatever glamor there is faded about ten years ago."

I'm sure Bellow did not anticipate his participation in the ultimate in glamor, the Nobel Prize ceremonies.

The Ultimate Hedonist

When I was writing sports in the early fifties at the *Chicago Daily News* a harried-looking young man in a frayed shirt came to the office and introduced himself. He said he had left *Esquire* and started a new magazine. Would I be interested in writing sports for *Playboy*?

He said he liked my writing, so I figured he was a smart editor. He showed me his first issue, with the nude picture of Marilyn Monroe in the centerfold. I suggested that I write under the name Jay Arnold.

I dropped off my articles at his near north apartment, and he sent me $100 for each one.

I liked Hugh Hefner. We had some things in common—both products of the state university, both journalists, both worked on the college paper, both relatively broke and raising young families.

In 1962 he sent a substantial contribution to my fund for retarded children, with a note, "An incredible lot has happened to us both in the seven or so years since our first meeting."

Our paths did diverge. Today I live in a suburban ranch house and he lives in a thirty-room mansion in Beverly Hills. He has

Mercedes limos in his garage and I have an aging Buick Century. Hef is with his thousandth or two thousandth or whatever woman companion and says he is the happiest man alive. I am in my forty-eighth year with my only wife, and wouldn't trade places with any person alive.

He told a friend of mine that not every woman he meets succumbs to his charms, but he has scored in the thousands, and enjoys his reputation.

"I have built here what could be viewed as a perpetual woman machine," he said to Bob Greene. "I don't go night after night looking for a new woman, but the women are here." Right. I saw thirty or so bunnies hippity-hopping around his mansion whenever I ventured inside.

Asked about his conquests, Hefner said, "Women, although they say they like a faithful and monogamous man, are very attracted to a man who has . . . had a lot of romantic experiences. The more experienced you are, the more desirable you are to a woman."

It also helps to be rich and live in a thirty-room mansion.

Now that Hef has cracked the big six-oh I believe he still feels in possession of his powers and is looking toward a fulfilled decade as a sexagenarian. (Will he still be chasing bunnies when he's eighty?)

Whatever his reputation today, Hefner was a very bright young editor, and a hard worker. He was years ahead of his peers in sensing what the public would accept.

His nudes led the way for imitators whose excesses and vulgarity made *Playboy* look like *Business Week*.

After Hefner purchased the Chicago mansion and moved his bunnies and a huge retinue into the place, I felt sorry for him. He rarely left the building. He had a huge bedroom with a circular bed and an endless supply of bedmates, though he tended to stick with one individual, like Barbi Benton, for a period of months or a year or two.

He ignored the clock, drew the shades, and slept and worked when the impulse moved him. During the street rioting at the 1968 Democratic Convention curiosity finally moved him out of his bedroom. He got dressed and ventured into the streets with a male companion. I was otherwise occupied in the rioting that night, but I understood that he encountered some uncouth demonstrators who either took a swipe at him or connected with a nonlethal blow. Anyway, he scooted back to his hutch and I don't think he emerged again until he climbed on his black jet and flew to California.

The magazine thrived while he personally supervised every word and picture that went into it. Other ventures faltered. A costly new magazine, *Show Business Illustrated,* failed, and the *Playboy* clubs got into financial trouble when they lost the take from the London gambling operation.

Hef was and is proud of his women, but he also has immense pride in one woman who has never appeared unclothed in *Playboy,* and who I think is more attractive than any woman who has graced his centerfold or bedroom.

His daughter Christie, who was a Phi Beta Kappa at Brandeis University, is immensely gifted and as personally as quiet and conservative as Hef is flamboyant. She is the top executive at *Playboy*. She has a brother who may be equally gifted, but is not as visible as Christie.

The children are a product of Hefner's marriage—the institution he discarded in favor of "living out my adolescent dreams as a kind of surrogate for a large part of the population."

So be it. To me, his greater achievement was fathering a daughter like Christie. Being a hedonist, he might have trouble understanding that.

George Halas

When George Halas, coach and owner of the Chicago Bears, was seventy, I visited him and asked questions.

Do you have a special source for your personal energy?
"Oh, nothing of consequence. I'll tell you . . . and you don't need to print this . . . but every morning I have a glass of water with a few drops of lemon. Kind of cleans out the pipes. Then a big glass of orange juice later, followed by coffee.

"But the main thing is instead of tearing out to lunch, I knock off in the middle of the day, get a thirty-minute nap. You know, I learned that from Thomas E. Wilson. Here was a man of eighty still running a big packing business. I just couldn't get over his freshness and vigor."

Is there a difference between generations of young men in character, ability, attitude, drive, and size?
"Wow! Gee, when you think in terms of Joe Kopcha . . . how he fought so hard to get that medical degree. He started us on our M.D.s, you know. He's a gynecologist in Gary now. Then there were Dr. Fortman and Bill McColl.

"I'll tell you. The guys today can exceed as far as playing ability is concerned. They're bigger, and have more speed. But only a few of them today . . . no, make that none of them today can exceed the men of yesterday in team spirit, in desire to play. These fellows were ferocious.

"For many years we had a maximum of eighteen players on a squad, and I was taking my life in my hands to make a substitution. These guys wanted to play, both ways, offense and defense. Now we have specialists. Who's the last one played both ways . . . I guess it was George Connor. There's a *man*."

What was the low point in your life?
"Uh, in 1932 we won the championship and lost $18,000 for the season. I ran out of money. I don't know if you remember those days . . . I couldn't get anything from the bank. I'd already taken my kids' savings accounts. I had to pay fellows like Nagurski and Grange with thousand-dollar notes."

Who were the great ones?
"Jim Thorpe. That fellow with Green Bay . . . became a baseball umpire . . . whatsisname? . . . That's it, Cal Hubbard. What a guy

he was! I'd be in the line and look up and see that man!

"And there was a fellow not too well known, but what an end he was. Ed Healy. Dartmouth, and then he played with Rock Island. We were playing them once, and I kind of took him out, and he got so mad he took a swing at me while I was lying on the ground. I moved my head or he would have killed me. His fist went six inches into the ground. Of course it was kind of muddy. I figured I wanted a man like that on my side, so we bought him for $100. We're close friends today . . . he has a farm out near Elkhart."

What is the best time in a person's life?

"Gee . . . right now. I'm enjoying it more than ever. That's right. I was seventy on Groundhog Day.

"Age is a state of mind, and my mind's fresh.

"I certainly didn't have any fun going to college at Champaign. I was on the varsity football, basketball, and baseball teams and taking engineering. I remember I was saving everything up for that last semester . . . light schedule . . . that was the semester Halas was going to have fun. And the war broke out and I had to cram and I got my degree in three and a half years and was in the Navy instead of in that glorious last semester."

I've written several times that Halas is a good loser.

"Well, that's for the public. Boy, I hate to lose. But there's no use alibi-ing."

Stanley Yankus

"The triumph of evil is possible when enough good men do nothing."   —*Edmund Burke, speaking to Parliament*

I first read that quotation on the wall of a farmhouse in Dowagiac, Michigan, several years before it became popularized in the sixties. Stanley Yankus, the farmer, was one of the most principled and admirable persons I ever met.

Yankus was the son of Lithuanian emigrants. He grew up in Chicago, worked in the stock yards and saved enough for a down payment on a $2,800 farm in Michigan.

He overcame a city man's ignorance of farming with sweat equity. When he was forty, in 1959, he farmed 100 acres. He had 5,000 chickens, and each week trucked about 12,000 eggs to a

That snake is as dangerous as a large worm, which accounts for my relaxed expression. I was with Marlin Perkins, then director of Chicago's Lincoln Park Zoo, bagging snakes in Louisiana bayou country. My attitude toward rattlesnakes was quite different. I stayed behind Perkins as we went through the swamps. When Perkins saw a rattlesnake, he went to it, held its head down with a forked stick, reached down, picked it up just behind the head, and stuck it in a bag secured to his waist. What guts he had.

wholesaler in Benton Harbor. This grossed up to $26,000 a year and netted $1,000 to $6,000 in 1959 dollars. That went to buy machinery.

Yankus puffed a cigar as he talked to me in his living room. (He read that cigar smokers don't commit suicide.)

"I experimented with different grains and found wheat and barley were best to use as feed," he related. "My 100 acres is divided into four fields, and I alternate wheat and barley. I grow about thirty-five acres of wheat a year, and give it all to the chickens. I also buy about $12,000 worth of chicken feed a year.

"My problem with the government isn't very complicated. In 1953 a man came into my farmyard and told me I couldn't grow wheat to feed my chickens.

"He said the government would let me grow only fifteen acres. I need at least thirty-five to feed the chickens.

"He said he'd fine me and show me I had to sign up with the program. I said if he fined me for just growing grain to feed my stock the people of America would rise up. They wouldn't let a thing like that happen."

It did happen. The government seized Yankus's bank accounts and fined him $5,000, which he had to pay or have his machinery confiscated.

"Now I could have signed up for this program," Yankus said. "That would have been easy. I'd grow less wheat, and the government would give me free money—much more money than I paid in fines.

"But I think that is wrong. It's as simple as that.

"I was brought up to make my own living. I have worked hard. All I ask is that I be allowed to make an honest living. I don't want government subsidies. I was not allowed to vote on them.

"As long as I live I've got to choose between right and wrong. I'm not going to stop now. Somewhere a man has to stand up and be counted. I have a choice of conforming, of taking public money for doing nothing, or of sticking to my principles.

"I can't surrender."

Yankus's day began at seven when he went to the big barn to clean the water fountains and mix feed. At the same time his wife started collecting eggs from the nests. They both worked in the barn, the fields, the garden, and the house until supper. After eating, Yankus and his wife, and their two older sons, thirteen and eleven, went to the egg room to wash, candle, weigh, and package the day's collection of eggs.

This routine went on every day of the year, including Christmas, Fourth of July, and everybody's birthday. They never took a vacation or a single day off. Their farmhouse was large and clean but the front porch was walled in and converted into an egg processing facility. Yankus was a good neighbor, served on the school board, belonged to the farm bureau.

"I've known all about the farm program," he told me. "My neighbors said I used poor judgment, that I was a fool not to sign up and get money while I could. All you have to do is stick your hand out and get it, they said.

"Well, I said you go ahead and get it. Maybe I'm not smart in grabbing all I can. But I honestly believe that if other people don't think the way I do, the country will be in serious trouble.

"It's got to stop somewhere. Everybody seems to have his hand out. Sooner or later we reach the point where everybody's getting something for nothing. Then who pays?

"I can't conscientiously leave a heritage like this for my children."

Yankus called the auctioneer and sold his farm. "I'm going to Australia with my family. I picked that country because one of my magazines listed all the nations by the amount of socialism they have, and Australia had the least.

"How does my wife react? She's full of fear. The older boy is like me—he likes a little adventure. The younger one is like his mother. He wants to stay. But we're going."

It would be nice to report that Stanley Yankus went to Australia and became a successful farmer. He wrote me ten years after he moved. "I'm doing all right. I learned how to provide my own living in Michigan, and I've learned how to provide my own living in the land down under.

"No harm has come my way—I'm not living in the midst of riots and violence. No bureaucrat or politician has been able to subvert one unfailing law—as ye sow, so shall ye reap."

Yankus worked as a salesman, kept a garden, saved money, and dreamed of having enough to buy a small farm. Finally in 1978 he closed a deal to buy a ten-acre almond farm thirty miles south of Adelaide.

Plans for his new house were due at his home when he died of a heart attack. He was fifty-nine.

Jane Addams

"During World War I, peace was Jane Addams's goal. It was in the lives of her neighbors at Hull House that she first had the conviction there could be peace in the world. For here all different nationalities, all different religions were able to live together as good neighbors."

I never met Jane Addams, but I knew Jessie Binford, her close friend. I asked Miss Binford to tell me about Jane Addams.

"Two weeks before her death, she was given a great ovation in Washington," Miss Binford recounted. "This is what she said in reply:

" 'I do not know any such person as is described here this

I did a nightly half-hour radio program on WBBM for two years with Fahey Flynn, reading a magazine here while I do the interview. Fahey was Chicago's all-time favorite newscaster, and a dear friend. He was sometimes criticized for being nothing but a newsreader, which he was. He figured that's what he was hired to do. But privately he was an educated, literate, sophisticated person whose erudition was not done justice in his chosen vocation. A former schoolteacher, he became wealthy when he changed vocations and read news.

evening. I think I have never met her. We all know much worse things about ourselves than anyone has ever said or printed about us. I have never been sure I was right. I have often been doubtful about the next step. We can only feel our way as we go from day to day. But I thank you all.'

"The world mourned her death," Miss Binford continued. "Her funeral was held at her home, and Hull House was her home.

"I remember an old Greek man who wanted to know what church she would be buried from. Catholic? Protestant? A synagogue? Greek Orthodox? Then he realized: 'At her home. Yes. She was all religions.'

"Thousands came to the funeral. I remember that Graham Taylor said, 'If you would see Jane Addams's monuments, look into the faces about you here.' And how true. For it was the people that counted to her, and it was her effect on people that mattered.

"She came to live in this neighborhood, one of the poorest. To her, Hull House was a home, not an agency, not an institution. And she was known as a good neighbor. Everybody felt she understood them.

"I remember an Italian woman who saw some beautiful roses Miss Addams had set on the table. The woman exclaimed, 'How did you ever keep those roses so fresh all the way from Italy?'

"You see, this woman had been a year in Chicago, but she had never seen a rose here.

"Miss Addams started reading clubs, a music school, weaving classes. But she managed all this without making Hull House an organized institution. She never had an office. She was never too busy to speak with someone. She had no staff. We were part of her household.

"People who met her once never forgot her, so great an effect did she have on them. After her funeral, I met a cabbie who asked if I knew her. He said, 'I did too, but I never saw her but once in my life.'

" 'When I was a kid selling papers near Union Station, a man asked me to deliver an important envelope to Jane Addams.

" 'I took a streetcar to Hull House. The door was open. I was a little frightened when they told me she was upstairs. I said I had to deliver the message direct.

" 'She had a warm fire in the grate. She didn't ask me who I was, or why was I out so late, or did my mother know, or why wasn't I in school. She talked to me like a grown-up, a person she cared about. Then she took me to the door and said goodbye. When I got a block away I started crying.' "

Said Miss Binford: "You see, she talked to him, probably for the first time in his life, just as though he were a real person. That's what she could do to people. It's hard to explain. But that cabbie, a middle-aged man, said as we drove to Hull House he just couldn't believe she was dead.

"I remember one forlorn little girl who had an illegitimate child. Miss Addams talked to her and gave just as much profound thinking, just as much attention to that little girl's grief, as though it were an international problem.

"Because to her it was an international problem. Everyone's life was so significant, significant enough to give it the very best attention. I have never felt such a profound mind.

"A short time ago, I talked to a group of social workers and I tried to express to them what really made Jane Addams so great.

"It was the feeling she gave to people. The feeling she understood exactly what made them what they were, whether they were the privileged rich or the beaten down.

"She understood."

Seeking the Magic of Billy Graham

6:25: The Great Hall of McCormick Place is an incredible sight as 35,000 chairs cover it from wall to wall. It seems like twenty football fields side by side.

Spectators already are filing in to hear Billy Graham. The last hammers hit nails. The PA system booms "Testing. Testing. One two three four." A staff member adds plastic ferns to the plastic flowers banking the podium with remarkably vivid hues.

6:40: "No, we didn't set up the chairs," says a McCormick Place maintenance man. "They were delivered Tuesday by chair rental outfits. Volunteers set them up. You should have heard them sing!"

7:03: Two thousand singers mass in stands behind the podium. Cliff Barrows apologizes for having to rehearse the choir. "I hope the rehearsal will be a blessing," he says.

7:07: I settle in a seat halfway back in the hall. A trim young girl walks by. She wears purple hot pants and a button reading, "Join the JESUS Revolution."

7:20: Half the people arrive carrying Bibles. Every character ever painted by Norman Rockwell, and all their relatives, are here.

7:35: In the special section for the deaf, fingers and hands waggle in spirited conversation. Behind them, headsets are adjusted by people in the sections labeled "Chinese" and "Español."

7:40: George Beverly Shea raises his arms. "Let us all join in singing 'All Hail the Power of Jesus' Name,' printed on the back page of your program." His baritone booms and the congregation sings loud. Most people don't have to look at the words.

7:45: The governor of Illinois states, "On behalf of the eleven million people in Illinois I am delighted to welcome Billy Graham. Tonight you are going to listen to one of the most important men in the entire world. I urge everyone who can to attend personally, and to listen, to testify, and to go forth."

8:05: I walk to the far corner of the hall as Myrtle Hall testifies in song. She is just a dot, about half a mile across a sea of chairs and heads. But every word is clear. She finishes and a man starts talking. He is almost invisible at that distance, but every syllable is clear.

I walk back to my chair. Billy Graham is speaking. "This is the first Crusade we ever started on a Thursday night. I was asked why. Well, we're paying the rent anyway, we might as well use the hall." I think he went on early for five minutes to accommodate the TV cameras' need for footage on the ten o'clock news. "I'll be back to preach," Graham promises.

8:11: Herbert J. Taylor, honorary chairman of the Crusade committee, talks finances. The budget is $540,000. "Where your treasure is, there will your heart be also," says Mr. Taylor. The ushers pass little white boxes for contributions. I fill out a small pledge to be charged to BankAmericard, on a form supplied in the program.

8:20: "Blessed Assurance, Jesus is Mine" is sung by the entire assemblage. The governor doesn't have to look at the words.

8:25: "I'm going to ask that we bow our heads in prayer," Billy Graham says softly. "Shall we pray?"

Then: "How many can't hear me? Lift your hand. We're doing very well. I see three hands. I guess the rest didn't hear the question.

"We are going to read from the twelfth chapter of the Book of Hebrews. I hope you bring your Bible every night. The Bible is going to be my text book. Not what the sociologists say. We've heard that. Not what the professors say. We've heard that. Not what the politicians say. We've heard that. What the *Bible* says!"

The words pour out, every syllable clear and loud. The acoustical system is superb. It allows Graham to stand back on the platform, gesture, turn to all sides.

I was there to try to understand the power of Billy Graham. I stop taking notes to try to better absorb what he is saying.

He talks about playing golf with Bob Hope and Glen Campbell. "I don't know what I was doing in that company," he says. "But you know . . . there was a young caddy there. That caddy came over to me and said, 'Brother Graham, do you think we could slip away for a few words of prayer?' Ten years ago you wouldn't have heard anything like that.

"Young people are marching for Christ! Young people are asking, What is the purpose of my existence? Why am I on this planet? I am at the mercy of chance. Do you know that one of every four songs of young people today talks of death or eternity?

"I want to tell you, God made you in His image. He gave you a purpose, and He gave you hope for eternity, because He loves you and He did it through Jesus Christ!"

Graham's voice lowers as he speaks of a businessman shot by a sniper in Chicago the previous day. "Now I don't know why he was shot, but I have an idea. He was riding in a Mercedes-Benz, and he was a have, and he was shot by a have-not."

Human nature hasn't changed, Graham said. Thirty-eight thousand coffee spoons were stolen from the Americana hotel in New York the previous year. Over 3 billion dollars worth of goods were pilfered.

"You must repent of sin! You must take Jesus! You have to be willing to turn from your sin—give it up. That's repentance.

"You must accept things that your intellect stumbles over. But your intellect has been visited by sin. You must do it publicly. Are you willing to say openly and publicly, 'I receive Christ?'

"Make this great and glorious commitment tonight and settle it forever. God is saying tonight, I am willing to come and live in your heart, and this is the start of a new life. You may say, Lord, I don't understand it all, but I repent, and I accept Your Son.

"In accepting Christ, you must read and study. You will receive Bibles. You must pray. God will answer your prayers. He may say yes. He may say no. He may say wait. But He will answer.

"You must witness. How? By a smile on your face. Rejoice! Look like a Christian. Act like a Christian. Go out of your way to make friends with a person of another race.

"And go to church."

Several hundred people walk to the front to receive Christ. Counselors attend them. Billy Graham walks to his seat. The service is over.

When Nixon was president, before Watergate, he came to the Tribune to meet with the editors and managers. I put on a coat and tie and sat one chair removed from the president. It made for nice pictures and something to tell the kids about, but if Nixon said anything worth remembering, I don't remember it.

The Least Interesting President

Many American presidents' reputations are better in historical perspective than they were in the White House. Eisenhower is increasingly appreciated for his low-key managerial style, his foresight in anticipating the arms buildup, and for the general well-being of the nation while he was in office. Observers took potshots at Ike because of his convoluted syntax, but now it appears that the sly President deliberately talked to reporters in twisted and tortured sentences to put them off. He knew exactly what he was saying—and what he didn't want to say.

As Watergate fades in memory Nixon's achievements in foreign relations counterbalance the Watergate negatives. The seriousness of the Iran-contra scandal makes Watergate look like what it was—a cheap burglary followed by a clumsy and stupid attempted coverup.

Herbert Hoover took abuse for presiding over the crash of the economy, although the elements were in place before he took office. Hoover was cold and seemed aloof. Some years after he left office I covered a speech he gave to suburban businessman, and found him a relaxed, informed, delightful person with an attractive, low-key sense of humor.

I was sitting in a Quonset hut in Guam when someone ran in and said Roosevelt was dead. My first reaction was, "Does that mean Harry Truman is president? God help us!" Truman, of course, fooled everyone, particularly Thomas E. Dewey. I remember Truman taking his morning strolls down Michigan Avenue with a couple of Secret Service men, and how graciously he shook hands with a line of cops at Midway Airport before boarding his plane.

Truman went back to his old home in Missouri and lived out his days with Bess in simple comfort. My other favorite ex-president did the same. When Calvin Coolidge left the White House in 1929 he and Grace Coolidge returned to their rented two-flat at 21 Massasoit Street in Northampton, Massachusetts. While they were away the rent was increased from $27 to $32 a month.

Coolidge wrote: "We like the house where our children came to us and the neighbors were so kind. When we could have had a more pretentious house we still clung to it. So long as I lived there I could be independent and serve the public without ever thinking that I could not maintain my position if I lost office."

If there were any Secret Service men around the Coolidge home, they weren't visible. Allison Lockwood, a professor at Montgomery College in Maryland, recalled his boyhood on the street where the ex-President lived.

"What my brother and I best recall of him were the shoe soles of the Presidential feet," Mr. Lockwood said. "Coolidge was an inveterate foot-propper-upper . . . and there he sat in the late afternoon or after supper, smoking his cigar, reading his newspaper, a straw hat tilted against the glare, feet up on the porch railing—much in the manner of our own fathers up and down the street."

One biographer called Coolidge "the least interesting of our presidents." Coolidge didn't care for pretense or publicity. He was self-conscious; he laughed little; he had nothing to do with the ladies; he paid little attention to dignitaries; he hardly ever called anyone by first name.

While president he saved practically all his salary. He had a sly sense of humor and a fabled economy with words. When his first presidential pay check was presented with some attempt at ceremony, Coolidge responded, "Call again."

I talked with Allan A. Seiler, editor of the Pike Press in Pittsfield, Illinois, who dug up some revealing quotes in little-known speeches Coolidge made when he was governor of Massachusetts.

- "The people cannot look to legislation generally for success. Industry, thrift, character are not conferred by act or resolve. Government cannot relieve from toil. It can provide no substitute for the rewards of service."

- "Don't expect to build up the weak by pulling down the strong. Don't hurry to legislate. Give administration a chance to catch up with legislation."

- "We claim the right of publicity. That is a remedy with an arm longer and stronger than that of the law. Let us know what is going on and the remedy will provide itself. The American people are prepared to meet any reasonable burden; they are not asking for charity or favor; fair prices and fair profits they will gladly pay, but they demand information that they are fair, and an immediate reduction if they are not."

- "Everybody must take a more active part in public affairs. It will not do for men to send . . . they must go. It is not enough to draw a check. Good government cannot be bought, it has to be given. Office has great opportunities for doing wrong, but equal chance for doing right. Unless good citizens hold office, bad citizens will."

On a January in 1933, Calvin Coolidge left his office at midmorning and was driven home. "There," Professor Lockwood wrote, "he fetched a glass of water from the kitchen, exchanged a few words with a hired man at work in the cellar, and went upstairs to die in much the same manner as he had lived—quietly, tidily, privately."

Heroes

My boyhood heroes were Admiral Richard E. Byrd, Charley Gehringer, and Bo McMillen.

My boyhood is so far away that I'd better tell who these men were. Byrd led expeditions to the North and South Poles when these were dangerous adventures. Gehringer was one of the greatest baseball players in the game, but because he moved effortlessly, and was quiet and modest, he didn't get the attention that came to more flamboyant players. His lifetime batting average was over .320.

Bob McMillen was a little ol' country boy who went to a little ol' college in Kentucky and set the football world back on its heels by whomping some of the eastern giants. Details grow dim, but I know I was convinced if Bo and his Praying Colonels could knock over mighty Harvard, anybody could achieve anything if he wanted it badly enough. That's what the boys' magazines told me when they eulogized McMillen. And Byrd.

A hero is defined as a man of distinguished valor or performance, admired for noble qualities. A heroine is a female hero.

Youngsters tend to latch on to some prominent person who assumes heroic proportions in their eyes. The conduct and attitude of their hero or heroine influence the conduct and attitude of the hero worshipers.

The hero is emulated in dress, mannerisms, and philosophy. Admiral Byrd was ideal hero material. Babe Ruth was far more prominent when Byrd was in the Antarctic, but Ruth was something of a lush and even the most naive youngster hesitated to pattern anything but his baseball swing after Ruth.

Entertainers attracted a huge number of hero worshipers, and still do in this generation, but I don't think they fill the bill. They should qualify under idol worship. Elvis Presley was an idol, but hardly heroic. The rock stars who generate such vocal and ostentatious worship today generally do not qualify as role models for young people.

The astronauts are the best hero and heroine worship material today. Admiral Byrd would be an astronaut today.

Not many politicians qualify. John Kennedy had the charisma that generated a fair amount of hero worship, but his personal life was less than exemplary. I can't see Reagan as object of hero worship, especially since the Iran-contra business. Jimmy Carter, Gerald Ford, Lyndon Johnson . . . no way.

Margaret Thatcher is powerful and an achiever, but hardly a person to generate hero worship. Mother Theresa and Albert Schweitzer led heroic lives in places remote from the United States and aren't adequately appreciated.

Paul Newman and Robert Redford are legitimate hero worship figures, because they are good-looking, pleasant, and are achievers outside their movie-making business.

I have trouble identifying current athletic greats of the heroic mold. Two likely candidates as this is written are Michael Jordan, an immensely talented and decently modest and personable basketball player, and Doug Flutie, who captured the hearts of sports fans as a college quarterback, and has the looks and demeanor to repeat his charm in professional football, if he is talented enough as a passer, which he probably isn't.

Television anchor people have the looks and brains and charisma to attract a lot of hero worship if it weren't that their off-screen lives have to be very private. They can't lead normal lives because people pester them anyplace they go in public. So they're virtual social recluses.

Martin Luther King, Jr. was probably the greatest object of hero worship in recent years.

I asked a number of people about their heroes and heroines, and found a pattern emphasizing movie and sports stars, but also someone else in another field.

A minister said, "George Washington Carver was a hero to me because he was a symbol of my race. He gave me the feeling all was not lost, and we could rise to great heights. General MacArthur was a symbol of integrity to me. I also admired Franklin Roosevelt because of his ability to inspire hope."

One fellow survived a case of hero worship of Paul and Dizzy Dean. It takes all kinds.

A professor told me: "I don't regard myself as a particularly religious person, but I liked St. Paul. I enjoyed someone who stood up and fought. I like his aggressiveness and his willingness to get involved. I also like Gabby Hartnett, and a grandfather who was a ship captain, and an uncle who was a teacher."

Uncles, aunts, and teachers and coaches make good hero material, and they are especially laudable because the worship comes from personal contact, rather than glamorization through the typewriter of a press agent or the eye of a movie or TV camera.

I met one of my boyhood heroes after I grew up. It was quite disillusioning. On the other hand, one of my current hero figures is Johnny Wooden. We were in the same outfit in the Navy, and I liked and admired him as a person. But the hero-worship came as I viewed from afar his career as the basketball coach at UCLA and his impeccable sportsmanship and behavior.

At the bottom of the list of potential heroes of young people are mothers and fathers, if both are living. They are much too close.

The Happy Brain

I may be off by a few hundred million, but by my calculations I have lost 1 billion, 340 million brain cells since I was 35, which is the age when you start losing these useful little body parts at the rate of 100,000 a day.

Not to worry. I still have 8,685,000,000 brain cells left. And since we use only 10 percent of our brain for thinking purposes, I'll continue my proper share of thinking.

Most of the rest is like a muscle, and thinking is the exercise. Enthusiasm maintains constant activity in the brain cells. People can be literally bored to death.

That's the reason many people go downhill when they retire. A friend of mine in Florida used to tell me that retirees came down and spent a year playing bridge, a year playing golf, a year drinking, and then died.

One of the most interesting people I knew was LeRoy Hasse, a clerk in an art store in Joliet, whose hobby was study of the brain. Many brilliant scientists have devoted a lifetime to learned research of the brain, and maybe a Joliet clerk isn't the best source for brain information. But Mr. Hasse knew his subject, and he had a knack for making it understandable to dumb laymen.

He certainly was an influence in my decision to buy a computer to exercise my brain when I left the *Tribune*. I'm now on my third computer and I think my brain is OK with its dwindling supply of cells.

In his younger days Hasse was assistant coach of an Indiana basketball team which won one game and lost twenty-four. "I thought there must be a better way to teach the kids how to play basketball," he told me. "That's when I began studying the brain, and I've been at it ever since.

"I learned we use about 50 percent of our brain for the automatic running of the body. We use about 10 percent for thinking. That leaves 40 percent unused most of the time."

I got acquainted with Hasse when he wrote me in praise of the high ethical standards of one of my personal heroes, UCLA basketball coach Johnny Wooden. Hasse also included about ten pages of information about his favorite subject.

He thought I should do a column on the brain, and suggested a number of scientists as sources. Instead it was a chat over coffee in Specht's art supply store in Joliet.

"Well, for starters," Hasse said, "ten neurons, or brain cells, can be connected in 1,267,650,500,228,229,401,703,205,376 different ways." He cited sources for all his facts, and this fact was from biophysicist Heinz Von Forrester of the University of Illinois.

"Problem—how do we get from 10 percent use of the brain for thinking up to 20 percent? I think we'll learn some day. But not in our lifetime. Maybe not for thousands of years. For now, it takes constant training, training, training."

He alluded to the chemical difference between men and women. "Women have three chemicals affecting their brains—estrogen, progesterone, and testosterone. Men have mostly testosterone with a little estrogen.

"These chemicals react in the center of the brain—the hypothalamus, which is the seat of emotions, and also of sexual behavior. My information is that women are smarter than men except during their menstrual periods, when they are only as smart as men."

He thought one of the best ways to live a longer life is to try to maintain your brain in a happy condition. It's happy when it's used.

Did twenty-two years of research into the brain lead him to the answer to winning basketball?

"I'm afraid basketball is best taught as a reflex art," Hasse said. "There's no thinking time. You react to the situation."

He was reading a book on Leonardo da Vinci lent by a friend. "Boy, do I admire Leonardo!" He enthused. "There's a young man who really knew how to use the brain.

"Did you know that Einstein, another of my heroes, said that the three things that guided him in life were kindness, beauty, and truth?

"Isn't that magnificent?"

More People
Nelson Algren

Algren's *Chicago: City on the Make* quoted in his introduction one of the worst columns I ever wrote. Then Algren wrote that this columnist "leaves the office early because his wife is having friends in for cocktails and you never can tell when an unattached chick might turn up."

I never met Algren, but I guess because I lived in the suburbs he fitted me in with his stereotype of all suburban men. I went home early every day because I came to work between 2 A.M. and 6 A.M.

Algren verbally bludgeoned virtually every institution and prominent person in the city in his book. But one fat target escaped any mention. Hugh Hefner's empire and mansion were a caricature so flamboyant, so publicized, and so vulgar they were beginning to embarrass even us Philistines in the suburbs. But not a word from Algren.

Algren did have a secondary career as a prop at Hefner's Temple of Gauche. Algren would find a place in a corner and glower as tourists nudged each other and whispered, "That's Nelson Algren, The Writer, in the corner, the one with the pipe." The food and drink were plentiful and free.

J. Edgar Hoover

The FBI chief needed somebody to blame for an alleged plot to blow up utilities in Washington and kidnap a White House official. Hoover told congressmen that the plotters were Philip and Daniel Berrigan, the two anti-war activist priests. At any given time I'd guess there were 100 nutty radicals sitting around somewhere in the United States plotting to blow up utilities, the White

House, or what have you. Sometimes they blew themselves up, but the White House and the utilities remain intact.

Hoover was pitching Congress for 1,000 more agents and an additional $14.5 million to battle the likes of the Berrigans, who had made the FBI look foolish by evading arrest for months.

The Berrigans committed a crime as a symbolic protest. They destroyed some records in a Maryland selective service office. After burning the records they stood around waiting to be arrested. After they were sentenced but before they entered prison, Phil Berrigan decided to carry his non-violent protest one step farther, and let the FBI try to find him.

He moved around the East for months, making monkeys out of Hoover's troops. They finally caught up and lodged him in the prison at Danbury, Connecticut, where the brothers were sitting when Hoover took his implausible cheap shot at them.

I wrote in my column the Berrigans "were in no position to blow up anything or kidnap anybody or defend themselves from the smears of a vicious autocrat."

I also wrote, "The most dim-witted law student would know that if J. Edgar Hoover had any evidence of a plot such as he described, it is his sworn duty to bring formal charges against the conspirators.

"Instead, he has chosen to dirty up people of whom he disapproves in the same way he tried to smear Dr. Martin Luther King, Jr. with the cheap-shot gossip about Dr. King's personal life."

It was tempting to suggest that at seventy-five Hoover was senile, but I don't think he was. "He is as vicious and as crafty as he was fifteen years ago," was my evaluation. "He differs from other septuagenarians in that instead of growing humble with age, he grows more arrogant."

The Berrigans were not really defenseless in prison. They were testifying to an ideal of the sacredness of human life. They chose to go to prison to dramatize their opposition to the sacrifice of thousands of American and Vietnamese lives.

"The Berrigans' ideal will live long after J. Edgar Hoover is dead and buried," were my words in 1970.

The Berrigans *and* their ideal live on, and as this is written they are facing another term in prison.

Hoover? History will judge. When William Webster moved into

Hoover's office in 1978, he performed a symbolic act. He moved the bust of Hoover out of the office.

Hoover had a file on me, which was dug up under the Freedom of Information Act by, of all people, Jane Fonda, whom I had interviewed during the Vietnam war. I didn't know it existed until after Hoover's death, and to my knowledge it had no effect whatsoever on my reporting or on any of my superiors' editing of my material.

Everett McKinley Dirksen

"And God created man" became, in the tongue of Senator Dirksen: "Then came the only creature that was created with intelligence, a soul, a personality, the prospect of divinity . . . there he was, this lonely creature . . . he had a beautiful home, if a garden can be called a home . . . God made it without the aid of the Housing Administration."

Dirksen didn't just talk—he played his booming bass vocal organ. Each vowel was caressed lovingly. He rarely used three words if it could be said in ten. He was the best orator I ever heard, and probably was the last of the great orators in view of what electronic amplification has done to politics and religion.

Dirksen was dedicating a school in Calumet City named in his honor.

"Can you imagine [*legato*] the army of fresh-faced, eager-eyed youngsters who will become the tillers of the soil of tomorrow or the technicians of tomorrow or the generals?

"I have tried [*molto appassionato*] to restore voluntary prayer in the schools of the United States [*fortissimo*], and if the Lord is willing and my spirit don't fail [*crescendo*], *I'll get it done in spite of the Supreme Court!*"

The crowd roared to its feet.

Dirksen talked with his audience, not at them. He loved being there. He was not condescending, and he had a rare ability to be self-deprecating without for a moment sacrificing his sense of dignity or importance.

Dirksen talked for thirty minutes and came out in favor of schools, children, prayer, soy beans, and America, and against draft card burners and low pay for teachers. There wasn't a person in the room who felt his time was not well spent.

Andrew Greeley

Father Greeley achieved recognition and material success when he wrote novels with heavy sexual overtones. As a non-Catholic I have trouble understanding the role of a Catholic priest as a writer of popular novels. Maybe the Catholics have the same trouble. Maybe the Archdiocese has the same trouble. But they can do something about it . . . I think.

Before the first novel—*Cardinal Sins*, I think it was called—Greeley wrote general columns that bounced in and out of Chicago newspapers. I had a rule never to quarrel with other columnists, but I broke it after one of Father Greeley's more preposterous pieces.

He wrote: "Anyone who has been sniffing around Catholic neighborhoods lately knows that Catholics are angry. What are they angry about?

"They're angry because they have discovered that they are the niggers of the seventies. They don't exactly like the role." His first evidence was the term "reform Democrats" used by Richard Reeves in an article about school busing in Boston.

Here is Father Greeley's interpretation of reform Democrats: "a newspaper name for a political movement that seeks to replace 'ethnics' with Jewish liberals, handsome WASPs and blacks with graduate school degrees. Any Catholic who survives is by definition a 'hack.' "

Two of Father Greeley's star witnesses were Ralph Ginzburg, the pornographer, and Madalyn Murray O'Hair, the voluble atheist of talk show fame.

If Catholics were to begin raising hell, it would be because of inflammatory rhetoric from this Chicago priest. My quarrel with Father Greeley was not that he was wrong. He and I both enjoy that privilege. His sin was that by propounding this idea he was encouraging it.

I've been deeply involved, personally and vocationally, in terrible racial and religious and neighborhood tensions. I've never known a time of less tension. Never have people of different religions in our community been more comfortable with one another than today.

No thanks to Father Andrew Greeley.

Henry Hyde is a conservative Republican congressman from Chicago's western suburbs. I am in almost total disagreement with his political and social philosophy. But he is genuine, sincere, and decent (although wrong most of the time), and we've been friends since his days in the state legislature, where he and Harold Washington were the dominant orators. Henry had a fund-raiser with Henry Kissinger as speaker, and as a side attraction he presented Irv Kupcinet and me with large trophies.

I have enormous admiration for Kup. He and I labor under the same handicap: neither of us is a particularly good writer. So we compensate by working harder and not overwriting—which pays in high readership and recognition. Kup worked harder than I did . . . harder than any newspaperman I know.

Dick Cain

The most interesting man I knew was Dick Cain, a compulsive adventurer. He was self-educated, literate, scholarly, and imaginative. I first worked with him when I was doing some basic muckraking and he was a vice cop. We put a crooked judge in prison and closed a lot of vice joints and he gave me material from his wire taps. He operated so close to illegality that he was constantly in trouble. He did a term in a federal prison for some kind of muscle job, and afterward went to work for Sam Giancana, the syndicate boss. Cain was executed by syndicate gunmen.

While he was in prison in Texarkana, Texas, he wrote me:

"Everything is just dandy. I am losing my hair, teeth, and charm at about the same rate. I don't know if you've written; my keepers are petulant about my mail. Anyone who reads or writes is suspect here.

"The censor had a terrible time with my use of the word 'flatulent' in describing bureaucracy. I was accused of harboring a dictionary!

" 'I Wisht I was a Country Girl Again' has supplanted the National Anthem on the prison radio. God and the Warden, the Apostles and the Lieutenants are equated on a chart, ostensibly a Christian table of organization. Wouldn't you know an agnostic would be exiled to the Bible Belt?

"I'm like Candide among the Bulgarians; Prometheus chained to the Caucasian crag, featuring, of course, the Vulture which eats out my liver each day.

"The doctor, a nice twenty-four-year-old boy who signed on here instead of escaping to Canada, is terrified at the sight of blood, but he's working toward becoming ill afterward instead of during.

"He *is* fortunate in that he has several inmate assistants who are experts at administering injections; the only drawback is the patient has to wrestle the assistant for possession of the hypodermic needle."

Commies, Anti-Commies, and Nazis I Have Known

The Russians Have Come

After the first Russian flight into space, a group of eleven Russian journalists visited Chicago. Someone decided part of their American experience should be dinner in a typical suburban home with a typical American family. I qualified with a wife who's a good cook, four children, and a police dog.

Only two came—Boris Burkov, the group's leader, a big, good-looking man who spoke no English, and the group's interpreter, Arkadi Ognivtzev. He went to school in England and had successfully overcome an English accent. Ognivtzev was rather short and elfish, and bubbling with good humor.

I picked them up in the Loop and headed north on Lake Shore Drive. It was a lovely spring day, the sun was warm, the buds were popping, the grass was at its richest green, and I drove past every church and school and university I could think of.

I quickly discovered we had to establish the price of everything, from the house to a quart of milk. My five-year-old Mercury convertible had cost $700 used. We put the top down.

"Your streets are so wide," Burkov kept saying. "Not like New York."

I told him: "We have lots of room to grow. This park we're driving on now is filled-in land. It used to be the lake."

This went into his notebook. We passed a fender bender. "All your cars carry insurance?" Burkov asked. "Not all of them," I reported.

We passed Mundelein College and Loyola University. "What do they teach? How many years do students attend? How many students? Do they give degrees?"

North into Evanston. "Does your wife have any help?" "No." "She does all the work herself?" "Yes." "Hmmmmmmm."

North through the Northwestern University campus. I stressed the great engineering school.

Bahai Temple in Wilmette was so impressive we had to stop to take pictures. Engraved on the Temple were the words "The Source of All Learning is the Knowledge of God. Exalted Be His Glory."

I told him I had been mayor of my village for four years. "How were you chosen?" "By popular vote—an election." "Did you have parties?" "Yes, local parties." "What kind of, ah, election? What kind of votes?" "I don't quite understand." "Ah, a secret ballot?" "Yes, a secret ballot. Real democratic."

We arrived at our house for a typical suburban dinner of beef rump roast, mashed potatoes and gravy, string beans, cantaloupe, a tossed lettuce salad, rolls, butter, jam, coffee, tea, milk, and chocolate cake.

The Russians seemed most impressed that the milk was delivered to the door, that we didn't have to boil it, and we could keep it as long as a week in the refrigerator. Burkov drank two big glasses of milk.

In the living room the Russians pulled out some presents for the kids. First was a postcard-sized picture of their pioneer astronaut, Yuri Gagarin. Then they gave the kids a charming wooden doll, several small medallions, one with a picture of Yuri, one with an Olympic runner, one with a rocket in orbit, one with a dove of peace.

Our typical suburban police dog hid under a bench in the kitchen and peered out at the strangers.

"What's the matter—she think we're Communists?" Burkov laughed.

The questions tumbled out, and whenever they involved anything tangible, "How much?" How much taxes do we pay? What does it go for?"

"Schools, parks, fire protection, police protection, water, streets."

"The children—what do they learn in school? Sewing, cooking?"

I said a little sewing, cooking, but mostly mathematics, English, history, civics, languages. "But the sewing, cooking . . . ?" they persisted. I had the impression they had been told American schools teach mostly sewing, cooking, and how to take a jalopy apart.

"At what age do they start school?"

"Five, usually."

"Too young. In our country, seven. Let them be children for a while longer. Let them be children."

Ognivtzev had a little boy just our boy's age. Burkov had two daughters, and hadn't been in the house two minutes before pulling out a stack of pictures of his daughters and grandchild.

We took a drive around town, zigzagging past every church and school. They looked silently at the house of the president of Amoco. Then we drove to a trailer park at the other end of town.

"How much do they cost? How many rooms? What kind of heat? How much rent for the space? Who lives in them?"

They jumped out to get pictures of the trailers.

Back to the house for coffee and talk. Burkov and Ognivtzev felt that while Russians know a great deal about American history and culture, and our writers and artists, we know little about them and their history and culture.

Russian school children know Mark Twain and Edison and Lincoln and Jefferson and Washington, they said. What do we know about Russian history? They cited Dreiser, Hemingway, Steinbeck, and Salinger as contemporary authors well read in Russia.

Driving back downtown the questions kept pouring out. "When was this highway built? What material? How long will it last? How often do you shop? Where? Does your wife go downtown often? Why?"

We swung toward the brightly lighted Wrigley building. "What is Wrigley?" Burkov asked. I said it is a man who makes chewing gum.

"I saw the American basketball team in Finland," Burkov said. "After that I assumed all Americans chew gum."

We parted friends. A quarter of a century later the relationship between the U.S.S.R. and the U.S. hasn't improved much at the top governmental levels. But the American and Russian people have come to know each other better. And the nuclear bombs are still under control.

Gene McCarthy wasn't running for any particular office when he dropped in for a visit. I always got along well with renegades and nonconformists and free thinkers and oddballs. Maybe it was because they made good copy, as opposed to the establishment types.

The Entertainer

Toward the end of the Vietnam war John Wayne made a brief documentary movie called *No Substitute for Victory*. He toured the country, showing the film in schools, entreating his listeners to rally behind the war. Said Wayne in the movie: "If there should be another seventeenth parallel, we should not plead with the Communists to get back, but warn them and do it once. *To hell with world opinion!* Only then will this great nation of ours survive."

When two men in front of a supermarket offered to sell me tickets to the film, I suggested if I wanted advice on wars I wouldn't go to John Wayne for it.

I had nothing against John Wayne personally, but he was in a position to influence public opinion to a degree incompatible with his experience and knowledge. He was a strong young man during World War II, but he spent it in Hollywood playing in *A Lady Takes a Chance* when his countrymen were being killed defending this nation.

I brought up his war record because no man can write totally clinically, coldly, objectively on the subject of war without being influenced by his own participation, or failure to participate, in military service.

When Wayne stood before an audience they were seeing the heroic Sergeant Stryker storming the beach at Iwo Jima. He was the firm-chinned Navy captain standing on the cruiser's bridge as Japanese shells burst around him. He was the gutsy Green Beret captain, or the Flying Leatherneck.

In Wayne's wars it was all so simple. In play-acting wars, we're the good guys. God is always on our side. The good guys always win, and all bullet holes are small and clean and all deaths are heroic. This was true until the resurgence of interest in the Vietnam war in 1987 and the movie *Platoon*, made by a man who fought in the trenches in Vietnam. The blood was real, not catsup.

I posed some questions to John Wayne:

• Is it worth having 5,000 more Americans killed in order to keep the military rulers of South Vietnam in power?   ( ) Yes.   ( ) No.

• Should we increase taxes as much as 20 percent to raise an army that will make sure the military junta of South Vietnam remains in power?   ( ) Yes.   ( ) No.

• Should we risk a nuclear war with the Soviet Union to prevent South Vietnam from uniting with North Vietnam? ( ) Yes.   ( ) No.

• Is it moral for Americans to destroy villages and towns and kill civilians in order to kill enemy soldiers in these communities?   ( ) Yes.   ( ) No.

We'd always been right, and God had favored us through our brief history as a nation. But my limited study of Christianity did not persuade me that God reserves special grace for inhabitants of the continent of North America.

Nazis

We always seem to have a handful of haters and malcontents around who call themselves American Nazis. Since World War II they've been a pitiful joke.

But before that war the American Nazi could give you the shivers. Their rallies attracted thousands. The Chicago unit alone had 125 young boys saluting the swastika and drilling and learning Nazi ideology. Parades in New York drew tens of thousands, and a Nazi rally filled every seat in Madison Square Garden.

I covered a Deutscher Tag rally in the picnic grove at Riverview Park which drew 30,000 men, women, and children July 1, 1940. The Chicago Nazis, called the German American Bund, were one of the sponsors.

It was difficult to say what percentage of the 30,000 were sympathetic with the Bund. Many were old Germans who came to sit around the picnic tables and drink beer and talk about the good old days in the fatherland.

But the Bundists were busy. The swastika fluttered from a flagstaff. The band played "Deutschland Uber Alles" and the Horst Wessel song. The crowd cheered when Adolf Hitler's name was mentioned. Arms were raised in a Nazi salute.

I watched all this with the feeling it was unreal. I got chills seeing the scar-faced Bund leader, Otto Willumeit, strutting through the crowds. Mayor Kelly not only attended, he made a speech. He said "everything that is said here will be in the spirit of real good fellowship."

The German consul in Chicago got into the spirit of real good fellowship with an accolade to Adolf Hitler. The real reason for the defeat of Germany's enemies, he told the throng, was that "they haven't had a single man who might be compared as a statesman and general to Adolf Hitler, who alone is great enough to bring peace to Germany and the world—a peace based on honesty and the neutral rights of nations."

A few months earlier Hitler had brought his peculiar brand of peace to Poland.

When we entered the war most of the men at the picnic or their sons put on American uniforms and fought against Nazism and fascism.

A couple of decades passed before a new generation of crackpots surfaced and called themselves Nazis. Their leader was George Lincoln Rockwell.

The Nazis had a headquarters on Ohio Street in Chicago. I assigned my toughest reporter, Mike McGovern, to infiltrate them. Mike tried several times, and was rejected. Then he borrowed a friend's black motorcycle, and roared up to the door of the Nazis' house. They poured out to see the black cycle and its black-clad driver. Mike was in.

He not only was accepted, but four days later he stood at attention at the headquarters as a bodyguard for Rockwell as the "commander" addressed his miserable little band.

Mike answered phones at the headquarters and chauffeured the Nazis on errands. He learned a lot about American Nazis. They were a miserable little band of misfits—humorless, hateful, and afraid. They also were very untidy.

Mike nearly gagged when he ate with them. After each meal they dumped their dirty dishes in the bathtub. At the next meal when they needed a dish they'd go to the tub and pull one out of the dirty water. One Nazi ate from an ash tray.

The episode ended with a brawl on the street in front of the headquarters with two Nazis going after one of our photographers and another reporter. In the melee Mike jumped on his black steed and sped away.

It made a great, front-page series. Mike later took his brand of Chicago muscular journalism to the *New York News*.

The next manifestation of local Nazism was the infamous Frank Collin, leader of a gang of juvenile delinquents who gained the attention they so desperately sought by proposing a march through Skokie. Collin was as much a threat to Chicago as a warthog, but the media made a big thing out of the Skokie incident, and he got the notoriety he wanted before he was hauled off to prison for molesting boys.

In 1986 some homegrown Nazis found kindred spirits in the Ku

Klux Klan and a new media epidemic shaped up. The Klan can get TV attention by wrapping large wooden crosses in burlap soaked in gasoline and lighting them and prancing around in their white sheets.

The media can make them or destroy them. The crackpots and haters can stand anything but being ignored. They are no more a threat to American society than were Frank Collin or George Lincoln Rockwell—unless the media, and television in particular, pay attention to their madness.

A generation ago a minister named Gerald L. K. Smith was viciously anti-Semitic and seemed to be making headway. The Anti-Defamation League asked the media to quarantine him, to stop giving him space, even when most of it was critical. The media cooperated, and Gerald L. K. Smith became a nonentity.

Personal

I Lose a Friend

For years I was considered a little strange because I came to work early in the morning. A primary reason for coming in early was to enjoy the company, friendship, and professionalism of Ralph Hallenstein.

Ralph worked from midnight to 8 A.M. as night editor at the *American*, and from 6 A.M. as day news editor when we both moved to the *Tribune*.

Ralph had a flawless news sense. Columnists tend to lose contact with the nuts and bolts of newspapering. I overcame this by clumping into the newsroom before dawn, grabbing a place on the news desk where I could work and pester Ralph. It was a pleasant learning experience.

We had a thing going about smoking. Every chance I got I took a crack in the column at cigarette smoking. Ralph smoked constantly. I don't know how many packs a day, but he'd start his shift with four packs piled on the desk in front of him.

There's lots of give-and-take in a newspaper office, and I laid on him hard for smoking. He gave back. He chuckled every time I put a dig at smoking in the column. But he never changed a word.

A couple of years after we moved to the *Tribune* I went on vacation for a week. When I came back I knew Ralph had stopped as soon as I got near his desk. The blue haze was missing, and Ralph without a cigarette in his hand or mouth was as obvious as Ralph without a right arm.

I heard a lot of kidding—the usual raucous humor aimed at anybody trying to break the habit. Ralph just smiled.

Later in the day he walked over to my desk. "I didn't want to talk about it out there," he said, "but I'll tell you why I quit. I had a physical exam and they found a spot on my lung. I'm going into the hospital next week for an operation."

It was like a kick in the stomach. The best I could offer was platitudes: "You're lucky you had the exam and they caught it early. You're tough."

There followed several months of physical and mental hell—operations, chemotherapy, radiation, hope, and despair. He made it back to work for a couple of weeks, but was too ill to continue.

Ralph died at the age of fifty-three. His best years had been ahead.

The tobacco industry spends billions creating the image of a cigarette smoker as a manly outdoorsman or a beautiful girl dipping her toe in a sylvan pond.

Each day 250 Americans die of lung cancer. Eighty percent of the cancers are caused by tobacco.

My image of the smoker is not the Marlboro man. It is a dead friend.

Blessings

When my children laughed—and they laughed often—life held no greater blessing.

They had health, love, shelter, food, security, and hope.

What did I do to give them these?

They lived in a fine home, but I didn't build it. Carpenters came and put up the walls, and plumbers built it, and electricians and concrete men and painters and laborers.

On a farm somewhere in Illinois or Wisconsin, farmers got up before dawn to tend their cows and get the milk my children would drink. The milk would be pasteurized and made safe in a dairy, and a trucker would deliver the milk to a nearby store.

At a loom somewhere women wove the cloth that was made into coats to keep my children warm.

When they were thirsty, they turned a knob and pure water came from the tap. Somewhere in the lake men were watching to make sure this flow of water didn't stop.

A hospital was near our home. I did nothing to help build it. But every minute of every day people there were ready to take care of my children if they needed help. There were people ready to speed them to a hospital in an emergency any time I picked up the phone and called for help.

A block away was a church. I did nothing to help build it. But my children went there, and learned moral and ethical values which helped guide their lives.

They had bicycles I didn't build. They had food protected in a refrigerator I didn't build. They rode in a car, walked on carpets, slept in beds that were made by others. They went to schools built by our neighbors.

Literally millions of American men and women are devoting their lives to protecting my children and theirs from foreign powers who would enslave us.

My little niche in life, my tiny, feeble, almost ridiculous assignment that helped me compensate for what I was getting, was to put down my thoughts six days a week and see them printed in a newspaper.

Even here I was totally dependent on others, from the men who chopped down trees to make paper to the kid on a bike who threw the paper on the front porch. Without them my forum would have been a soap box in a park. If someone had built a soap box. And made a park.

I could live in the woods, exist off the land, and see no man, and ask nothing. But I chose to be part of an organized society which, despite its flaws, can provide a blessed life.

Giving thanks on Christmas or on Sundays isn't enough.

We should ask: What am I getting? What am I giving?

Merry Christmas

Christmas is not my favorite day. One December 25 a few years back was probably the worst of my Christmases, but it was not unrepresentative.

I was on my back all day with the flu. So was my wife. Our Christmas dinner was a cup of broth.

Two of the kids had been home but went back to college early Christmas day to study for exams.

The TV conked out Christmas eve. The phone also went dead, but the phone company had a man out to fix it within three hours. This was before the government broke up AT&T.

Our eldest phoned from San Francisco that she was just about over her pneumonia. The previous Christmas she fell off a cliff in California and broke a foot. The Christmas before that she had been suffering from Bell's palsy. Christmas before that we had spent at her bedside in Presbyterian-St. Luke's Hospital. She was suffering from exhaustion from her medical studies.

Suicides go up in the Christmas season. Loneliness is more intense at Christmas than at any other time.

The most common reaction Christmas night of women responsible for family eating is "Thank God that's over."

Customarily I conclude our family observation of Christmas by putting my arm around my wife's shoulder—if we're both ambulatory—and saying, "Well, it could have been worse."

I have stopped lying at the office December 26 to all the cheery inquiries, "And how was your Christmas?"

"It was awful," I reply, if it was indeed awful.

Ed Lahey

In 1938 Eddie Lahey, a *Daily News* reporter, was named the first Nieman Fellow for a year of study at Harvard. Eddie was the best reporter and newspaper writer I ever knew. He was a streetwise intellectual, and he dazzled the Harvard academics with his side-of-the-mouth contributions to their practical education.

I was hired from *City Press* to fill the vacancy left by Lahey. That is, everybody else moved up a notch and I came in at the bottom. Eddie returned to the *News* after his year at Harvard.

When John Knight sold the *News* to Marshall Field III, Lahey stayed with Knight and became head of the Knight newspapers' Washington bureau.

Eddie used to check in periodically at Sacred Heart Sanitarium in Milwaukee for seven to ten days of rest and think. In 1960 I planned to drive up for a visit and dinner at Mader's.

I got a note from Ed in Washington: "Forget about the Milwaukee trip. Have had a pretty horrid visitation in the past twelve hours. Blood out of its course. The night was never so long.

"This morning, after some indecent prodding, the doctor said the hospital right away, exploratory surgery tomorrow morning. If I'm lucky it will be an ulcer. . . . If you know any prayers, say a few for an orthodox coward."

Lahey was the kind of a man who at a time like that would write a note to a friend canceling a dinner date.

Ten days later I received a copy of a letter addressed to John Knight, to Knight's editors, and to me. It described the events following his "horrid visitation."

"Thursday, November 10 . . . First sign of a lesion in the hydraulic system appears at 11 A.M. First reaction, panic. Second, maybe it will go away.

"Friday, November 11 . . . Still there. Dr. Bill Argy says to meet him downtown. He prods fore and aft, painfully, and shows alarm. Argy calls a Dr. H., who says to get me to Doctor's hospital that afternoon.

"Dr. H. is a mature man, regarded in his profession as tops in urology, the first one or two men another doctor calls on a urological problem. His competence and experience are unquestioned. This fact is relevant in view of later developments.

"Saturday, November 12 . . . I am taken to surgery early. Two and a half hours later, while emerging from the anesthetic, Bill Argy tells me I have a malignant tumor.

"Dr. H., the top man in the surgical exploration, tells my family that the cancer, which is in the bladder area, is very active. A biopsy is rejected from two reasons, he explains. First, there is no uncertainty to be cleared up by a biopsy. Second, a biopsy could only serve to spread the active cancer.

"November 12 thru November 15 . . . Sitting here in the bedroom of my apartment, this period seems like an improbable nightmare, the kind I have periodically when the bad guys on TV are trying to gun me down. . . . I am inclined not to discuss it . . . but since I disturbed the routine of others with this incident, I'll try to report these three days—and nights—with a minimum of mawkishness.

"My first desire when the roof fell in was for spiritual assurance. I felt like the boy who said his prayers only when he slept in a folding bed. I told the first priest who came to hear my confession and bring me communion that I could not help feeling hypocritical in my sudden spiritual panic. He was very good about rejecting this thought.

"I asked God desperately to save me from one of those long, dragged-out terminal situations, where the family is agonized and the savings account fractured before the patient dies.

"I said I didn't want to be no Job, to let him go to his church, and I'll go to mine. I kept repeating that all I wanted was a quick and merciful death, with a minimum of inelegance about it. . . . I was supported in this course by a priest friend who assured me that I wasn't dogging it by such a prayer.

"I was reminded frequently those days that the only real division in the world is between the sick and the well. . . . Also, thinking of all the death I had witnessed, I was reminded that death is something that always happens to someone else, like an automobile accident. We all, in the presence of a dead body, are saying beneath our breath, 'I'm alive.'

"My personal affairs, slender as they are, were put in order by Arthur Goldberg, who brought over a couple of his office girls to witness my will. Art told me of an interesting phone conversation that day with John Kennedy. He was speaking off the record to an intimate who might be dead in a few days, and I'll leave it at that.

"The affection of my family and the concern of my friends and associates made a deep impact on me. For a guy who doesn't like the human race, I was touched at the number of people who were praying for me.

"Wednesday, November 16 . . . I was taken to surgery at 10 A.M. . . . I was peculiarly at peace. I was completely agreeable to going out the back way. Dr. H., before we went to the post, said he felt that he'd bring me back to my room. I told him not to make a federal case of it. I wanted a quickie.

"2:30 P.M., Wednesday, November 16 . . .

"I was coming to, after four and a half hours of anesthesia. My friend Dr. Bill Argy was patting my arm.

" 'Ed, there's no malignancy,' he was saying.

"The less said about the anti-climactic days that followed the better. One friend sent word, 'Tell the bum to send back the flowers.' An eighty-year-old Jesuit in Annapolis, who had seriously been praying to be taken as my 'substitute,' sent word, 'Look, Ma, no cavities.'

"I remained trussed in artificial plumbing thru November 17 and 18. The discomfort was irrelevant. I was in a daze, felt like a real faker, tried not to think about anything.

"A doctor friend of many years, Mike Kennedy, had popped in every morning before opening his office. Mike has a strong religious bent. He told me guardedly of a couple of experiences with his own patients, one of them a glaucoma victim whose recovery Mike is still unable to account for in his clinical experience.

"Finally Mike said: 'If I were you, I'd plan on some act of thanksgiving. I talked to Dr. H. and he says that on last Saturday you clinically had a cancer.'

"End of case. I quit while I'm ahead. No questions, no beefs. I feel that perhaps I have been granted a gift of some years that I might not have had.

"And my thought right now is that I'd better damn well use them wholesomely and productively."

Ed Lahey lived nine more productive and wholesome years.

Addendum

I discussed Lahey's experience with the minister of my church, Jim Spicer. "I am a child of my time, and have sipped just as deeply of the heady philosophical wine of logical positivism," Spicer responded.

"My first reaction to anything that can't be weighed, measured, tasted, or smelled is suspicion.

"However, while I was a chaplain at Billings Hospital at the University of Chicago I encountered two or three situations very similar to that your friend describes.

"The doctors I worked with were competent men, and perhaps

equally important, painfully honest men. The most we could ever do or make out of these situations was to kind of stand and look at each other with no comment.

"I was never sure what happened, but I was sure of a couple of things. One, these experiences make sophomoric nonsense out of small minds who really operate as though they believe that given enough time, enough monkeys, and enough typewriters, they can solve all the world's problems.

"It allows me to be ultimately and honestly open and seeking in all dimensions of life. You really don't have to push reality once you have learned to appreciate it.

"The second thing that has come to me is that there is a reality which you can point to which is significant in itself, namely, this man's experience of being dead and then suddenly alive.

"There is a depth and power in this experience which defies understanding from the outside. All the buttons and gadgets in the world pale into insignificance when one such rich human experience comes to light."

The Numbers Game

Have you ever figured how many numbers you have? In the dark ages before the computers began taking over, we were identified by a first name, an initial, and a last name, and usually a home address. That was enough.

I took an inventory of my numbers one day. To the bank I was 0711-2030-555-013. The utility knew me as AT64ED6932A2. At church for fiscal purposes I was number 487.

I was employee number 22149 at the newspaper, but my pay check identified me as 1:010/3031:9/00 022 1. I was 4147 in one union and 32-727-555-782 in the other. To my health insurer I was 21051881. The other insurance companies knew me as 3277368, 3309979, 879452, N6872388, V-31-55-44, 25-383-400, 17-383-293, 16-108-441, and 21-288-309.

Number 334-10-1686 is my Social Security tag. I paid my real estate property tax bill as number 04-34-212-004.

The U.S. Navy carried me as 139-282, N2-723-883, 359584. To the Department of Agriculture I was 36-064, to the phone company

724-1015-110-B. In one office in New York I was F848, in another SK6614. To the mortgage company I was 6-018-234, and the savings and loan, 407-961.

I subscribed to a number of periodicals, all of which identified me with designations like MABE9J1645NNIR212.

The University of Illinois Alumni Association once knew me as J. A. Mabley Journ.'38. They bought a computer which made me number 1-200-155-715-441-900 '08 Journ. They not only depersonalized me, they knocked thirty years off my graduation.

I haven't even begun to list the numbers of all the credit cards that have been sent to me. They'd take another page.

Are we better off being numbers instead of names? Business assures us that this system is more efficient, and it would cost far more to do business the old, pre-computer way.

If that's so, why was everything so much cheaper then?

Animal Tales

Pal

My most recent dog was a large German shepherd. Our only problem with Pal, other than his large appetite, was that he loved everybody. He was sure all visitors came only to see him. He wagged and shook and celebrated not just his family and visitors, but anybody who happened to walk past the house.

He didn't jump on people, but he leaned a lot. His only enemies in the world were squirrels and sparrows, and I'm sure if he ever caught up with one he'd have licked it.

The neighbors' children didn't understand why I didn't want them playing with Pal unless I was present.

It was because I trust no dog alive. I've had dozens of dogs and loved them and spoiled them. But it is a dog's instinct to bite when he is angry or afraid. We humans have domesticated these animals and have this instinct under control in most dogs. But the instinct is still there, dormant, in every dog.

Children are especially vulnerable. Their faces are at about the level of a large dog's head, and are an immediate target. Children aren't strong enough to fight off a large dog, and most haven't been taught how to handle dogs.

As soon as a child can reason, he should be taught when coming near a dog to let the dog approach him, rather than going up to the animal aggressively.

We had a nice little dachshund that let our kids maul and push him around when they were small. There never was a problem because they didn't hurt the dog, and he had a gentle nature. But when he was seven or eight years old he unexplainably began snapping at neighborhood children. I replaced him fast.

There wasn't much regulation of dogs when I was growing up. It was fun having them chasing around with us in the streets. I have no quarrel with the present necessity to license and leash dogs. But these laws were written for mostly wrong reasons. Suburbanites didn't want dogs trampling their gardens and messing their lawns, and city people didn't like picking their way through dog leavings on sidewalks and parkways.

The danger of dogs came from the other end. It's truer than ever because more people are buying and breeding dogs for protection. Some breeders mated German shepherds with timber wolves to get stronger attack dogs.

Dogs are a nuisance and a worry and an expense and they get hair and dust all over the house, so why have them? I'm the wrong one to ask. I just like animals.

They handle life better than most humans. They are loyal and affectionate. They always get up and wag when you come home. Pal seemed more interested in whether I brought someone home with me.

Some people love their dogs more than they love humans.

Do Pets Have Extrasensory Perception?

Can your dog or cat read your mind? Can it respond to your unspoken command?

Probably. When the Illinois Center for Psychological Research held a roundtable on "Animals and ESP" I got curious enough to ask some experts.

There likely is communication between man and animal that is not dependent on voice, gestures, or even facial expression, psychologists believe. A lot depends on how you define ESP.

"Many of the things we attribute to ESP are no more than a difference in ability to sense and perceive the thousands of things going on around us," said Dr. Jack Tuttle, veterinarian for the University of Illinois extension service.

"Animals appear to have more ESP than humans do. For example, a dog barks as soon as a burglar sets one foot on your property. The animal senses it, smells it, or hears it. Animals sense forest fires before people can detect them. Animals get agitated before earthquakes in California.

"I'm convinced that some animals are able to read minds by sensing emotions in a way we can't yet measure. Animals—especially dogs—know immediately the emotional level of their owner, regardless of whether the owner says or does anything.

"They're also positively attracted to people they will have the most interaction with. They can sense more about us than we can about them.

"I can read the minds of my dog and two cats. I can tell by my dog's eyes when he's asking for something, or just looking for affection, or doesn't want anything at all.

"If ESP is possible in humans, it's got to be in animals also. To me, ESP means the ability to sense or perceive above and beyond others.

"A dog's sense of smell is ten thousand to twenty thousand times greater than a human's. A dog can smell a female in heat five to ten miles away.

"It's amazing how animals can perceive the subtlest changes in humans. There's a story about a horse that could add and subtract by tapping out answers with a hoof. Finally someone figured out the horse was so willing to let the trainer be responsible for its survival that it would do anything the trainer commanded.

"As soon as the horse reached the right number, it would see the trainer's eyes relax, and it would stop."

Some people have experimented at home by throwing two different colored balls on the floor and trying to get their pet to pick up one color through telepathy. Instead of saying it, thinking it.

There are documented cases of people leaving or losing their dog hundreds of miles from home, or of moving to another state and leaving their dog behind. Through some instinct we do not understand, the animal finds its way to its family.

Waterhole Ike

Mark Cowley, owner of Waterhole No. 1, a saloon in Golconda, Nevada, read how a race horse named Secretariat was syndicated, with shares of stock being sold to the public.

The rest of this story comes from a phone conversation with Cowley.

"This is a small town . . . only forty-five or fifty people," Cowley said. "In our little bar we talk about everything that's going on. We have to create our own entertainment.

"When I read about Secretariat I decided to syndicate a pig. I sold shares for one dollar apiece and we bought a young pig and named him Waterhole Ike.

"Word got around and I had to print up three hundred stock certificates. The stock was selling so fast I called a meeting to elect officers. I nominated myself president and seconded the nomination with a proxy of a guy who was too drunk to know what I was doing.

"The money got to be too much for the cigar box, so I opened a bank account in Waterhole Ike's name. The bank wanted a Social Security number so they could report the interest to the government.

"So we applied for a card for Waterhole Ike, and HEW sent one. I have it in the vault here—530-80-4623. Then another bank wrote Ike a letter offering higher interest, so we switched. Later they sent him a letter saying he was eligible to borrow up to $25,000.

"I checked with Social Security and told them I had a friend who was an alcoholic. He really is, you know. I pour all the beer that people leave in their glasses into a big bucket. We have to breed him early in the morning because by half past ten he's had two or three gallons of beer and is in pig heaven. The curl even goes out of his tail.

"Anyway, Social Security said my friend was entitled to help. All I had to do was sign the papers. Then I checked with welfare. I said I had a friend who was out of work and had ten dependents. They said he was entitled to $633 a month plus food stamps.

"But I didn't apply for either program. Ike doesn't want any government handouts. He's not that kind of pig. He can take care of himself. He's kind of a middle-class pig.

"This is the first year he's had to file a tax return. One year he earned $400, and then he made about $1,200. He actually earned more than that, but he had a lot of expenses. He's got a pretty fancy red, white, and blue pen.

"Besides the stock sales, Ike gets an income from stud fees. He's a pretty good stud. He had twenty-five sows last year. He gets $25 or the pick of the litter.

"He didn't actually pay any taxes this year. He was eligible for a credit of $71 in his Social Security account and a cash rebate of $19. He filed as self-employed and an unmarried head of a household.

"Unfortunately, all forty-five people in town are mad at me because they're afraid Ike will make Golconda so popular that property taxes will go up."

Cowley insisted he wasn't trying to poke fun at society. But he said it with a little lilt in his voice . . . laying on that country bit . . . "Gee, I don't know what you mean. . . ."

At War with Nature

The blue jays and robins ate most of my raspberries. The raccoons got all the grapes. The robins got so many strawberries I pulled out all the plants. The squirrels ate so many peaches that I cut down the tree. The plums are gone—squirrels, birds, or both. The rabbits no longer can eat my beans because I put up chicken wire around the bean patch. The blue jays, squirrels, and bugs fight it out for the apples.

Nobody bothers the tomatoes.

Such are the delights of gardening in my particular corner of the suburbs.

I wrote frequently about my crops and wildlife, and have been asked if I'm still at it. Well, yes. And so are the birds and beasties.

As this is written we're entertaining six raccoons each evening—four babies, two adults. A possum joins them every few nights. Each spring brings a new brood of raccoons. They didn't bother us, and they're awfully cute. A manx cat that lived wild used to eat with them, but she decided it looked warmer inside and she moved in.

Assorted squirrels and chipmunks and all kinds of birds complete this urban animal preserve, in a built-up residential area only eighteen miles north of the Loop.

Two deer walked across our front yard on a recent dawn. We're a couple miles from a forest preserve, and I have no idea where they were going. Friends near the forest preserve say the deer eat a lot of their trees, shrubs, and gardens.

I put a fake owl in the garden and the birds perch on it. A fake snake in the garden has frightened the bejeepers out of several visitors, but it amuses the wild life. I saved the grapes from the raccoons one year by putting a radio with a talk show near the vines all night. The following year the raccoons spit out the grape seeds on the radio.

I haven't even mentioned the insects and what they do to food and flowers. But they're not very cute. Not like raccoons and chipmunks.

More Shorts

WHERE'S THE FIRE?

Long before the government broke up AT&T, small communities had switchboards, and usually the operator recognized everyone in town by voice. "Hello Helen. Would you ring the hardware?"

In Coal City whenever the fire alarm sounded at the City Hall or fire station, the central office switchboard buzzed to life with everyone asking, "Where's the fire?"

In one instance the operator replied that it was so and so's house. The next day, a full twenty-four hours later, the central switchboard buzzed, and with no introduction whatever, the caller of the previous day asked,

"How'd it start?"

HOW'S THAT AGAIN?

When a Milwaukee man wrote to disagree with my opinions on the John Birch Society, I wrote back to the return address on his envelope. My letter was returned by the post office, with this stamped on it:

"Authorized Time For Forwarding Has Expired. Please Advise Your Correspondents of Your New Address."

Was this message intended for me? If so, how could I find the man to learn his new address if the postal service wouldn't forward my letter? If the message was for him, why was it sent to me?

MI AMIGO JOSE

For seven or eight years, each December an envelope came to my office containing a note and several one hundred dollar bills—from three to seven of them—for the retarded children.

There was no return address, and the notes were signed "Su Amigo Jose." The notes were on dime-store paper, in an unsophisticated hand, and always carried gentle messages of love and concern for others.

One December came a letter from Jose's sister-in-law with his last gift—$250.

"In life," she wrote, "Jose didn't want any plaudits or recognition for his good deeds. He gave away his money. His sisters, with whom he lived, say he wouldn't want recognition after his death, either. In respect to his wishes, let him remain as he always signed . . . Su Amigo Jose."

He wasn't a Latin. He was Polish.

EVERYBODY'S A DOCTOR

When I was a TV critic I had to watch soap operas once in a while. There was one in which most of the characters were doctors. The lady doctor loved the man doctor, who impregnated a nurse, who was suffering the dread disease aspodistritis.

Years later when I had turned respectable a bad back forced me to be horizontal for a week. During this enforced confinement I turned on a soap opera. A lady who's familiar with these things filled me in.

"He's a doctor," she explained, "and so is she. They're in love. Those other people are doctors too, but they don't have any lines because the union charges more if they speak. They glide around taking temperatures and injecting saline solution and wiping foreheads, but they never say a word.

"The nurse is pregnant. The man she's treating is a doctor who got some unknown disease while searching for Compound D in the Lithium project."

If you think the world is moving too fast, turn on a TV soap opera every five years. Nothing changes except the names of the diseases.

THE PLUMBER'S POLL

The TV industry didn't like me after I visited the water-pumping station at Michigan and Chicago avenues and found that a large part of their audience was in the bathroom while the commercials were on. That was true in 1963 and it's probably true today.

My Plumber's Poll was delightfully simple. When a lot of toilets are flushed at one time, the water pressure in the city pumping station goes down. In the good old days of television they had commercials on the hour and half hour, not every twelve or fifteen minutes as they do today.

The engineers noticed the pattern on their pressure charts, and had no trouble tracing the cause.

The first big dip on this chart was at 7:30 P.M. January 1, 1963. The Rose Bowl game ended then. The next big dip was for the 8:30 commercial, then another at 9, one at 10, and so on.

I offered this service at no cost to the television industry, but they didn't want it.

EARLY TV

A young lady in an Uncle Sam suit played "God Bless America" on water glasses filled to different heights. This performance had a certain primitive appeal when I saw it on a television screen in a Chicago saloon in 1947. The men at the bar eyed the screen dolefully, entranced by the motion but unmoved by the message.

Playing drinking glasses filled with do re mi fa sol portions of water was early evidence of the ingenuity of Chicago television, which was to bring the city fame as the point of origin of bright, uncomplicated, literate, and immensely entertaining television programs.

James C. Petrillo was the czar of all union musicians. He regarded this new offshoot of broadcasting with suspicion. Naturally he forbade his musicians to perform before the cameras.

The city's lone TV station, WBKB, now WLS-TV, was trying to entertain fifty thousand set owners and countless barflies for eight hours a day without spending much money and without using union musicians or scabs. An astonishing array of ukulele and harmonica players suddenly became TV stars, augmenting piano players, high school choirs, seals which honked out "My Country 'Tis of Thee," and of course, the young lady with the musical water glasses.

Chicago had eight thousand saloons, and every one had a TV. If only five customers were watching at any given time, that meant forty thousand sets of eyes, however glazed, were intent on the screen. In the forty thousand homes which boasted TV sets, neighbors, friends, and relatives swarmed in to watch the box. Everybody knew if you had a set because of the aerial on the roof.

A survey of set owners found only 3 percent who called the medium "disappointing." A CBS vice president was staggered. "That's as small a percent of 'disappointing' as anything I know, even sex," he said.

EPISCOPALIANS MAKE BETTER COFFEE

Religion doesn't have to be grim. An Episcopalian sent me a copy of "What Episcopalians Believe" from the *Anglican Digest*.

Episcopalians believe it is wrong to vote for a political candidate on purely religious grounds unless he is an Episcopalian.

Episcopalians make better coffee than almost anyone.

Episcopalians believe in the importance of confession and frequently confess their sins, particularly when confronted with the evidence.

Episcopalians generally are suspicious of rectors who have spotlights trained on their pulpits.

Episcopalians believe in ecumenism because they want everyone else to become just like Episcopalians.

Episcopalians listen to sermons with great interest, except when they're thinking about something else.

Episcopalians wouldn't trade jobs with their rectors, but would like to trade vacations with them.

Episcopalians believe in miracles and sometimes expect them, particularly during stewardship drives.

Episcopalians who have never been on vestries claim they don't know what goes on at meetings. Episcopalians who have been claim they don't know either.

Episcopalians enjoy church suppers and will pay as much as a dollar for the privilege of bringing the family to one.

Faces in the City

Urban Dialogues

"Me and Eddie got on the el at Sixty-Third Street. I was sort of intop . . . intopsicated and Eddie almost had to carry me on. I'd drunk a pint of gin with a girlfriend. But Eddie was sober.

"We headed north and Eddie started pushing people around like he always does. He knocked a woman down and beat her on the head for nothin'. He didn't rob her. He gets like that . . . wild. I tried to stop him but I was too gone."

Buck, nineteen, chubby, nearly illiterate, sits in a police lieutenant's office, drags on a cigarette, and talks. He has five sisters and a brother. His mother is dead. His father is "somewhere in the city." He quit school at fifteen. His pal Eddie is nineteen, surly and untalkative.

Buck: "At Thirty-Ninth we changed trains. We seen this man and this girl in the train and I asked them for a quarter and he give it to us.

"Eddie started pushing people around. Then he came up to this man reading the paper and started hitting him. I came up to the man and said, 'I'll stop him hittin' you if you give us a dollar.'

"The man pulled out his money clip and me and Eddie snatched at it. It dropped to the floor. This guy right by us started to move and I said set down or Eddie give it to him too. Eddie gets like that. I don't have no nerve to do nothin' when I'm sober.

"I didn't hit the man with my fist or nothin'. I sort of pushed him. It was Eddie hit him.

"Yeah, it was my razor Eddie had. It was old and busted and I'd thrown it away, but Eddie picked it up. He said it still had some good."

Their victim, a dentist, was struck with such force that his head broke a car window. Twenty or twenty-five people in the train did nothing to interfere.

What if the dentist had put up a fight?

"Well, Eddie's one of them chicken guys. If the man hadn't been so easy he probably wouldn't have robbed him. Eddie never do it alone, he needs someone with him. But if the man hit at Eddie, I might have helped him fight.

"We got off the train and went over to a tavern. I brought a pint of gin and Eddie had a beer. I was trying to tell Eddie about the purple lights. The lights in there was purple and they make white shirts look purple. He don't get it.

"We took a cab later and I kind of don't remember. We got picked up by the cops and spent two days in the bullpen, on suspicion or somethin'. The judge turned us loose and said don't go hangin' around street corners no more.

"Eddie got picked up and stooled on me. I knew him since reform school. We hung around together and robbed newsstands. I remember a couple days before that dentist, I was with him at Sixty-Third and Dorchester. He said, 'Let's get that old lady's pocketbook.' I said I didn't want to. He went over and knocked her down and hit her and run down an alley.

"I felt sorry for the lady, she was heavy and old, and I went over and helped pick her up. Then the police come and say which way that guy go, and I say down the alley.

"I guess I just shouldn't hung around Eddie and his gang. I'm supposed to go in the army. I signed up to go straight. I thought it might do some good. Now I guess I ain't going."

Buck was right. He went to prison.

The time when this took place is irrelevant, because it was a common story in Chicago for a quarter of a century. As this is written the Chicago police have just established a transit detail with some twenty-five uniformed policemen riding el trains and buses to protect the passengers and drivers.

The Indians

The Sons and Daughters of the American Revolution and other good Americans were observing Thanksgiving over festive tables while some of the Sons of the People They Took the Country Away From were pounding a bar at the Jackpot Saloon on Skid Row.

"They came over on the Mayflower and they had a Bible in one hand and a rifle in the other and they stole every *&$#@*&%& thing we had," shouted Hugh, a Chippewa.

"But we can still laugh," said Ben Shigwadja as fellow warriors grunted approval and hoisted another shot. "No matter what they took we can still laugh. A guy can stick a gun in my ribs and I'm going to keep on laughing."

The line for turkey dinner at the Harbor Light was so long these Indians repaired to the shelter of the Jackpot and the nourishment of a four-bit bottle of wine. Joe Whitefish. Felix Recolette. Johnny Standingbythedoor, Mike Dodgingwolf, Yellowhorse, Bill Adams. Bill Adams??? "I don't where my father got *that* name," Bill Adams said.

"There are a lot of Indians on the street. I know twenty-five and that's only a small part of 'em."

Hugh wouldn't tell his last name because his father was a chief. "You're just down here for kicks," he grumbled to the visitor.

Trouble in Park Ridge

Park Ridge is a suburb nestled between the Chicago city limits and the world's busiest airport. Most of the complaints from Park Ridge are about the planes descending over their rooftops. Chicago benefits from the airborne noisemakers and Park Ridge suffers. Park Ridge is a nice town and doesn't allow booze to be sold and it was there long before O'Hare was and it isn't fair.

Otherwise Park Ridgers (Ridgians?) behave pretty much like other suburbanites. A group of residents wanted to bell all the cats and fix all dogs and cats so there would no more puppies and kittens within the Park Ridge limits. Kind of an offbeat idea, but no worse than an ordinance passed in the Chicago City Council prohibiting starlings from flying over the forty-eighth ward.

A public hearing was held in the public library basement on a proposal for new laws to make cats and dogs stay home. An alderman who owned an Airedale presided. The 100 present were divided about equally between people who loved dogs, people who loved cats, and people who hated both.

Cat owner, woman: "My cat doesn't need a license. She has clean habits."

Cat owner, man: "Remember the black plague? In the dark ages people destroyed their cats. Do you know what happened? The rats ravaged the city, and the plague spread. If a cat is not allowed to roam, he cannot properly police the rats.

"If you start licensing cats, next it will be parakeets and goldfish. I violently object to bells and ringlets around a cat's neck. It would be detrimental to his health and welfare. If a cat, on the roam, catches a bird, that's his God-given right as a cat."

Taxpayer, man: "Would this be a tax or a regulation? Why the three-dollar fee? Isn't that a tax?"

Alderman: "It would be for the bookkeeping. You must not get angry, people!"

A man with glasses: "Who owns the squirrels in Park Ridge? If Park Ridge owns them, I'd ask the city fathers to confine them to City Hall. Squirrels are a nuisance. Every morning when I wake up there are two on my roof chewing the wood."

Man, neutral: "Why not license all pets? I mean *all*. Raccoons, squirrels, elephants. I might decide to buy an elephant some day."

Woman, whispering to visiting reporters: "Gosh, would Mrs. —— have a hemorrhage if an elephant did his business on her lawn."

Voice: "What about snakes? Why not bell them?"

Businesslike man: "I'm not against all cat owners. I don't want to hurt them all. I'm against one woman and one cat, which messes everywhere. If we could regulate those two without bothering anybody else, I'd be happy."

A Boy Scout: "We have a very productive cat, and every four months she has five or six kittens. She has been doing this for the last three years. If you pass this law will I have to get a license for every kitten?"

Sympathetic adult: "Good question. The kid would shoot a year's allowances on licenses."

When the Nazis took over Greece they ordered all the dogs and cats killed so the rats would multiply. Today Park Ridge, tomorrow the world.

The Market for Gypsy Girls

A gypsy girl called me on the phone. "Please help us. We don't want to be bought and sold. Nobody helps us. If they knew I was talking with you they'd beat me."

I asked a policeman youth worker about the gypsies.

"A nice little gypsy girl in her teens, good at fortune telling, properly uneducated, will bring $3,000 to $4,000," he said. "I'd guess about $50,000-worth of girls are sold here each year.

"Fathers selling their daughters in marriage is one of the quaint old-world customs that came across the Atlantic. Why, a gypsy father would be ashamed if he couldn't get money for his daughters. We've been trying for years to do something about it. We try to check the ages of the girls and there aren't any records. No marriage records, either. They tell you all the papers burned in a wagon fire in Tennessee.

"There is no wedding ceremony, really. The bride's father just puts a white bandana on the girl's head. That's it. Once in a while a girl is sold to a gadzo—that's a non-gypsy. But the contract isn't considered binding, and sooner or later the girl wanders back home.

"It's important that the girls be kept out of school. If they go at all, they usually are pulled out by the third or fourth grade. Learning is dangerous. The girls who do manage to learn about the gadzo world revolt against their assignment in gypsy life to steal and wait on men. Television is dangerous too.

"The girls are so scared of getting hurt they keep quiet. The one who pays the money—usually the father-in-law—has the power over the girl. She has to earn back the money he spent on her. Sometimes the husband doesn't see her until the wedding."

This took place in the sixties. One of the pluses of television is that it has helped educate the gypsy girls. The selling of girls is fading as the older gypsy generations die.

The Crime Fighters of Old Town

Old Town is a neighborhood of a few blocks near Lincoln Park. The residents have saved and upgraded an area of old homes. The community has individuality and character, this being true of both the structures and the occupants.

To prepare for the winter crime season they held a town meeting in the large back room of a neighborhood tavern. Most blocks had one or two "eyes" to keep a constant lookout for prowlers or suspicious-looking strangers. Many had laid in a supply of knives, clubs, guns, locks, watchdogs and burglar alarms.

The district police captain said some thieves use beer can openers to get into cars. One gentleman said the winos are making hotels of abandoned cars. He pronounced it *weenoes*.

After the meeting coffee was served and burglar alarm salesmen took over. A woman approached the reporter.

"I've been watching the people in the room," she said. "You seem to have a sense of humor. Don't you think we're just a bunch of nitwits sitting here exposing our plans? I saw two men. They looked just like burglars listening, and they quickly left before the coffee was served.

"I have some small knives, one in each room, but the trouble is I don't remember where I put them."

A salesman's siren went off. "Oh dear, if they don't stop, I shall have to leave," said the lady. She left.

A man: "I have a dog. That's the best alarm. A mutt. His mother was rather indiscriminate in her tastes."

A salesman explaining a pocket-sized alarm: "The idea is that when the thief snatches the purse it will scream for you. He'll think he's carrying a time bomb or something and drop it. Purse snatchers are rather stupid anyway—it's not an easy type of work."

Our advice to burglars: stay out of Old Town. There's not that much to steal, and you're liable to get shot, stabbed, bitten, slugged, clubbed, slashed, scared, or talked to death.

The Garbageman

"This guy," said Gertrude Stacy proudly. "He has some sense, I dunno, call it ESP or what, but he can look at a garbage can, and some instinct tells him if there's something worthwhile in it."

The walls of Alex and Gertrude Stacy's flat in Ravenswood were lined with shelves holding artifacts, *objets d'art*, knickknacks, cups, vases, mugs, plates, pitchers, and some beautiful copper and brass ware which were black when Al hauled them out of the garbage and which glistened after he cleaned them up.

Al had ten years driving a garbage truck in the forty-seventh ward on Chicago's northwest side. He had a knack for finding objects of some value or use to persons other than the thrower-awayer. In fact he frequently accepted orders from people in the neighborhood. When the local kids flooded a yard for ice skating, Al and his coworkers provided skates for the whole gang. No problem. No charge.

I chatted with Al and Gertrude at their kitchen table. In a corner were three huge plants Al coaxed back to life. A dog growled at me from a corner of the kitchen: "I got him at the police station." I glanced at an illuminated Old Style beer clock over the stove. "Yep," Al grinned. "And I have a nice Bud sign and a Hamm's sign that when you turn it on the water starts rippling.

"You should see my garage," he added.

I noted that in Australia garbagemen were highly respected and are called "garbos."

"That's good," said Gertrude. "You know, here it's the young people who really respect the garbagemen. They do honest, necessary work. And the children . . . why . . . they follow Al and the others down the street.

" 'Find any toys Mr. Stacy?' they'll yell."

"There's a little girl, six, on my route," Al said. "Her mother says the first thing she hears our truck, nothing will do until she comes and says hello. There's an Airedale the same way, has to come out and sniff and wag at us."

Al took pride in his work, and talked trade with other garbagemen when he traveled to California or Salt Lake City or wherever.

"I'm not complaining," Al said, and his wife smiled.

They also had a snow-white cat, and I didn't ask where it came from.

Party at Hef's Pad

When I was midwest correspondent for a documentary series on National Educational Television, we did one half hour from the Hefner mansion in Chicago.

That was an interesting experience, but I had more fun when I got an unexpected invitation to a party at the mansion.

The starting time was 1 A.M., which I guess is Hefner's afternoon. I hadn't been up past midnight in ten years, but I felt a compulsion to attend. The house on the Near North Side had become a Chicago landmark, and how could I be a Big Columnist if I'd never been to a party at Hef's pad?

The house is built along the dimensions of a United States Court of Appeals. A Frain usher sat in the lobby checking in the guests. He was one of fifty-five employees in the place. Four of these were security officers whose duties included protecting from attack the many Bunnies in the hutch.

The Frain man directed me up a flight of carpeted stairs to a hall where two young ladies behind a counter were checking wraps.

Festive sounds came from the left. I walked down the hall into a large room. This was it. The room is about half the size of the Palmer House lobby. It is paneled in wood and was full of furniture and people who looked as if they had been picked by a Hollywood casting director.

Near the entrance sat a young woman with hair falling around her shoulders. A man named Benny was leaning toward this girl and flicking something off her bare and ample chest—crumbs, dandruff flakes, cigar ashes, whatever.

Farther along in the room a young woman and a young man sat in unanimated conversation. Her bare legs were crossed, and the young man idly tapped her knee to see if her leg jumped. It didn't.

Thirty or forty people stood holding glasses filled with liquid, simultaneously talking and keeping an eye on everybody else in the room.

A magnificent sound system filled the air with jazz. The ceiling was ringed with photographic flash lamps. Three young men hustled about taking pictures, with each shutter click setting off the lamps. It was a little like being in a violent electrical storm, with jazz instead of thunder.

A small door at the far end of the room led to a narrow stairway, which led downstairs to a small swimming pool, the humidity of which would destroy any hairdo. Three males and one female were romping around the pool somewhat like porpoises.

Another small door led to another small flight of stairs which led down to a barroom which was quite dark, but, I sensed, full of people. A window in the wall revealed the water in the swimming pool. It was murky, and if there were any human forms in it, I couldn't make them out.

I wandered back to the ballroom and the thunder and lightning. Food was being served in a small adjoining room. It was now 2 A.M. and I hadn't eaten since six. I approached the buffet table. It was loaded with orange juice, frying eggs, and sweet rolls.

"What's this?" I asked.

"Breakfast."

"Yesterday's or tomorrow's?"

"Yesterday's. We serve dinner at 3:30."

I said thanks and left hungry. The lady behind the food table was the prettiest and brightest-looking person in the place. She, and most of the bartenders and servers, had master's degrees. They were teachers, and this job was their moonlighting.

I had toured the place, it was 2:30, and I was tired and hungry. I said good evening to the host and started out the door.

Approaching the stairway to the lobby I heard a female scream . . . not in terror, but not "ha ha" either. Kind of like the way the girls screamed in the movies when Harpo Marx chased them.

Two girls came racing around the corner, one pulling herself from the grasp of a man I had been told was Shel Silverstein, a Sophisticated Artist.

As they disappeared around the corner, the girl was pulling away.

Big Mama

Big Mama was a West Side lady built along the lines of Mama Cass. Her heart was as big as her body. The last time I saw her she was propped up in her living room. Her legs had given out. Her house was filled with kids and adults she was feeding and sheltering. She had written me to ask for help at Christmas for her flock. Kenan Heise, my assistant, and I scrounged some stuff and took it to Big Mama.

Kenan and Arthur Allen, an officer of Public Aid, founded the Neediest Children's Christmas fund, primarily as the result of Allen's work and Kenan's visits to many like Big Mama.

Kenan quoted Big Mama in his book, *The Death of Christmas.*

"I got twenty-four kids on this block who won't have no Christmas," she said. "I could give it to them if I had it. I don't have it.

"When I used to work, I used to help people paying rent and buying them clothes and getting kids presents. I just loves to give things.

"I don't know nothing worse than being too poor to give something. It aches your heart. I just feels like a dog. The kids next door. I used to Santa Claus them. Now, I can't do no Santa Clausing. I can't give them nothing.

"Most everything I got, I gets from secondhand stores. I haven't had no new clothes in ten years. Right now I don't have one piece of underwear. Not a slip. Not a pair of panties. I wear size fifty-two and you don't get things size fifty-two secondhand at Salvation Army.

"Still, I'm glad God has been as good to me as he has. People ask me if I gonna make it. I think I has made it. I'm sixty-five and I'm filled with the Holy Ghost.

"Christmas is the birth of Christ, and it is best we accept that.

"When you exchange gifts, there is no blessing in that. It is no good. I never gives anything to anybody who don't need it.

"I been in the market and I seen an old man or an old woman order two pork chops and then tell them to take one back when they saw how much it cost. When I had money, I told the butcher to give them six pork chops and I pay.

"We're all children at Christmastime. I need clothes. I need panties. I'd like to be able to pay some of my bills. I'd like to get something good to eat."

The Checker

My worst problem at the supermarket is the jerk who goes to the ten items or less counter with 12, 15, 20 packages in his basket. Or her basket.

We normally don't give much thought to what might irritate the checker. This has always struck me as one of the toughest service jobs, even after they've got all the gizmos at the register.

A lady who spent five years checking at a supermarket told us she dearly loves 98 percent of the customers. But, oh, that other 2 percent.

There's the shopper who puts bread and pies in the bottom of the basket and then piles canned goods and five pounds of sugar on them, and complains because the bread and pies are crushed.

She not only complains, but sometimes goes back to get replacements and leaves the crushed food for somebody else.

The list of irritators is long:

• The customer who comes in five minutes before closing and wanders around buying fifty-dollars worth of groceries.

• The one who says put all the order in one bag, and then decides she needs two bags.

• The one who complains there is no bagger. (The checker is unhappier about that than the customer).

• The twenty-item customers in the express lane always have a reason ready: "I'm in a hurry." "The kids will be home for lunch in five minutes." "I'm on my lunch hour." (They spend twenty of the next thirty minutes next door looking at dresses.)

• The man who blows El Stinko cigar smoke in the checker's face. After he has dropped ashes on the vegetable bin.

• The person who waits until the checker has rung up the entire order, and then starts to look for her pen and checkbook. Why can't she have the check ready, except for the amount, wails the checker.

• The customer who takes her anger out on the checker because the mail was late that morning, or she had a fight with her husband, or the car wouldn't start.

• The person who puts his cart in line and then runs all over the store getting more items to put in it. I had thought checkers didn't notice that sort of thing.

• The person who doesn't say she has food stamps until everything is rung up and the tax is put on. Then the checker has to separate the items and take off soap, paper products, and pet food because food stamps are food only.

• The shopper who puts an item in his cart, then changes his mind, and leaves it wherever he happens to be. This includes ice cream, meat, and other perishables.

• The ones who give the checker dirty looks when she has the audacity to close for a break or go home at the end of her shift.

• People who confide their personal problems.

• The lady who waits until the checking is finished, and then goes to the desk to cash a check for more than that amount, leaving nine people cooling their heels in the line.

• The shopper who screams bloody murder when the checker hits the wrong key and rings up thirty-five cents for a thirty-four cent item, but never makes a sound when the mistake is twenty-four cents instead of thirty-four in favor of the customer.

• The customer who leaves the cart at the counter for somebody else to take care of. The customer who leaves the cart three blocks away.

• The customer who complains about prices. The checker usually runs a household herself and is as distressed about the prices as any of her customers.

I asked my friend the checker if all this was bad enough to make her want to quit. "Oh no," she answered. "I'd be bored to tears sitting in some office with nobody to talk to."

Home Life

The Woman in the Home

NBC showed a TV special saluting ten Women of the Year. The ten were an opera singer, two women in TV, a governor, a day-care director, a writer, an Olympic diver, an anthropologist, a judge, an Indian affairs specialist, and a President's wife.

Among 100 million American women NBC couldn't find one woman worthy of symbolic recognition for raising children and maintaining a home.

This observation is not going to generate one of those cutesy-pie pieces on blowing tiny noses and putting on snowsuits and chauffeuring to Little League. I just feel that every one of those ten was probably nominated by a public relations person or agent. Women whose lives are devoted to their homes and families don't have press agents.

We've never been able to come up with a suitable vocational designation for the woman at home. "Housewife" and "homemaker" don't do it. "Domestic maintenance supervisor" is facetious. I don't know the proper word. But she is the woman who makes a career of staying home, bearing children, raising children, cooking, cleaning, shopping, making the home comfortable and attractive, and symbolically, standing in the door with a cheerful greeting for returning members of the household.

She's the one who pulls it all together and makes it work.

These days many women have two jobs—home and away. But there are enough making homes to justify recognizing it as a full-time vocation.

NBC could come back with figures on how many children their Women of the Year have borne and how beautifully they manage their own households. I'd want accompanying statistics on how many maids and cleaning ladies and nannies they collectively have employed. Also, how many have at their disposal public relations agents to assist in informing the world of their achievements.

The home career women don't have agents. They don't even have a voice. If one writes a newspaper column or has a radio or TV voice this act automatically disqualifies her as a pure home careerist.

The mechanical skills of the home careerist—cooking, handling the accounts, driving, cleaning, shopping—aren't hard to master. But the human relations aspects—teaching proper values, maintaining both harmony and discipline, generating a warm and loving atmosphere—these are skills as challenging as holding a high C or smiling into a TV camera or conducting a large women's club meeting.

Whenever someone speaks for the home careerist, it usually drips with condescension and/or whimsy.

One woman I know (intimately) has gone through hell at times managing her household and coping with family crises. She has met them with courage. She mastered the mechanics with good cheer, raised her children skillfully and lovingly, and now presides over a home that anyone might envy.

Yet periodically she'll sit back and say, "I feel so useless. What have I accomplished?"

She gets little appreciation for her accomplishment. She watches a television program saluting Women of the Year and feels inadequate. NBC needs a special to fill an hour and a women's magazine needs a promotion, so they choose to glamorize ladies who make their livings in politics and the theater and in academics or the women's movement.

That's fine—but why ignore the most important women in America?

I printed these opinions, and generated an unusual response. The depth of feeling on both sides surprised me. In fact, I didn't know there were two sides. Here are some of them:

From Dee Taylor of Chicago: "Your cheapest shot of all was the implication that something was lacking in women who employ baby-sitters and cleaning ladies, or that they could not possibly have achieved their status because of their own talent, hard work, and dedication, as you men do, but as a result of publicists who had to beef them up.

"As long as we still do our own wash and scrub our own floors we are 'real' women . . . feminine. Tell me, Mr. Mabley, if 'homemaker' (which obviously sticks in your throat, too) is such an exalted, glorious career, why aren't more men entering into it?"

Susan Kennedy, Kenilworth: "Why must communications media, so-called liberationists, and female professionals feel it their responsibility to lecture us housewives on topics of self-worth, places in life, goal-seeking, assertiveness, and the like?

"We do not ask, nor seek their opinions, nor do we parade ourselves around boasting of our excellence in child-rearing, cleaning, laundering, advice-giving, and maintaining domestic tranquility. But by God we do need frequent words of praise and understanding from husbands such as mine and writers such as you!"

Bonnie Lake, DeKalb: "Showering mothers with honor is what produced that social travesty, Mother's Day, where all the year's self-sacrifice is supposed to be taken care of with a $9.95 bunch of roses.

"If the professional mother is like most—narrow-minded, socially retarded, intellectually squelched, tranquilized, socially useless outside her little fort—then she is to be rescued, not honored."

Maggie Minchow, Hinsdale: "You can help other husbands and fathers realize that were it not for the little women at home, they would not be (in business) where they are today. The married man has it over the single man for advancement. Why? The company gets two for the price of one.

"So make that paycheck out to both of them. Banks should require both signatures to cash that check, pay Social Security to both, make equal contributions to pension plans, any other payroll deductions to both—as long as the wife is a full-time homemaker.

"In this society, the greatest recognition for a job well done is the paycheck. Knowing you have earned your salary goes a long way in giving self-respect. It is easy to drop a wife, easier than to fire a teacher or a union man. And of the three, the one who can't file for unemployment compensation is the wife."

Bonnie Lake again: "If your wife has any brains or sensitivity, she is angry. So is the woman down the block. The only ones not angry are those whose spirits were broken so long ago they are numb.

"Ask yourself what self-respect you would have if your role was that of a domestic: stewing hours in the kitchen to serve the food only to have everybody else retire to watch the Super Bowl while you were left with a bunch of dishes with spinach clinging to them."

My mother was a professional—a concert pianist, on the road much of the time. Two of my daughters have jobs in business and are raising small children. A third daughter is a physician, and our daughter-in-law works. I've lived with these viewpoints and experiences all my life. Each of the women in my life was or is fulfilled in her choice of pursuits. My wife has further perfected her skills in managing our household. She still is spirited, and is not angry.

The Father as a Pal

Teenage lament: "My father just wants to be a pal to me. Who wants a forty-year-old pal? I wish he'd start acting like a father."

Forty-year-old father: "O.K. I'll act like a father, the old-fashioned kind who took no nonsense from any of the kids. Make 'em toe the mark. Give them discipline for their own good."

Teenager: "He's a tyrant. Our home's like a concentration camp. Who wants a father like that? Why can't he be a pal?"

Are there any parents alive who have contemplated their grown children and not asked, "What did we do wrong? What would we do different if we had it to do over again?" I suppose there are some who think they never made a mistake in guiding their children to adulthood. But I never met them.

It is very difficult to be a successful father, at least successful in the eyes of your offspring. This is normalcy and there's no use fighting it.

Give your teen too much allowance and you're spoiling him.

Give him less and you're depriving him. Let your teen use a charge account and you're pampering her. Don't let her use a charge card and how's she ever going to learn the value of money?

Insist on music lessons and you're a tyrant again. Don't insist on music lessons and the poor child is growing up culturally deprived.

There are little mundane tasks in every household that have to be done. How many parents have surrendered abjectly because through hard experience they've found less energy is expended in doing the dishes themselves than is expended in acquiring the services of one teenage dishwasher?

If a boy comes home dirty he's all boy. If he comes home clean something's the matter with him. If a girl has a lot of dates she's boy crazy. If she doesn't have a lot of dates, something's the matter with her.

Turmoil is normalcy. What else could be expected from a creature that insists on blasting rock radio, drinking Cokes, and eating fries? You wonder about your child if he never brings friends home, and if he brings a lot of friends home they all seem to detour through mud or slush on their way to your living room rug.

A minister friend whose occupation was dealing with teenagers gave me this analysis:

"A teenager has to find out who he is. But to do this, he first must find out who he is *not*. That's why you find him constantly trying something new, experimenting, daring, trying on this personality or that one, always reaching."

Finding who he is not can be painful, but there's no better way to find who he is.

I talked with a family service counselor in the western suburbs. People said to him, "You don't mean to say we have these kinds of problems here in Hinsdale?" or Glen Ellyn or Naperville or on through the corridor of prosperous suburbs.

They have problems in abundance, beyond the common ones I touched on.

"These parents should sit in one of our caseworker's chairs and face these youngsters as they come in for help," he said.

I grew up in the heart of the city, and I suppose there were a lot of these kinds of problems. But I and my friends weren't aware of them. Maybe life was better for being simpler then.

But I raised four children in the suburbs, and worked with youngsters, and of course visited with scores of parents.

We have problems in the suburbs. In abundance. Far more than I was aware of in the city.

There are fewer teenage problems in communities which have clung to old-world customs, and particularly the customs of the authority of the father. I'm unfamiliar with the family discipline practices of most Asians, but they must be doing something right. Look at the scholarship grants and academic achievements of high schools and marvel at the number of Asian names.

I'm not arguing for a paternal iron hand, though this would settle a lot of problems. But the more Americanized we get, the less stomach we have for cracking down on the kids. The path of least resistance is to not argue with them and hope for the best.

Kids want discipline, though superficially they resist it. This might be a topic for discussion tonight when mom and pop clean up the kitchen.

The Sound and the Fury

Stock tip: Hearing aids. When the rock and roll generation gets older they'll be so deaf they'll need artificial help to hear.

The villain is amplified music. Volume seems to be equated with good. I avoid these sonic booms like the plague, but some of the amplification is unavoidable. Cars full of youngsters whish past and the noise of their radios can be heard a block away. I'd think it would addle their brains.

Yet of all the achievements of our teenagers, none impress me more than their ability to concentrate on homework while the radio or tape deck crashes out 85 decibels of musical hysteria.

My kids used to sit with their heads in a book, writing out Spanish translations or figuring logarithmic curves. No less than ten feet from their ears "the beat" was beating out—a steady, unintelligible flow of cannibal rhythms, interrupted every three minutes by an announcer whose salary was scaled to the volume of his pleas to buy skin cleansers.

I was outraged at this approach to homework, and waited

patiently for their grades to suffer. Then I'd pounce and confiscate the boomers. It didn't happen. Their grades didn't go down.

A Southern Californian, John E. Hoffman, earned a doctorate in education by examining study habits. Part of the study was testing 281 eleventh grade pupils while music blared at 85 decibels. That's a noise equivalent of the Chicago Symphony pounding out Richard Strauss's "Thus Spake Zarathustra," or just 5 decibels less than a pneumatic drill tearing up Michigan Avenue.

Students of higher-than-average intelligence scored as well or better on examinations during the noise than they did in a quiet room. Superior readers performed more effectively under loud noise than poor readers.

Dr. Hoffman tried an explanation. "Teenagers like the radio, record player, or television turned on loud at any time because they want to feel the sound. They want to participate, to actually feel the beat.

"They do it when they study because this puts them in a good mood, and thus they are more receptive. Also, forcing themselves to learn under this form of stress increases their concentration, and the superior students seem to learn more rapidly."

I also believe in the idea, untouched by Dr. Hoffman, that many youngsters know how much their parents hate the blasting, and it's a form of protest, or defiance, or independence, or meanness, or whatever.

"Feeling the beat" helps explain the volume at rock concerts. They can feel the vibrations.

Noise is a curse of the '80s. I'm writing this near an open window in my house, exactly ten miles from O'Hare Field, directly under the flight path toward a main runway. Every couple of minutes a jet roars by overhead. It's loud, but not loud enough to stop conversation as it was when I lived six miles from the airport. Millions of people living near airports from Atlanta to Los Angeles are cursed with this noise pollution.

I avoid noisy restaurants, but I judge from restaurant reviews that in the trendy places it is mandatory that the noise level be high enough to make normal conversation impossible.

It's hard to escape the noise at home. A vacuum cleaner generates 73 to 81 decibels. A TV with average volume is 68, except during commercials, when I think it goes to 80. A dishwasher churns at 69, an air conditioner and air filter fan unit at 57. The stove vent fan, dishwasher, and garbage disposal all going at the same time create 91 decibels.

An article in the *Journal of the American Medical Association* called the modern kitchen "a miniature transient simulator of old-fashioned boiler factories."

The only noise outrage which has improved is the diminishing numbers of squawk boxes, portable radios which were carried about the streets and parks blasting musical garbage at 100 or more decibels. They were as polluting in their way as smoke in its way. They have been replaced to some extent by portable tape players with headsets. That's a break for neighbors and passersby, but I often wonder what it's doing to the hearing apparatus of the person whose head is between the headphones.

We'll know more in five or ten or fifteen years. Watch the sales figures for hearing aids.

Do It Yourself—at Your Own Risk

One of the kids walked through the living room into the kitchen and announced: "Water's coming out of the ceiling."

Sure enough, water was coming out of the ceiling, dripping onto the piano. Water also was coming down the walls and onto the drapes and on the rug.

I ran upstairs and sloshed into the bathroom, where a faucet was wide open.

I had been repairing a downstairs leaky faucet, and turned off the water. My wife in the upstairs bathroom turned on the faucet. Nothing came out. She left the faucet open and came downstairs. I finished fixing the downstairs faucet and went into the basement and turned the main water valve back on.

That was the worst of a bunch of negative results in half a century of doing it myself. We had little choice when we were building families and homes and yards in the era now designated as the baby boom. What with the costs of children and rents and mortgages and transportation we did it ourselves or it didn't get done.

My second worst disaster was the Concrete Episode. I was adding a room to the back of the house, and saved a few hundred bucks by doing the footings, or wall foundations, myself. I dug three feet down through rock-hard clay, making a trench much too wide. But I built wooden forms with the proper dimension.

Came the big day and the ready-mix truck pulled up, swung the trough over my empty forms, and the concrete began pouring out.

I was feeling proud as the forms got two-thirds full. Then they collapsed.

The driver was just great. Instead of standing there laughing, or smirking, he was sympathetic. We decided the only thing to do was keep on pouring. We filled the wide trenches to the top. That room has the widest foundation in town. But not the neatest.

In the Navy they taught me to keep one hand in my pocket when fooling around with live electricity. If you touch a live wire with one hand and the other hand touches a conductor, the electricity goes through your body, and that smarts.

I have such respect for electricity that I won't touch a live wire. To me it's a rattlesnake waiting to strike.

I was wiring a wall plug in an upstairs room after carefully removing the basement fuse. My screwdriver touched the plug, there was a blue flash, I jumped three feet. When I was satisfied I was still alive, I looked at the screwdriver in my hand. The tip had melted into a ball.

I had pulled the wrong fuse, and neglected to test whether the wires were hot when I exposed them. Cheap lesson.

This can be encouraging for young do-it-yourselfers. Things do go better. I was trying to think of any disasters in recent years, and they've been happily trouble free. Of course as you get older there are fewer things that need doing. The last floor tile I laid a few years ago went on with very little mess. This was in marked contrast with earlier confrontations with floors, tile, and black goo.

Is there any amateur floor tile layer who hasn't cursed the sight of that goo coming up in the cracks between the tiles? You cover the floor with the cement, spreading it out evenly with just enough to stick, but not enough to come up between the cracks. Then you get on your knees and lay the tiles, carefully and snug against each other, press them tight—and up creeps the black goo.

I understand they now sell tile with stickum on the back. Also there is a vast supply of prepasted wallpaper, which is great unless you live with a housekeeper who shops everywhere for *just the right* paper, and finally finds it, and of course it is not prepasted.

The only times I hung wallpaper upside down I discovered the error after a few courses were up. And on the subject of upside down, anyone who tries to paper a ceiling is mad. The battle cry of ceiling paperers is "Help!" Usually followed by "Grab the other end!" coming from a head draped with a strip of pasted paper.

Painting ceilings is easier, but it involves two standards of vision, one normal vision, the other *super*vision, and that word is intended in both connotations.

I have normal vision, and recently finished the kitchen ceiling with a coat of paint advertised as "One Coat Absolutely Covers All." The kitchen ceiling wasn't very dirty, and it was white over white, and I finished and felt pretty good until *super*vision came to inspect.

"When are you going to do the second coat?" she asked. "What do you mean second coat?" "To cover the lap marks." "What lap marks? I don't see any lap marks." "Right there, those lap marks. Can't you see them?"

Don't argue with *super*vision. I rolled on another coat of "One Coat Absolutely Covers All."

I will never again try to lay oak flooring. It's a cinch for carpenters, but oak is an extremely hard wood, and in laying tongue-in-groove, unless you hit the nail exactly on center, it will bend rather than penetrate. I must have bent five hundred nails and hit my thumb a dozen times flooring one room.

Well, these were some of the bad times. Modesty prohibits my listing the projects that went reasonably well. And if we hadn't been able to do all those things ourselves, we'd be living in a shack.

The War Zone

Ike on War

Three statements by President Eisenhower:

"Every gun that is made, every warship launched, every rocket fired signifies, in the final sense, a theft from those who hunger and are not fed, those who are cold and are not clothed."

From Ike's farewell address January 17, 1961: "This conjunction of an immense military establishment and a large arms industry is new in the American experience. . . . We recognize the imperative need for this development. Yet we must not fail to recognize its grave implications.

"In the councils of government, we must guard against the acquisition of unwarranted influence, whether sought or unsought, by the military-industrial complex. The potential for the disastrous rise of misplaced power exists and will persist."

A letter from Ike to his close friend, "Swede" Hazlett: "Some day there is going to be a man sitting in my present chair (the White House) who has not been raised in the military services and who will have little understanding of where slashes in their estimates can be made with little or no damage.

"If that should happen while we still have the state of tension that now exists in the world, I shudder to think of what could happen to this country."

Professor Stephen E. Ambrose, an Eisenhower biographer, wrote, "Ike feared that an arms race with the Soviet Union would lead to uncontrollable inflation and eventually bankrupt the United States without providing any additional security.

"In Ike's view, the more bombs and missiles we built, the less secure we would be, not just because of the economic impact, but because the more bombs we built, the more the Soviets would build.

"In short, Ike's fundamental strategy was based on his recognition that in nuclear warfare, there is no defense and can be no winner. In that situation, one did not need to be superior to the enemy to deter him."

• • •

I was a Christian, and a reasonably active one, when the Vietnam war began. I went to church every Sunday, paid my dues, served on a few boards.

Ten years later I wasn't quite sure what I was. I no longer attended church. I had little faith in a religion which made only the feeblest protest while Christians in airplanes dropped bombs that killed men, women, and children by the thousands. Instead of the Bible I was reading the *New Yorker,* which protested, "Our souls have withered. Day by day, we are turning into monsters. For a hundred reasons, and for no reason whatever, we are blowing men, women, and children to bits with our bombs, and we can't feel a thing."

We are primarily a theistic nation. "In God We Trust" is printed on our money. Our pledge of allegiance proclaims "One nation, under God."

Until Vietnam we had won all our wars. We took it for granted that God was on our side. Our wars were "just" wars. We grew powerful and prosperous and won wars with God's help.

What happened in Vietnam? Maybe God was trying to tell us something. Could it be that God loved those brown-skinned human beings as much as he loved us?

• • •

After World War II we compensated for the death and destruction of our enemies by sending them our wealth to help rebuild their nations.

A number of Christians and Jews brought twenty-five young women disfigured by the Hiroshima atomic blast to this country for medical help. It was a symbolic act of penance and mercy. It was in keeping with our national character.

Vietnam changed us. We became bullies. We ridiculed and persecuted and jailed people who felt so deeply about the war that they participated in demonstrations about their beliefs.

In December of 1972 as we prepared to pay homage to the Prince of Peace, we reached new depths. We mounted the most horrible barrage of death in the history of warfare.

As our fire and steel and explosives devastated a tiny Asian nation that was no threat . . . no possible threat . . . to our well-being, most of us turned away from the suffering for which every one of us bore some measure of responsibility.

It was so easy to tune out the war, because we were immersed in the pleasure of wrapping Christmas gifts and making plans to bring joy to our children and the poor, as our tributes to Jesus Christ.

My disillusion with the Christian church was heightened by the fact that the one man with the power to stop the killing, the man who ordered his planes and his ships to rain death on our brothers in the eyes of Christ, this man was a Christian, who attended church, who received spiritual guidance from the Reverend Billy Graham and the Reverend Norman Vincent Peale and from that very symbol of American Christian rectitude, the *Reader's Digest*.

The pulpits rang on Christmas day with pious hymns of gratitude for our blessings and with tributes to our greatness.

All I felt was shame and despair.

The Bomb

The Atomic Scientists of Chicago sprang up almost spontaneously after Hiroshima and Nagasaki. One of my first assignments after I got back to the *Daily News* after World War II was to go to the University of Chicago campus and report on the emergence of these physicists from their private, unpublicized world.

"We felt a need to get together publicly and talk about things that we had discussed privately in our classified lunchroom," recalled physicist Alex Langsdorf, a member of the original group of two hundred, and later its chairman.

"We knew the world would never be the same. We felt that scientists should be interested in the social consequences of science and should share in community life.

"We knew, for instance, that if the Germans had the bomb, and dropped it in Lake Michigan, radioactive water would splash on Chicago.

"We speculated on when the Russians might get the bomb. Some said fifty years, some said one hundred. A few said never.

"The most frightening guess was that they'd have it in twenty years. People who said that were considered radical."

The Russians exploded their first atomic bomb four years later.

The scientists who developed the bomb originated the movement to control or abolish atomic weaponry and war. They founded the influential *Bulletin of the Atomic Scientists*. It was contrary to all their scientists' instincts to take to the public forum. Nevertheless they wrote articles, made speeches, organized discussion groups, and sought in every way possible to stimulate a chain reaction of public opinion.

But it took years . . . really decades . . . before the seeds that they planted grew into a sizeable and influential mobilization of world opinion and realization that a nuclear war would probably end civilization as we know it.

"This involves a very long-range feeling of responsibility toward the human race," Langsdorf said. "It involves a thousand years from now on the genetic time scale, forty years from now on the cancer time scale.

"It's difficult for most people to take in their thinking. You lie awake at night thinking about a sore tooth or your child's problems in school or bills. You don't lie awake thinking about genetic change doing away with the human race three thousand years from now.

"Personally, it is my hope that a stalemate might go on so that we could avoid bombing for five hundred or a thousand years. Maybe by that time we will have enough travel so that we can develop friendship.

"If it's so easy to drop a bomb on the other side of the world, it is easy to travel there, if the government will let you.

"I think when the ordinary people of one country get to know the ordinary people of another, they don't seem quite so sinister."

Langsdorf's wife, Martyl, designed the famed clock on the cover of the *Bulletin*. When she created it, the time shown was ten minutes to midnight. When the Russians exploded the bomb it moved to five minutes to midnight.

In 1958 it was at two minutes before midnight.

Albert Einstein and Leo Szilard, a brilliant physicist with a passion for truth and reason, persuaded President Roosevelt that the Germans might develop the atom bomb if we didn't get it first. Dr. Szilard had the foresight to anticipate the consequences of our failure to have the bomb, and he had the scientific brilliance to play a key role in creating the bomb.

He helped save the nation with the bomb, and then devoted the last years of his life to saving the nation *from* the bomb.

In 1962 he visited the college communities at Chicago, Harvard, Swarthmore, and Western Reserve and asked for reaction to his proposal to establish a Council for Abolishing War, or perhaps a Council for a Liveable World. It would have two principal functions—to lobby in Washington, and to work for the election of Congressional candidates who were in basic agreement with the Council's goals.

The response was strong and enthusiastic, and today the Council may be the most influential single private entity working toward arms control.

How persuasive was Szilard? I offer my own testimony. Journalists are supposed to stay out of public movements and public affairs and thereby maintain objectivity. I went down to the Chicago campus and became cochairman of the Chicago organizing committee. I make no pretense at lack of prejudice on the subject of abolishing nuclear arms.

Said Szilard: "I, personally, find myself in rebellion against the fate that history seems to have in store for us, and I suspect that some of you may be equally rebellious. The question is, what can you do?

"To abolish war is a tall order, and I speak of it with reluctance. It has been apparent, however, ever since the end of the war, that the bomb would pose a problem to the world for which there is no precedent and which cannot be solved short of abolishing war.

"The Council would speak with the sweet voice of reason, and our lobby could see to it that they shall be heard by people inside the administration and also by the key people in Congress.

"Would they be listened to, if they were not able to deliver votes?

"The minority for which they speak might represent perhaps 10 percent of the votes, and 10 percent of the votes alone would not mean very much, just as the sweet voice of reason alone would not mean very much. Still, the combination of 10 percent of the votes and the sweet voice of reason might turn out to be an effective combination."

Sneaky Ways to Start a War

When nuclear tests were being conducted in the atmosphere, a blast 250 miles above Johnston Island in the Pacific put out street lights in Hawaii, 800 miles away. More accurately, it was the EMP, or electromagnetic pulse, which put out the lights.

A nuclear bomb exploded 250 miles above the United States, or above Europe or the U.S.S.R., probably would knock out the electronic equipment on the land below. "Probably" because nobody knows for sure. Nuclear explosion tests in the atmosphere were halted before adequate research on EMP could be conducted.

The Johnston Island incident was called *radio flash*. Scientists subsequently figured out that the high-voltage atmospheric pulse generated by a nuclear explosion causes electronic disruption.

Picture the scenario after a blast high over the North American continent. Computers would become inoperable, and so would communications systems and factories and radar and aircraft and probably your late-model car. Without computers, without electronics, without communication, the military and everything else below would grind to a halt.

The *Guardian* of London gave this description:

"A single shot unleashed 300 miles above the atmosphere and incapable of producing any other damage on earth could disrupt unprotected electronic systems. Emergency radio systems are highly vulnerable, as are telephone lines, unprotected computers, and virtually all equipment containing sensitive electronic and wire circuitry."

While the major powers are bankrupting themselves building more and bigger bombs and bombers and submarines and aircraft carriers and star wars defense systems, little attention has been given to another simple and unorthodox way to cripple or destroy a nation. That is carrying an atomic explosive device into a city and placing it in a bus station locker. It could be detonated by a remote radio signal.

The major powers aren't likely to intentionally generate nuclear warfare because they know it is suicidal. But the atomic scientists have a favorite theory, the "Laughing Third." A small nation could make a bomb and either explode it 250 miles up, or put it in a locker in New York City or Moscow.

The target nation would not know the source of the bomb. Submarines probably would start shooting nuclear missiles at somebody somewhere, if they could get instructions.

Meanwhile, the small nation could send troops to take over the target nation.

It probably won't happen. But it could. And one of the madmen who periodically take over governments may think it worth a try.

Poopery

&%$#@*?>{*%!~#@!!!!!!

Clark Gable said "damn" in *Gone with the Wind* and caused a small sensation. In the fifties the word pregnant was used in a movie *The Moon Is Blue,* and the movie was banned in some communities because of pressure from religious groups. Richard Burton and Elizabeth Taylor were considered daring for using three or four basic cuss words in *Who's Afraid of Virginia Woolf?*

Then came the protests of the sixties generated by the Vietnam war. The rebellious young demonstrated their defiance with marching, extreme music, and extreme language. They went all-out with gutter language to offend the establishment, or their parents, or authority, or whoever. Their own press was foul with bad language. Then the college press picked it up. Then it began to seep into the general press, and became the norm in much popular entertainment.

Many liberated young women seemed to feel that repeated use of deleted expletives was one measure of their new independence. So they salted their conversations with their limited but forceful swear words.

I never did hear imaginative swearing after I left the Navy decades ago. Men in the military frequently have time on their hands, and there were no women around in a war situation. One form of recreation was boasting of how long this guy or that guy could cuss without repeating himself.

In 1967 I posted this notice on our editorial room bulletin board:

"With the increasing permissiveness, it is necessary that we carefully consider the use of obscenity, profanity, and vulgarity in our paper.

"As a general rule they should be avoided. There are exceptions. When a Chicago Seven defendant used a barnyard expletive in court, the Field papers used the word, the *Tribune* and *Chicago Today* newspaper did not. *Time* magazine did not. There was some justification for use of the word. It was a judgment call, and I agree with our decision.

"When Truman called the music critic a son of a bitch, almost all papers used S.O.B. I imagine today the majority would spell it out.

"Profanity, vulgarity, and obscenity are offensive to many readers. Many parents have no objection to it in adult reading, but do not want it presented to their children as part of normal speech.

"Profanity is a crutch, oral or written. It is a cheap and easy way to convey an emotion. It takes a great deal more skill to convey an idea without the use of vulgar language. *The New Yorker* magazine is an example of good writing which rarely resorts to profanity or vulgarities.

"It will be difficult for writers and interviewers concerned with the theater and movies to eliminate these vulgarisms, but unless they are absolutely necessary to communicate an idea, they should be avoided.

"The people in the arts are relatively sophisticated, or have a veneer that passes for sophistication, and are not offended by this kind of writing.

"But this is a mass circulation newspaper, read by tens of thousands of children. It is a challenge to write with taste and style and communicate simultaneously with the sophisticated, highly educated, and discerning reader and the less sophisticated, less formally educated reader."

The young reporters and copy editors didn't like this one bit, but the publisher happened by and saw the notice on the bulletin board, and added his approval.

I've never heard a clergyman swear. They have an outlet to express their disapproval, distaste, and disgust at obscenity. We in more secular work fear ridicule or being called nicey-nice, and confine our opposition to the living room or dining table.

Men and women in the media like to appear worldly and sophisticated. Objecting to profanity and smut doesn't fit the image, so there is very little objecting. I'm old enough so that I don't care if people fail to find me worldly and sophisticated, and I'm stubborn enough to resist the erosion of standards of decency and verbal expression that prevailed two generations ago.

A Wheaton clergyman, John D. Jess, had some business cards printed with the caption "Ten Reasons Why I Swear." The reasons:

- It pleases sensitive people.
- It is a mark of manliness.
- It proves I have self-control.
- It indicates how clearly my mind operates.
- It makes my conversation so pleasant to everyone.
- It leaves no doubt as to my good breeding.
- It shows I have more than an ordinary education.
- It is an unmistakable sign of culture and refinement.
- It makes me a very desirable personality among women and children.
- It is my way of honoring God who said, "Thou shalt not take the name of the Lord thy God in vain."

On the reverse side of this card was printed:
"Profanity—a method of making ignorance audible."

The Power of the Mind

A French psychotherapist, Emile Coue, had several million Americans in the twenties chanting over and over, "Every day in every way I'm getting better and better."

He claimed if we repeated these words with conviction every day we'd get better and better.

I was a schoolboy and decided to go along with adults and try it. I'd faithfully chant it a dozen or twenty times every morning.

I haven't the vaguest idea whether I got any better . . . or worse.

This was an early manifestation of the power of positive thinking which has gained increasing recognition, though in somewhat more conventional form than chanting. Clem Stone's version is PMA, or Positive Mental Attitude. Some psychologists refer to the power of positive thinking.

A respectable number of physicians practice holistic medicine, which expands medical treatment to include the whole person and his or her mental attitude.

Preston Bradley, the great pastor of People's Church, didn't use labels, but his life and preaching were founded on positive thinking and love and concern for others.

He spoke of Emile Coue in historical context, relating to the power of the mind to influence physical well-being and mental stability. Bradley said that merely chanting "Every, day etc." without conviction didn't work. Coue said "a confident voice" was necessary, and would send this power into the subconscious and eliminate ideas tending to cause distress and disease. Coue said he was not a healer, but taught others how to heal. He claimed organic changes brought about by the power of suggestion.

It was not clearly defined whether "better and better" applied to one's frame of mind or morale or determination, or could include such matters as a stubborn toothache or a common cold or failing eyesight. Coue believed in both mental and physical control.

Millions believe that cures can be brought about without resorting to physicians or other scientific practitioners of the healing arts and sciences. They believe God can cure through divine intervention in response to prayers or unspoken faith.

I've been told by reputable doctors that 80 percent of the patients who walk into a physician's office are going to get better regardless of what the doctor does.

There also is new evidence that the body contains elements that counteract pain, and that the human will can trigger these elements into action.

It is also theorized that the mysterious pain-suppressing power of acupuncture is actually a physical release of the pain-counteracting element in the body. Orientals found that by inserting tiny needles strategically in the body, severe pain could be relieved, and a patient could undergo radical surgical procedure without suffering.

The effectiveness of acupuncture is documented beyond reasonable doubt, but American medical science remains skeptical. The consensus among doubters is that the patient is under some form of hypnosis.

Norman Cousins's use of the curative powers of laughter has been well publicized. But most doctors aren't comfortable with anecdotal accounts of unconventional cures. Medical records are loaded with cases of recoveries from illnesses diagnosed as incurable and hopeless. The patients and their loved ones usually attribute the recovery to divine intervention, to the answering of their prayers.

Their doctors are simply mystified.

There is persuasive argument that science knows as much about the working of the human mind as we do about what exists in the rest of the universe.

Are Good Manners Out of Style?

Many men still are uncomfortable walking down the sidewalk with a woman when she is on the curb side. We used to automatically hop, skip, and jump around a female companion to make sure we took the curb side. Now the feminine companion may be offended by this maneuver.

I took my puzzlement to an officer of the National Organization for Women. "Helplessness of women, not mutual respect, is implied in some of these customs," she suggested. "When politeness reflects a concern or mutual respect, I have no problem with it. God knows there isn't much of it left."

Is standing aside to let a woman off an elevator first just an obsolete ritual or an acceptable sign of respect? Should a male be uncomfortable when a businesswoman picks up the lunch tab? Do many men still stand up when a woman enters the room? Has the common courtesy of the fifties become male chauvinism of the eighties?

Early in '87 the *Wall Street Journal* took a survey of American courtesy, or lack of it, and printed the results on the front page under the headline: "Rampant Rudeness. In the U.S. Today, 'Common Courtesy' is Contradictory Phrase. Boorish Behavior is the Norm; Blaming 'Me Generation.' "

People fight over access to public phones. They fight for a cab. They let doors slam in the face of people behind them. They talk and eat popcorn in theaters.

"No doubt about it," concludes the *Journal*, "small, everyday courtesies among Americans these days seem to have gone the way of finger bowls and hand fans—rarer in everyday usage than an 'After you, ma'am' on the New York City subway system."

They allow there probably is more courtesy in the South and in smaller cities and towns. I tend to suspect social surveys conducted by inhabitants of New York or Washington, or which use as a frame of reference the conduct of passengers in the New York subway system.

I don't think things are as bad as the *Journal* implies. It goes in cycles. Wearing offensive clothing is a form of discourtesy, and there has been a 180-degree turn in dress among the young, who now lean toward dressing for success.

Courtesy is consideration for others. It takes many forms. The absence of structured manners or etiquette does not mean absence of courtesy.

Thoughtfulness means holding the door for another, helping a stranger, replying to a letter, asking "Do you mind if I smoke?", eating quietly and neatly, not using obscene speech, and being cheerful instead of grouchy.

My generation gap shows in my dislike of swearing in mixed company, or women swearing at any time other than when they hit their thumb with a hammer. Profanity is coarse, crude, and discourteous. Intolerance of it is difficult with its new profusion in movies, conversation, books, newspapers, and tapes, and some feminists' conviction they should swear as much as men.

Attire is a symbol of one's self-respect and attitude toward others. The dirty, ragged clothes so many young people wore in the late sixties were symbols of defiance and anger. Clothing and personal hygiene improved with the end of the protests.

Ages ago I attended a state university and lived with a group of young men who required that freshmen wear jackets and ties to class and that everyone in the house wear jackets and ties to dinner except Fridays and Saturdays.

Male and female students enjoyed social occasions called dates, and put on formal clothing to attend dances. We didn't boo at athletic contests. This may sound like the student body was nicey-nice, but they were tough enough. The football players played sixty minutes each game. Gang fights took place regularly. Most of the students gave good accounts of themselves in World War II.

Courtesy—concern for others—was a very conscious part of our education.

I have never encountered any evidence that it hurt us.

Movies Were Better than Ever

"If you are over thirty-five, chances are you hardly ever go to movies," wrote a movie critic recently. These young critics claim possession of what one of them calls "the liveliest, most consistently relevant art form in today's world."

Movies are no more lively and relevant today than they were fifty years ago. Some of the spokespersons of the younger generation believe that sex and movies were discovered about the time they reached adolescence.

We did have Andy Hardy movies. But. . . .

I was a grade school kid when I was carted to a theater showing *Potemkin*. "Now there is a movie," my parents told me.

Not much later Victor McLaglen appeared in *The Informer,* one of the finest pieces of theater ever put on film.

Sure, *Min and Bill* and Busby Berkeley musicals occupied the screens, but so did *Citizen Kane* and Robert Montgomery in *Night Must Fall* and two Barrymores in *Rasputin* and Paul Muni in *I Am a Fugitive from a Chain Gang*.

Gentleman's Agreement struck a blow against anti-Semitism in the forties. One of the first anti-war films was *What Price Glory?,* followed by Lew Ayres in *All Quiet on the Western Front*.

Good movies? Garbo in *Ninotchka*. Garbo in anything. Leslie Howard in *The Scarlet Pimpernel*. Bogart in *The Maltese Falcon* and *Casablanca*. Ray Milland's *Lost Weekend*. Olivier and Fontaine in *Wuthering Heights*. *Gone with the Wind*. *Grand Hotel*.

My wife and I used to go to fifty, seventy, maybe ninety movies a year. Lately we see maybe ten or twelve a year. We're not watching much television.

What's happened?
Maybe they're not making movies like they used to.

The Service Man's Dream

When I reported that there were twenty-four different electric motors making things run in my household, a number of readers said I was a piker, that I was in the horse and buggy age.

Here are the motorized devices in one Park Forest household:

Vacuum cleaner, window fan, air conditioner, kitchen exhaust, furnace blower, electric drills, saw, sander, grinder, shaver, hair dryer, hedge trimmer, edger, barbecue, clothes dryer, washing machine, clocks, food mixer, can opener, knife sharpener, electric organ, floor polisher, refrigerator, sewing machine, and mangle.

Another man in Lake County had all these plus a dishwasher, garage door opener, deep well pump, an electric train, movie projector, cream whipper, and an electric fingernail filer.

How in the world could we exist without those motors? Everything's relative. For a few years we owned a small farm in upper Wisconsin. An aunt had lived there alone year 'round, and we took it over when she got old.

It had *one* electric motor, for the refrigerator. No inside plumbing. No running water. Heat from a stove in the living room. It wasn't luxurious, but it wasn't that hard, either, to adjust to going outside for water, wood, and to use a hole in the ground. And Aunt Clara—all ninety-five pounds—lived there through the tough Wisconsin winters.

Should the Old Be Allowed to Vote?

When I was fifty-five, I wrote: "All persons should lose their voting privileges at retirement age or age seventy, whichever is earlier."

I also maintained: "Anyone who migrates to another state after age fifty-five should lose his or her vote."

I have reached seventy. Do I still think I should lose my voting privilege?

Maybe. A pretty good case can be made both ways.

When I read the proposal to deny the vote to the aged in the *New Republic*, I thought it was a put-on. But thirty-seven-year-old Douglas Stewart, associate professor of classics at Brandeis University, was serious.

We like to believe old people are wise, benign, and tolerant.

Aristotle said their chief characteristics are greed, cowardice, resentment over the cheats of life that did not turn out as planned, and the consequent desire to punish somebody for it.

Stewart makes his case: "The old, having no future, are dangerously free from the consequences of their own political acts. It makes no sense to allow the vote to someone who is actuarially unlikely to survive, and pay the bills for, the politician or party he may help elect."

Stewart got turned off by old people when he returned to his native California as a visiting professor at the University of California, San Diego LaJolla.

LaJolla is a colorful town to the ocean north of San Diego, occupied by many rich retirees.

"Old people on the streets refuse to give students directions or even speak to them," Stewart observed. "Businesses refuse them service. The local press prints an endless stream of abuse directed at them and the university. The cops lose few opportunities to threaten students found off campus." The air smokes with hostility.

California, of course, was overwhelmed by migrants who preceded the present invasion from Mexico. Most of whom were from the Bible Belt. Old and getting older. They brought their money and fundamental politics with them.

They began taking the state away from the people who built California, who made it a state so attractive that the migrants deserted their homes and lifelong roots in Nebraska and Tennessee and Illinois.

Academics were especially sensitive to what happened to the superb state university system built by native Californians. Rising generations could get excellent tuition-free educations without regard to wealth or social origin. It was a poverty program that really worked.

The new Californians were infuriated by these universities. Their leader, a migrant from Dixon, Illinois, named Ronald Reagan, imposed tuitions and cut funds. The new Californians were pleased to simultaneously save money and penalize radicals.

The universities' prestige, created by billions of dollars and immeasurable dedication, was diluted.

The invasion is far greater in Florida, which has to regard the mass in-migration of the elderly with mixed feelings. The retirees bring their money, which is good, and their voting power, which isn't so good. They've come in such numbers that they have become a dominant political force.

An interesting power held by the aged is to help deny voting privileges to eighteen-year-olds. The old tend to equate youth with giddiness, fatuity, and herd instinct. But if we deny the vote to the young (though we make them fight our wars) on the grounds of immaturity, is it reasonable to consider denying the vote because of senility?

Seventy-year-old persons have had forty-nine years of voting privilege to shape society into the form most pleasing to them. Their votes after seventy will shape society for the young, and create obligations and conditions for which the aged are not accountable.

I have howled editorially for decades about the national debt, but it still is the creation of my generation and our young-looking old leader, Reagan. It is a devastating legacy to leave to the young. An appropriate penalty would be forfeiture of our voting privilege.

AC/DC, Heavy Manners, and Skankin' Lizard

My generation has unconcealed difficulty trying to understand the music and entertainment of our adolescent children. We assume it is another manifestation of revolt against parental authority, via culture shock and ingestion of stimulants. But it's lasted so long it certainly is wearing thin, We surmise with horror that maybe they like the stuff for itself.

Earlier in this decade a rock group called AC/DC performed at a Chicago arena. Their appearance was heralded by the ringing of a large bell on stage and the sound of fireworks tossed from the balcony by members of the audience.

The *Tribune* rock critic called the show a fairly mundane performance. The focus was on a guitarist named Angus Young, whose gimmick, the critic reported, "is that he styles himself as a perpetual schoolboy in disgrace, dresses in short pants, and frequently lies down on the floor and rolls around and kicks."

Well, we ancients recognize that easily enough. There's more.

The guitarist topped his performance as he "removed his red velvet jacket, white shirt and—in a final dramatic high point—turned his back to the crowd, bent over, and dropped his red velvet knickers."

Mr. Young achieved stardom after the previous star of the group died of choking on his own vomit after a drinking bout. He followed the precedent of the drummer of the group Led Zeppelin.

About the music of AC/DC. The *Tribune* critic said, "The songs all sound alike." Perceptive.

Attractions scheduled to follow AC/DC at the arena were listed as Shoes, Duke Tomatoe & the All-Star Frogs, Amuzement Park, the Kind and the Rage, Heavy Manners, and Skankin' Lizard.

The *New York Times* reviewed an AC/DC performance and commended lead singer Brian Johnson for his ability "to sustain a bansheelike scream without losing his voice. . . . AC/DC explicitly equates making music with making war."

It's fair to say few people over forty-five are able to understand the appeal of a group of young people who perform on amplified instruments, and are acclaimed for the ability to sustain a banshee-like scream and for the dramatic highlight of dropping one's pants.

"Generation gap" is a catch-all phrase for the lack of understanding and communication between age groups. It's nothing new. My best friend in high school and I used to listen in his house to radio broadcasts of popular bands—Casa Loma, Duke Ellington, Benny Goodman, the Dorseys, Count Basie.

His father was an opera impresario. Dad would walk into the room and growl, "Why do you listen to that . . . that *garbage*?" If he was near our chairs, he'd bop one of us on the head. It was a playful bop, but it rattled my teeth.

What will it be like when the kids in the AC/DC audience have children of their own and are subjected to whatever are the musical fads of the year 2015? Will the AC/DC of that generation perform with electronically amplified field artillery pieces as their main instruments? How will they top the dramatic climax of dropping their pants?

To legitimize the revolt against parents, each generation must exceed the excesses of its predecessors. One's imagination boggles.

The Best Years

What are the best years of our lives?

That's a standard question of inquiring photographers. The answer usually is the age of the person asked—seventeen, twenty-five, forty-five, sixty-five, whatever.

What about the first year? They can't ask babies, but how do you beat having everything done for you? You get plenty of sleep. People fuss over you and don't demand anything in return but a smile. You learn a lot. If you want something you holler. You don't worry about war, money, discrimination, or inflation. Those come later in the "best years."

Circumstances beyond one's control determine good and bad years. I spent the blue-ribbon ages of twenty-six to thirty in a Navy uniform, and believe me, those were lousy years. The thirtieth year was pretty good because I was still alive.

Any year with illness, accidents, domestic problems, or job difficulties is a bad year.

Putting aside these circumstances, and assuming normal progress through life, the usual answer is the right answer. Now is best.

The years following the completion of one's education can be tough—getting into a vocation, deciding on marriage or single living, finding a place to live, finding friends, starting a family, getting acquainted with the joys and terrors of raising children. They are years of great highs and dreadful lows.

The years after forty or forty-five are less complicated.

I am impatient with young people who look on being in the fifties, sixties, or seventies as something undesirable, with seniors who dye their hair red or blue or black to try to hide their age, and with the lady in *Redbook* magazine who used turtle oil to try to look thirty instead of thirty-five. "Eighteen to thirty-five are the best years of a woman's life," proclaimed *Redbook*. Bunk. They're the skinniest years.

When I began work in Chicago as a reporter, I was a very smart cookie. I knew all the answers. You had only to ask me.

But I also found that every time I learned an answer, I discovered two more questions. The older you get, the more you know and the more you realize how little you know. Age brings knowledge, useful experience, and a comfortable humility.

As I got into my twentieth and thirtieth years of columning, my writing became calmer, more reasoned, more tolerant. I was aware that a writer attracts attention by attacking any available target with vitriol and wild swings and sarcasm and cynicism and loaded adjectives.

For longevity, though, responsibility means durability. I was much more shrill in the early days. I was aware some people were saying, "Mabley's lost his zing." It was partially true, depending on how you define zing. The compensation was that I was still writing columns after turning out 8,000 of them, and the *Trib* kept me on a couple of years past mandatory retirement. I think they couldn't find a younger guy who could turn out six columns a week.

You have to go back only a generation or two to a time when forty was over the hill. It was mid-life crisis, so serious that a man wrote a best selling book called *Life Begins at Forty* to help those over forty overcome the blahs.

Grandmothers used to look like grandmothers. Now they look like Jaclyn Smith. But yuppie copy writers still turn out endless ads and pictures and commercials and stories picturing seniors doddering through the golden years. smiling benignly at their grandchildren, strolling hand-in-hand toward the sunset, stopping along the way at a restaurant for dinner before five o'clock at reduced rates.

I switched from volleyball and softball to tennis at forty-five. Even then people were reacting, "Are you out of your mind? You want to have a heart attack on the tennis court?" I still play today, four or five times a week, with young and old and in-between. The only casualty I've seen in thousands of sets was one snapped Achilles tendon, on a man in his thirties.

When you get into the sixties and seventies doctors tend to blame aches and pains and other distress on age.

"Face it," they'll say. "You're getting old."

That's a cop-out. I went through youth and middle age with an endless affliction of minor physical problems—a lot of headaches, a back that almost left me a cripple, a lot of holes in my teeth, and almost constant sprains, bruises, and aches from sport participation.

I suddenly realized when I became a sexagenarian that I'd never felt better, never been healthier. I finally got smart enough to start eating sensibly, take off ten pounds of lard, get the right vitamins, organize my exercise, think healthy, and stand straight.

The Ultimate Salesman

Two door-to-door magazine salesmen managed to get into a residential hotel in Evanston during the dinner hour. They knocked on the door of two sisters, aged eighty-three and ninety-one.

They were admitted. They quickly found that the sisters were religious. One of the salesmen told the sisters he was studying for the priesthood. Money from the magazine sales would go to the Jesuit fathers, he said. He mentioned names of priests in the area.

The other man said he lost his parents, and had spent ten years in Boy's Town, and now was studying at Creighton University in Omaha.

They were such nice looking young men, and obviously devout, that the sisters decided to subscribe.

One of the women bought a thirty-year subscription to *Esquire* and eighteen-year subscriptions for *Ski* and *True Detective*. She wrote out checks for $100 and for $149.50.

Her sister, ninety-one, bought ten-year subscriptions to *Argosy*, *High Fidelity*, and *Infant Jesus* for $133.50.

One of the salesmen cashed a check at the desk on his way out. The clerk called the Evanston police, and an hour later the two salesmen were in jail, charged with operating a confidence game.

I spent a good part of my time warning people against cons like this. In fact, a week before this happened I'd written a column warning against unscrupulous magazine salesmen. I suggested that the column wouldn't deter them. It didn't. But I hope jail did.

The Importance of Being Number One

"Once a nation ceases trying to be Number One, that nation will not be a great nation. Let it not happen to America," one of our Presidents stated in response to what he saw was an erosion of ambition by Americans.

Question: What does being Number One mean? The richest, the most powerful, the most compassionate, the nation with the best reputation in the world community, the winner of the most Olympic gold medals?

Is number one tangible or intangible? Do we have to be number one in everything—science, nuclear weapons, space, chess, aid to other nations, trade deficit?

Or is it enough that we strive to do our best? That we sacrifice building one aircraft carrier to become the number one force for peace? To be first to find a cure for cancer rather than first to get to Mars?

Suppose you were a coach on the American Olympic track team and the President exhorted you to enhance American prestige by winning the most points, by coming in number one.

Just before the races you discover that your main opposition is using undetectable drugs to stimulate their runners.

You could use the same drugs with little fear of discovery, and probably win the gold.

What do you do? Is the team which wins the race with stimulants the real number one, or is it the team which comes in second without cheating?

I wonder about the answer of those American coaches who parrot Vince Lombardi that "Winning isn't everything—it's the only thing."

The *Wall Street Journal* editors suspected that the President (it was Nixon) might be right about the changing attitude toward being number one, and commissioned Trendex to take a national poll.

To no one's surprise they found that being first matters less to younger Americans than to the older generation.

Being first in military preparedness is an acceptable goal to most, because among world powers in the nuclear age there is no second prize for defense. The winner takes all.

Only half of those questioned believe the United States should try to be number one in sports, and just a shade over half would have us strive for supremacy in space exploration. Russia was first in space, we were first on the moon. Both nations survived this .500 average without visible scars.

I think this indifference to primacy reflects disillusionment with American priorities—the glaring disparity in government concern for educating children and caring for the ill versus expending billions for bombs which could blow up the planet three hundred times over.

Most people are not defeatist. There is a general desire to strive for perfection, or at least to do one's very best, without worrying what other people or nations are doing.

The debate is good if it does nothing more than cause some of us to reexamine our values. We want to be great, but greatness doesn't necessarily lie in star wars or the estimated time of arrival on Mars.

It lies in the condition of all human beings, not only relatives, friends, and American citizens.

The Sporting Life

Good Sports, Bad Sports

At halftime at the Ohio State–Illinois football game in Columbus in 1937, the Illini coach was presented with an illuminated scroll:

> To Robert C. Zuppke. Aggressive always, in a quarter century of loyal and distinguished service to the University of Illinois; moulder of men in the stern discipline of football; stable in victory, sturdy in defeat; resourceful and courageous, with undaunted determination to give his own best and to exact the best in others; teacher, leader, honest exemplar of the competitive spirit as fundamental in the American way of life—
>
> To you we dedicate anew the inscription carved high on the tower of our own Ohio Stadium, scene of classic combat with your teams: "For friendship through contest."

After the presentation, the 240-piece Ohio band formed a "Yea Zuppke" that filled the gridiron.

Such a ceremony would be difficult . . . no, impossible . . . today. Try to picture Illinois similarly saluting Woody Hayes, the recent

Ohio coach, or Michigan's Bo Schembechler being given a plaque by the student body of the University of Iowa.

Three years after the Zuppke ceremony Cornell University beat Dartmouth, but films later showed that Cornell scored the winning touchdown on an illegal fifth down. Cornell forfeited the game. "We have done the right thing, the clean thing, and this will live with us," the Cornell president told the team.

In 1972 Miami beat Tulane under identical circumstances, winning on an illegal fifth down. Miami officials shuffled their feet, hemmed and hawed, and announced it would be "inappropriate" to forfeit the game they won illegally.

This is a reasonably good measure of the change in sportsmanship and ethics in big time athletics.

Now major college football and basketball are a business in partnership with the advertising industry, i.e., television. Winning is essential to commercial success. Losing is failure. Winners get TV contracts.

Ninety-nine percent of media sports coverage is directed toward the 1 percent of athletes who are in the business of professional sports, labeled as major college, or labeled as professional.

The biggest value in non-professional sports lies not so much in winning, but in learning how to lose. It is sickening to see pro sports heroes take defeat with sunken chests and hung heads and whining alibis.

I can make my point better by going to some of the most successful coaches and athletes.

Don Schollander, who won four Olympic swimming medals: "Contrary to what Vince Lombardi said, winning is not everything. It may be important to a select few, but it is participation that is good for individuals, for society, and on the local level."

Bob Cousy, all-time great Celtics basketball player: "It's wrong to break rules and it's wrong to teach young people that you can break the rules and get away with it.

"If a young man's teachers—his coaches, athletic directors, college presidents—are teaching him by example that the way to success is breaking or evading the rules, it is only logical for that young person to assume that this is the way other respected members of society conduct their lives and that this is the way he should conduct his own."

Joe Paterno, Penn State football coach, to the graduating class: "We set high goals. My squad even has to listen to me quote Browning: 'A man's reach should exceed his grasp, or what's heaven for?'

"We play with enthusiasm and recklessness. We aren't afraid to lose. If we win, great, wonderful—and the alumni are happy for another week. But, win or lose, it is the competition which gives us pleasure."

Fran Tarkenton, former Minnesota Vikings quarterback, now a successful businessman: "I'm not going to allow my son to play small-fry football or baseball or any sport run by adults supposedly for the kids. Kids today are getting tired of structured sports, of playing the foil to adults. I think they really want to go out in the back yard with a few friends and just have a knockdown, drag-out game among themselves. Kids want to be kids."

John Wooden, who retired leaving a record unparalleled in American sports, to his UCLA players in practice: "No, no, no! Some of you are just standing around watching. Play your man tight before he gets the ball. Goodness gracious sakes, use the head the good Lord gave you."

Wooden didn't drink, smoke, or swear. I was in a Navy unit with him for several years and never knew a finer gentleman. Panhandle Eastern Corporation in 1986 ran a series of ads quoting "perennial leaders in their professions." Wooden's philosophy deserves repeating:

"Many people are surprised to learn that in 27 years at UCLA, I never once talked about winning," stated Wooden. "Instead I would tell my players before games 'When it's over, I want your head up. And there's only one way your head can be up—that's for you to know, not me—that you gave the best effort of which you're capable. If you do that, then the score doesn't really matter, although I have a feeling that if you do that, the score will be to your liking.

"I honestly, deeply believe that in not stressing winning as such, we won more than we would have if I'd stressed outscoring opponents.

"There's not great fun, satisfaction, or joy derived from doing something that's easy. Failure is never fatal, but failure to change might be.

"While it may be possible to reach the top of one's profession on sheer ability, it is impossible to stay there without hard work and character. One's character may be quite different from one's reputation.

"Your character is what you really are. Your reputation is only what others think you are. I made a determined effort to evaluate character. I looked for young men who would play the game hard, but clean, and who would always be trying to improve themselves to help the team. Then, if their ability warranted it, the championships would take care of themselves."

Let 'Em Drink Beer

When I was writing sports I covered the World Series and heavyweight championship fights and a countless number of major events. But nothing I covered aroused more interest than my battle with the Chicago Stadium over water fountains.

I got thirsty after the first period of a Blackhawks–Montreal Stanley Cup game and set out on a search for water. I was there as a spectator with my wife. If I'd been covering the game in the press box the Stadium would have provided me with any liquid I desired.

As a spectator I began my quest. I didn't want beer, I didn't want scotch, I didn't want pop (especially at Stadium prices). I wanted water. The law says water shall be available in any public place seating over four hundred people. Unfortunately, the law was passed after the Stadium was built, and the Stadium owners had enough clout to get in a grandfather clause exempting their building.

There were no water fountains. I covered the place top to bottom. I even sent my wife into the ladies room to see if there were any fountains. She found a dirty drinking glass on a dirty sink. That was it for twenty thousand hockey fans.

I wrote about the absence of water at the Stadium and started a controversy that lasted a good ten years. It was a delightful thing for a reporter to have hold of, because the facts were irrefutable, there was no defense, and readers were enchanted.

Arthur Wirtz, who owned the Stadium, was a proud and stubborn man and he wasn't going to put in water fountains and mess up his beer sales just because of some pipsqueak sportswriter.

It was fun trying to pin down the Stadium officials.

One Stadium spokesman told me—and this is an exact quote, "Well now Jack, you wouldn't want to drink water like you get out on West Madison Street would you? Honestly now, do you think if we put in fountains anybody would drink that water coming from West Madison and all that?"

"Nobody complains about it," said Don Murphy, their publicity person. "I don't drink water. Anyway, I think there are cups in the johns."

Murphy and I inspected the johns. No cups. "Well," said Murphy, "if we had cup dispensers it would be just another thing for somebody to break or steal. Why don't you talk to Mike Wirtz?"

Mike Wirtz: "Oh, I'm just in charge of maintenance. Why don't you talk to Bill Horstman? He's the manager."

Bill Horstman: "Oh, really? No water fountains? Why don't you talk to Arthur Wirtz?"

Howard Hughes was easier to talk to than Arthur Wirtz.

I heard they eventually put in a drinking fountain at the Stadium. I don't know because I've never been back.

In the Cubs' Locker Room

Walter Jacobson's first newspaper job was as my assistant at the *Daily News*. I'd met him when he was a batboy for the Cubs and I was writing sports. I was curious about a batboy's view of these professional athletes. Here's what Walter reported:

"Roy Campanella was the greatest guy in the league. He called me 'Muscles.' I weighed 140. Jackie Robinson always seemed to have a chip on his shoulder.

"Robin Roberts is one of the most intelligent men I've ever met—not loud and vile like many of this teammates. Stan Musial always sat by himself. He seemed to be thinking about his restaurant business.

"Roy Smalley was a wonderful friend. He was really hurt when the fans booed when his name was announced in the lineup. 'They just won't give me a chance,' he'd say, and I'd hurt too.

"Eddie Miksis was unbelievably crude. Every other word was profane. What really bothered me was the way he and others screamed at opponents. I won't say the words they used, but they referred to race and religion.

"This from guys who'd been my idols.

"It was kind of a shock to see chain-smokers and beer drinkers and potbellies and caved-in chests.

"My favorite visiting teams were the Dodgers and Redlegs. The Dodgers were on top, and acted like the best. Duke Snider was the classiest man in the league, in looks, dress, and mannerisms.

"Rogers Hornsby managed the Redlegs and he was mean and crude. He made me sit in the bullpen so I wouldn't talk to the players. Eddie Stanky was the wildest manager. He'd tear things apart when he got mad.

"Ed Waitkus and Willie Jones of the Phils were good to be with. Waitkus was always willing to talk about the time a girl shot him in a Chicago hotel room.

"The Phillies had songfests in the clubhouse after they won. The Dodgers and Braves drank beer. It was always fun to be around after a victory. After a loss, everybody sat around looking blank and not saying much, mostly cussing.

"The Braves were new in Milwaukee and their popularity swelled their heads. Eddie Matthews was the most conceited man in the league, and Logan was a close second.

"Once I accidentally broke the handle of Del Crandall's bat and he swore and screamed like I'd cut off his arm.

"All the players except the Giants fooled around in the dugout and clubhouse. Lighted cigarette butts were put inside the belt loops, chewed gum rubbed into hairy arms, shin bones hit with bat handles. The Cubs and Braves seemed especially playful.

"Most of the managers—Cavarretta, Durocher, Stanky, Hornsby—were cold and nervous and I tried to stay away from them.

"I was paid two dollars a day and worked from nine in the morning until six at night and I'd do it again ten times over."

(That was before Walter started getting paid half a million dollars a year to do Channel 2 newscasts in Chicago).

High Five

The handshake in sports became obsolete sometime in the early sixties. The quick palm slap with a teammate after a winning basket or home run or quarterback sack was refined into the high five which is now the dominant greeting. Giving skin is also common in normal social situations.

Ray Meyer, DePaul basketball coach: "I saw the handslap come in during the early sixties. In basketball it used to be a one hand slap. I called it a lazy way to shake hands."

Brent Musburger, sports telecaster: "I'm pretty sure it originated with major league baseball. I think it started after a home run. My bet is it started with Mays and McCovey."

Policeman Randall "Lefty" Martin: "I think it came through sports because I can remember they did it after a strike in the bowling alleys when I was a kid, and that was twenty-five years ago."

A lawyer: "It was the black musicians back in the thirties. I saw Louis Armstrong do it for years."

Rich Falk, Northwestern basketball: "I remember using it back in high school. It's cool. It's a type of congratulations. It's also a quick greeting—like a little wave when you pass someone in a car."

Ernie Cox, newspaper photographer: "When you greet someone it isn't really a slap. You just let your palm slide across his and say, 'Hey, what's happenin'?' The guy tells a boss joke or gives a good answer, then you slap the palm of his hand with the back of your hand."

Red Saunders, musician: "It's been around for a long time. It means everything's right, an approval of any kind of situation. When it first started out, they said, 'Gimme some skin!' And it definitely originated with musicians. Like most fads, it happens, and nobody knows how it originated."

George Ireland when he coached Loyola's national basketball champions: "I have my own version which I taught the kids—just skin instead of a handshake after a basket so they can get back on defense right away."

I play a lot of tennis and was once in an exhibition match against Bill Cosby and Frank Parker. My partner was an old pro, George O'Connell. They creamed us. Cosby is an excellent and enthusiastic player, and a good sportsman.

In 1966, before professional tennis became a big-money industry, Butch Bucholtz was one of the top ten pros coming to Chicago for a tournament. I'd watched the best pros, and was convinced I couldn't score a single point against one of them.

Playing Football Without a Helmet

Athletes today are bigger, stronger, faster. Better? Maybe. How would the 1987 Bears do against the 1942 Bears? Where would Bronco Nagurski fit in with the 1987 Bears?

I cringe at the ferocity of tackles in football today. Linebackers hit the quarterbacks like missiles. It's fashionable to write that oldtimers were tougher than today's players. Possibly tougher. But not better. The average pro today is fifty or sixty pounds heavier than the early pro players, and he hasn't sacrificed quickness or

As a publicity hype for the tournament, a match was set up between Bucholtz and me, to see if I could score a point. I had to caution him to play as if I were Rod Laver and not a neighborhood hacker, or the experiment would be meaningless.

We warmed up for ten minutes, and he won the serve.

On his first serve, he double-faulted.

I'd won my point.

We played four games. I won one, but I think if he'd been playing all out I'd have had trouble taking five points in a set. But it was fun.

speed for size. There are a lot of three-hundred-pound players. The Fridge has demonstrated that it takes more than sheer weight to play at the top.

Who's to say one generation is tougher than another? Improved equipment and civilizing rules make for fewer injuries today.

Yale football players in the 1800s were getting their brains addled because they didn't wear padding or helmets. In 1890 the Yalies started letting their hair grow for protection during the fall football season. It was nice padding, but unfortunately it also was handy for opposing tacklers to grab.

They didn't tackle cleanly around the legs then. Linemen didn't crouch or play low. They mostly stood bolt upright and crashed into one another with arms flailing. You couldn't make the line unless you were a good boxer or wrestler.

I wasn't there. This information is from John W. Heisman, the player and coach after whom the Heisman trophy was named.

The flying wedge was so brutal it was one of the first maneuvers to be outlawed. Harvard inaugurated it in 1892. "Nine players withdrew about twenty yards from mid-field," Heisman said. "At a signal, in two lines they started simultaneously and at full speed, converging at one point. They worked up a stupendous mass momentum, and the interference they gave the runner behind them was something wonderful to behold and terrible to stop.'

Players were permitted to grab hold of their own runner any way they could, and to push, pull, or yank him down the field, in much the same way as the Fridge tried to toss Walter Payton over the goal line in a 1985 game. In 1985, of course, this was illegal. But in 1890 some halfbacks had leather straps, like luggage handles, riveted on their pants to provide firm handholds for their teammates.

Today there is a neutral zone between the two teams as they line up to put the ball in play. The opposing linemen crouch facing each other across no man's land.

Originally there was no zone between the teams. There was an imaginary line even with the ball, and the players stood ready to bolt into action right where they imagined this line to be. More often than not a difference of opinion arose as to where these nose-to-nose gladiators imagined the line to be, and some of the most spirited action took place in the charging, pushing, and wrestling when the teams lined up. before the ball was snapped.

The neutral zone was introduced in 1903 to reduce bloodshed.

Games consisted of two forty-five minute halves, and only four substitutes were allowed on the squads. And of course all players played both offense and defense. This was true into the thirties.

When the ball went out of bounds, it wasn't automatically brought in. The two teams lined up at right angles, and the ball was thrown onto the field, to be won by the strongest and swiftest pursuer.

There were no five-yard stripes on the field, and no linesmen or line sticks. The referee kept track of the distance by dropping a handkerchief where he thought the ball was last put into play. One of the crafts of a good football team was kicking the handkerchief toward the other guy's goal while teammates engaged the referee in a discussion of the rules.

They weren't the good old days, necessarily, but they certainly were interesting.

Knute Rockne, the famous Notre Dame coach of the twenties and thirties, was a link between the old-timers and the modern game. The standards of conduct he established for his athletes still prevail at South Bend. The university's image would be enhanced if the students at televised games would reduce their boorish behavior and conduct themselves by Rockne's standards. But that's another problem.

Knute Rockne, Jr., was browsing through his father's belongings and came across a list of what the coach called "the correct mental qualifications of an athlete." See if they're applicable today.

Scholarship: The player should first be a good student. Do not neglect studies. Your first purpose should be to get an education.

Habits: Good habits are only doing those things that help and not doing those things that will harm or hinder.

Ambition: Keeping an eye on the future, always trying to improve oneself. Interest and spirit sometimes outweigh natural ability.

Attendance: Anything worth doing is worth doing well. Try not to miss a day of school or practice.

Sportsmanship: Good sportsmanship means clean and fair play. Treat your opponent with respect.

Losing: You can be a hard but good loser. Any coach or team that cannot lose and treat their opponents with respect has no right to win; a poor sportsman generally tries to amuse the spectators with his self-styled clever wit by making abusive remarks, which on intelligent spectators act as a boomerang.

Winning: If you are the rightful winner, be willing to take credit for it, but keep in mind that it was only your time to win and that your winning was probably due to conditions or a reward for your sacrifices; a kind word or handshake goes a long way toward forming a lasting friendship, and does not change the score.

Service: Students should always consider that they are receiving far more than they are giving. Their best efforts for their school are none too good.

The Present and the Future: Give your school the best that you have, and the best will come back to you. Your success in the future depends on the present. Build well.

Learn from Losing

Is it heresy to suggest it is more important to teach high school and college students how to lose than how to win?

Coping with victory isn't difficult. The win itself induces a generous euphoria, a sense of achievement, and often in today's society, tangible profit. Living with winning calls for minimal training.

Dealing with defeat is difficult. Learning how to cope with defeat is important because unless you lead an extraordinarily blessed life, you are going to encounter many defeats.

Everybody loses sooner or later. The magnificent Michael Jordan rode to glory with an Olympic basketball medal, and with a national college championship team. He learned how to deal with losing when he became a professional ball player.

It is exceptional when an American champion professional baseball or football team repeats the following year.

George Halas was a winner. He achieved everything good that football has to offer. He was tough. He won graciously. But he impressed me most when he lost, as he did a lot in his final years. No whining. No excuses. Halas's jaw stuck out and he vowed he'd do better, that he was going to win again. And he did lay the foundation for another world championship before he died.

I knew of only one major athlete who never suffered defeat. Rocky Marciano won all his heavyweight fights, but fate decreed his life would end tragically early in a plane crash.

Educators recognize the value of athletic competition by allotting generous blocks of time to physical education and intramural competition. They rationalize the excesses and commercialism of football and basketball by using part of that income to subsidize the rest of the athletic program.

It's a sorry rationalization, and has contributed to the dollar madness that infects both professional and college sports. Greed, empire building, and an irrational drive to win at any cost are degrading athletics at all levels where an admission fee is charged or television is involved.

Sixty-four top college basketball teams enter the NCAA championship tournament every year. Sixty-three of them will come out losers. Most of these players will be crushed by their "failure."

The evil of big time, big money sports and their insane emphasis on winning permeates down to Little League baseball and football fields. The kids are assaulted with a constant TV display of pushing to win because the victory means a World Series check, a Super Bowl payoff, endorsements, bargaining for a $2 million contract.

A Little League umpire in my suburb quit and told the local paper why. "The majority of the players I found to be pretty good kids," he said. "The managers and coaches aren't unreasonable unless they lose a heart breaker. I think it's time those managers and coaches start thinking about the kids instead of the games.

"Parents are the worst. The parents on both sides yell constantly at the umpire. In one game after the home team scored two runs in the last inning to win, the manager of the losers swore at me using every name one could imagine.

"And this, I suppose, is setting an example of good sportsmanship for the kids."

Psychology Today reported a survey of more than a thousand players, parents, and coaches involved in Little League. In many cases they found the game was taken away from youngsters and used to satisfy adult egos.

Parents should sign the kids up and then leave them alone, the researchers believed. "When a boy comes back from practice or a game, his parents should ask, 'Did you learn something today? Did you have fun? These are more important than 'Did you win?' "

The young players praised their coaches for knowledge, but most said the coaches yelled too much and were bad losers.

More than 95 percent of the 531 kids interviewed said they were more interested in having fun than in winning. Seventy-five percent said they'd rather play on a losing team than sit on the bench with a winner.

Boxing Should Be Abolished

If some twenty-fifth century archaeologists from another planet try to reconstruct twentieth century civilization by digging through the ruins of planet Earth, they might reach this deduction:

"For entertainment, the Earthians had huge arenas in which they gathered by the thousands. In the centers of the arenas were rope enclosures they called rings. Two men would be put into a ring and would fight until one beat the other senseless.

"The mob would cheer wildly as one contestant was about to be knocked unconscious. At times, one man would be beaten to death by his opponent as the mob screamed approval. Millions more watched the execution in their homes through a device they called television."

In our sophisticated civilization of the 1980s we look with scorn at savages who entertained themselves by trying to kill one another, or who made human sacrifices to their gods. But we condone this entertainment by supporting it with our attention, our money, and government supervision.

The apologists for boxing say why not abolish football, which also kills, or auto racing.

The difference is that boxing is the only sport in which the goal is physical injury to the opponent.

All life is a hazard. You gamble on being killed when you walk out the front door every morning.

The argument against professional boxing is moralistic. Should we countenance a degrading commercial spectacle in which the objective is to disable, maim, or kill?

What purpose is served by professional boxing? The people who make money are the sleazy promoters, the managers, and the members of the advertising industry involved in commercials relating to TV fights.

Boxers are killed, injured, left soft in the head, and in most instances, broke.

The owners and apologists for boxing argue that it helps poor boys, that young men who might otherwise spend their lives digging ditches or washing cars are enabled through fighting to make good livings and lead decent lives.

Muhammad Ali made and retained a lot of money. He also shuffles and mumbles. Joe Louis made millions and was a pitiful hulk in his final days in Las Vegas, exhibiting himself in night clubs to make enough to eat. Chicago fighter Johnny Bratton was on top of the boxing world when I was covering boxing. The last I heard he was living on the streets after spending time in the mental hospital at Manteno.

These were champions. Add to them the thousands of punch-drunk ex-pugs who fill the skid rows and mental hospitals and relief rolls and you get an accurate picture of the character-building and economic benefits of professional boxing to the young men who do the fighting.

I firmly believe in the value of amateur boxing, and deplore its weakening. I boxed a little in college and in the Navy. Amateurs fight with big pillowlike gloves. A kid who puts on a pair of gloves gets physically tough, learns sportsmanship, and paradoxically, learns gentleness. Rarely is an amateur boxer, or even a neighborhood kid who puts on the gloves, a bully.

Boxing was illegal in most states until 1918. It was made legal by the argument that we should encourage the development of the art of self-defense among our young people. It's a valid contention. Why not teach boxing in high schools and college?

When Illinois Senator Paul Simon was serving in the Illinois legislature he introduced a bill—which obviously didn't pass—to make boxing illegal in the state.

"Professional boxing is a sport only in the sense that Nero's throwing Christians to the lions was a sport," said Simon. "Boxers are killed every year, and this hits the headlines. But what does not make headlines are the many boxers who end up punchy. The constant pounding on the head results in severe damage to the brain.

"By comparison, bull fighting and cock fighting—which we outlaw—are relatively humane.

"I know of no legislator who wants to outlaw high school or college boxing, or who wants to outlaw the Golden Gloves type of activity, where young people with well-padded gloves learn to box.

"But there is no comparison between these things and the professional blood bath which some would like to drape in the honorable toga of a sport."

The 1968 Democratic Convention

The Riots

There was about one policeman or National Guardsman or regular Army soldier in Chicago for every demonstrator, approximately 20,000 on each side, when the Democrats assembled in Chicago to nominate Hubert Humphrey to run for President in 1968.

The Yippies and the Movement and assorted other protesters against the Vietnam war threatened to have 100,000 to 150,000 demonstrators on the streets. Wild threats were made: Lace the water supply with LSD. Dynamite natural gas lines coming into the city. Take over a gas station, pump gas into the sewers and set it afire. Put agents into hotel kitchens and put drugs in the food for delegates. Take jobs as taxi drivers and kidnap delegates after they came in at O'Hare. Have a mass stall-in on the expressways.

It was all bluff, but no responsible police force could ignore it. Daley's people took the threats pretty seriously, and mobilized the immense counterforce. The problem for the protesters was that the talk of violence scared tens of thousands from coming to Chicago. When word came that motorcycle gangs were on their way a week before the convention, word went out across the country through the underground newspaper network: "Stay away from Chicago."

The 100,000 turned out to be 20,000—but these included some crazies and a substantial delegation of experienced and skilled demonstrators. They found real patsies in Chicago. My own stories warned about their technique, which was to taunt the police into what the Kerner Commission accurately labeled a "police riot."

A Barnard college coed described the tactics used in a New York demonstration. "The protesters rushed police lines in front of the Waldorf Astoria, then fell back into the crowd who were watching them. The police, unable to tell the demonstrators from the spectators, tore out at everyone."

The morning of the biggest riot in Chicago, Wednesday, August 28, which began in front of the Conrad Hilton, I wrote a final warning:

"A simple strategy, as old as revolution itself, is to turn the people against the state, and to make the police hated. The next step, scheduled today, is to get the police swinging clubs in Loop crowds in the hope that innocent onlookers and passersby will be swept up in the police charge.

"The whole show is being run by revolutionaries who have hardened their techniques in New York, at the Pentagon, at Columbia, in Oakland, and at Berkeley.

"They are very dangerous. If they weren't, we wouldn't have all these troops in Chicago. We are playing their game. We are reacting exactly the way they want us to react. And we should stop calling them hippies. The hippie joke is over."

The first score for the radicals came at 6:20 P.M. Wednesday when they taunted National Guardsmen blocking the Congress Street bridge into shooting tear gas. The wind was off the lake, and the gas blew onto Michigan Avenue, into the Congress, Blackstone, and Hilton hotels, and several blocks into the Loop where people held their faces and ran into stores and buildings to get away from the stinging fumes.

With the nationally televised rioting well under way on Michigan Avenue, a group of demonstrators started moving toward State Street. This generated their second big score—worse, in my mind, than the Hilton rioting because there were no TV cameras on State Street, and little restraint on the police.

Policemen started beating pedestrians on State Street. They repeatedly swept the sidewalks. Six to ten uniformed men with night sticks would form a line and sweep everyone out of the way. "Move! Move!" they shouted.

People who had been watching *Rosemary's Baby* in the Roosevelt Theater wandered innocently out of the theater and wondered what the excitement was about. Clerks working late, scrub women, tourists, students getting out of classes at Roosevelt University—all the people you'd find on the street on a Wednesday night.

They were caught in the sweep, lured into the trap by the radicals, who taunted the police and ran. Across from the Palmer House a line of policemen chased twenty-five or thirty pedestrians. The policemen walked at a near-trot, nightsticks extended, shouting: "Off the street! Move! Move!"

If people ran it started a panic and other policemen came running. If they walked they were overtaken and risked being slugged. I was caught in half-a-dozen sweeps, and narrowly escaped being slugged. This was open season on reporters.

Scores of spectators under the Palmer House canopy watched in horror as a policeman went animal when a crippled man couldn't get away fast enough. The man hopped with his stick as fast as he could, but the policeman shoved him in the back, then hit him with the night stick, hit him again, and finally crashed him into a lamp post.

Clergymen, medics, and this crippled man were the special pigeons in this riot. At State and Adams a night stick cracked the head of a clergyman who didn't move fast enough. He was lying in a store doorway, bleeding heavily, when I left. Any attempt to intervene would have brought a severe beating.

As I walked away a policeman across the street cracked a clergyman across the back because he walked instead of ran.

It sickened me to have to report this police rioting, because I was and am on the side of the police. I went out that day to write exactly what I saw. I thought my report would bring credit to the police.

Ninety-eight percent of the police were fine. Man after man handled situations decently and firmly, responding like pros to provocation that was unbelievably vile. But the brass didn't have all of their men under control, and rioting is contagious.

Scores of demonstrators were arrested and injured. Many, maybe most of them, were asking for it. The tragedy was that the police officials fell for the stupid trap of beating up innocent citizens. They were too arrogant to believe the warnings. Their intelligence was lousy and their judgment worse.

I was the editor in charge of covering the street disorders at the 1968 Democratic convention. It quickly became apparent that autos or foot power were inadequate to cover the action from Grant Park to Lincoln Park, so I brought my bike to work. I had two flags from a small mast. One read "PRESS," the other "RED CROSS"—for use as the occasion demanded. Dean Fischer of Time *liked the idea and got his bike out, too. An hour after this picture was taken in Grant Park, the worst rioting of the convention broke out down the street.*

Julie, Rennie, Abbie, and Tom

The trial of the Chicago Seven in Judge Julius Hoffman's court was hard to believe when it was going on, and in retrospect it's still hard to believe.

Judge Hoffman's sentencing of three of the defendants to jail for contempt of court demonstrates the flavor of the entire proceedings.

The contempt citation for Rennie Davis read:

On February 4, during the testimony of the witness Riordan, Mr.

Dellinger spoke out. In the ensuing disturbance, Mr. Davis inserted the following remarks:

> THE COURT: Take that man into custody, Mr. Marshal, take that man into custody.
> VOICES: Right on, right on!
> MR. SCHULTZ: Into custody.
> THE COURT: Into custody.
> VOICES: Right on.
> MR. DAVIS: Go ahead, Dick Schultz, put everybody in jail.

For those eight words Rennie Davis was sentenced to two months in jail.

The complete contempt citation against Tom Hayden read:

> On January 28, while the Assistant United States Attorney was making a statement to the court, Mr. Hayden rose and said:
> MR. HAYDEN: That is not true.

For those four words, Tom Hayden was sentenced to seven days in jail.

Now comes Abbie Hoffman, who was the loudest, boldest, most imaginative, and most profane of the defendants. Judge Hoffman's contempt citation against Abbie Hoffman read:

> On February 5, after the court had decided not to reinstate Mr. Dellinger's bail, Mr. Hoffman (Abbie) made the following remarks in the outburst which ensued:
> MR. HOFFMAN: Your idea of justice is the only obscenity in the room. You schtunk! Vo den! Shanda fur de goyem! Obviously it was a provocation. That's why it has gone on here today because you threatened him with the cutting of his freedom of speech in the speech he gave in Milwaukee.
> THE COURT: Mr. Marshal, you will ask the defendant Hoffman to . . .
> MR. HOFFMAN: This ain't the Standard Club.
> THE MARSHAL: Mr. Hoffman . . .
> MR. HOFFMAN: Oh, tell him to stick it up his bowling ball. How is your war stock doing, Julie? You don't have any power. They didn't have any power in the Third Reich, either.
> THE COURT: Will you ask him to sit down, Mr. Marshal?
> THE MARSHAL: Mr. Hoffman, I am asking you again to shut up.

MR. RUBIN: Gestapo!

MR. HOFFMAN: Show him your .45. Show him a .45. He ain't never seen a gun.

Abbie Hoffman's contemptuous statements continued for two and a half typewritten pages in this citation. Among his remarks to Judge Hoffman:

"You know you cannot win this [obscenity] case."

"I hear you haven't lost a case before a jury in twenty-four tries. We're going to get away too. That's why you're throwing us in jail now this way."

"You are a tyrant."

"The judges in Nazi Germany ordered sterilization. Why don't you do that, Judge Hoffman?"

"No I won't shut up. I ain't no automaton like you. I don't want to be a tyrant and I don't care for a tyrannical system. Best friend the blacks ever had, huh? How many blacks are in the Drake Towers? How many are in the Standard Club? How many own stock in the Brunswick Corporation?"

For all of these statements, Judge Hoffman sentenced Abbie Hoffman to six days in jail for contempt.

The Power of Aum

Lincoln Park, August 26, 1968, the week of the Democratic Convention disorders. Jean Genet, the French writer, opens a press conference by saying in French to Allen Ginsberg, poet and guru to the hippies:

"I took very much Nembutal last night to try to forget I am in America."

Ginsberg: "Ten people humming 'aum' can calm down one hundred. One hundred people humming 'aum' can immobilize an entire downtown Chicago street full of scared humans, uniformed or naked."

Ginsberg sincerely cared for the young protesters, and he really believed in the power of Aum. He was to get the opportunity to test it under fire.

Ginsberg provided one of the most unusual sights I witnessed in a week of remarkable sights. He was seated on the lawn in Lincoln

Park. In a circle around him, about twelve deep, were seated young men and women participating in the week's protests.

Ginsberg was humming, or droning, a note, which is spelled *AUM*, pronounced *om*. He held the note as long as one breath lasted, took a deep breath, and slid to another note.

The others hummed with him. I don't know how long their breaths held out, because I stood watching for only ten minutes.

Another witness pondered the reaction of the National Guard if they heard a loud humming noise coming down Michigan Avenue that night. Maybe the soldiers' defense would be a loud counter aum.

However, the showdown came in the park. In the midst of the maelstrom as police began to sweep demonstrators out of the park, Ginsberg stood on a hill behind the revolutionaries, humming as intensely as he could while the comrades at the barricades cried, "Kill the pigs!"

Then the police fired tear gas, and unless Ginsberg was up a tree, he was running along with the rest of us toward Clark Street.

Looking Ahead

Looking Back to the Future

In 1964 the British journal *New Scientist* asked 100 authorities on science and public affairs to forecast the state of the world in 1984.

These learned men said medicine would have conquered cancer, or be close to conquering it, by 1984. Heart diseases and viral infections would be near extinction, they predicted.

Planes, trains, and automobiles would be under automatic control with automation moving into virtually every field. We would have colonized the moon, and perhaps have men on Mars.

Underwater dams would harness the strength of the ocean currents for electric power. Submarine tractors would cultivate the floor of the ocean as a major new food source.

These projections were made on the basis of existing knowledge and ongoing developments. Obviously they missed a lot of targets. There was a remarkable lack of speculation on the growth of electronics.

Less scientific forecasts for the mid-eighties were put into a time capsule in a new *Look* magazine building in Des Moines in 1957. Carroll Shanks, president of Prudential Insurance, predicted disposable income per family would be $15,000 a year. Adman Leo Burnett said in 1987 men would still be wearing suits that were in style in 1959, and I will personally testify to the validity of that prediction.

Look's experts predicted 250-mile-an-hour automobiles. One adman said the human brain would be thoroughly understood. I think in his own mind was the concept of implanting in a consumer's mind an irresistible impulse to purchase a particular product on sighting it at the supermarket.

These authorities also believed the dread diseases—cancer, arthritis, tuberculosis—would be unknown. But they saw mental hospitals tripling in size.

All in all, these leaders in science and medicine and economics and business had very little concept of what was ahead for twenty years.

I doubt if today's predictors are any more capable.

(No one predicted there would be no *Look* magazine in 1984.)

In 1961 I wrote a facetious column predicting what the city would be like in 1981. I missed on most, like saying the national debt would be only half a trillion dollars. But I did come pretty close on one prediction: "A civic reception will mark the first two years in office of Mayor Smith, a Northwestern political science graduate whose great grandparents were slaves in Virginia."

In 1939 a Harvard professor said television would never become popular because watching it "must take place in a semidarkened room and it demands continuous attention."

Andrew Carnegie said in 1900 that in the new century the world would be purged by war. "To kill a man," he predicted, "will be considered as disgusting as we in this day consider it disgusting to eat one."

In 1950 the Associated Press did a half-century roundup of the best scientific thinking and made some projections. One they hit on the nose was "A housewife may use an electronic stove and prepare roast beef in less time than it takes to set the table."

But what a housewife! Anthropologists and beauty experts predicted that by the year 2000 the American woman would average over 6 feet tall, wear size 11 shoes, and have shoulders like a wrestler.

Predictors have had a few triumphs and a lot more wrong guesses, or scientific projections of known facts. I found no scientific projection that the superconductor of electricity would be perfected before 2000, and yet it is reality in 1987 and will virtually revolutionize the delivery of power.

Scientific breakthroughs and achievements in the last fifteen years of the twentieth century may equal or surpass the developments of the preceding two hundred years. Progress is coming in quantum leaps, and the major problem facing our society is to keep human beings in control of our own destiny.

The Lost Tribe

The writings and pictures in the ruins made it fairly easy to characterize this tribe.

It was a strange society. It believed itself the most civilized on the planet. But it followed customs and rituals little removed from primeval man.

Women were particularly ritualistic. They painted their faces with livid hues, using dyes and coals. They bound their bodies tightly, and made their feet misshapen by constricting them in tiny harness-like stilts.

Their dances were primitive, accompanied by a heavy beat from drums and some stringed instruments.

The chant was unintelligible even to the dancers, who gyrated in pairs, face-to-face, with strong sexual overtones. The music was so magnified that deafness was a common problem among the dancers and listeners in their later years.

For entertainment they frequently selected two of their strongest males, put them in a small ring, and cheered wildly until one beat the other into insensibility.

They elected tribal leaders who had power to exact tribute in the form of taxation.

Although, as noted, they regarded themselves as highly advanced, they followed jungle law in dealing with those who disobeyed their laws.

They put to death some lawbreakers, and caged others, some in lightless dungeons.

The weak and defective among the children frequently were hidden in out-of-the-way buildings and existed in conditions considerably worse than those of the pet dogs and cats of the tribesmen.

The absence of loyalty, or even of prevailing purpose, was observed in rituals of the society. Once a week these people gathered in a variety of temples, hung with rich offerings, and attended by priests of the rite.

The people worshipped a god of benevolence and love, but even in the temples, the women attended first to the dress of the neighbors.

On concluding their rituals, they would rush from the temples, frequently bumping into one another and cursing impediments, thus denying the loving kindness to which they had just given tribute.

Worship of sex had a more prominent place in their society than worship of the spiritual.

The best-known members of the tribes, far surpassing the priests and doctors, were blonde goddesses, selected for their mammary development. It would appear from the writings that these goddesses were immensely rich and quite inferior intellectually.

The strongest tribes tended to worship all light skin. The fairest of the people won easiest acceptance. The darker the skin, the more the person was shunned.

Those with the darkest skins were made to live in restricted areas and largely kept away from the places where the light-skinned tribesmen lived and worked.

Strangely, those with the lightest skin regarded it as a sign of distinction to darken their skin through exposure to sunlight.

This civilization discovered a means of self-destruction in what they called the twentieth century. Toward the end of the century they caused an enormous explosion which eliminated all life on the planet, called Earth.

The Land of Plenty

Picture an imaginary town. The world population of three billion is reduced proportionately to a town of 1,000. This town has 60 Americans, with the remainder of the world represented by 940 persons.

This hypothetical community was figured out a couple of decades ago by Dr. Henry Smith Leiper, a leader in the Congregational churches. The precise figures have changed, but the principle remains.

Some 330 residents would be classified as Christians. Two hundred and thirty would be Roman Catholics, and fewer than 100 would be Protestant Christians.

At least 90 townspeople would be members of the communist party, and 370 others would be under communist domination.

The town would of course be integrated, though it would be marked by many ghettos. The 303 whites would be a distinct minority to the 697 non-whites.

The 60 Americans would have fifteen times as many possessions per person as the others in the community, and they would produce 16 percent of the town's food supply.

The Americans would eat most of what they grew, or store it in their sheds at great expense if they couldn't eat it themselves. They would eat 72 percent above the maximum food requirements.

Hunger is relative, but it can be said conservatively that a third of the people in the town would go to bed hungry every night, and perhaps 100 would be near starvation.

This disparity in the food supply and its distribution understandably would lead to a lack of affection among the hungry toward those who had to figure out ways to grow less food.

The Americans would have a disproportionate share of steel, fuel, coal, electric power, and general equipment.

More than half the people in town would be hearing about Karl Marx, Lenin, Stalin, and Khrushchev, but half of the population would never have heard of Jesus Christ or what he taught.

The American families would be spending some $850 a year for arms to guard themselves from attack by their neighbors, and to assure they could wipe out their neighbors in case of attack.

At the same time they would be spending less than four dollars a year to share their religious faith with other members of the community.

The 60 Americans would be well-off and so would about 200 others representing western Europe and the wealthy classes in South America, and a few favored classes in South Africa, Australia, and Japan.

But the majority of the 1,000 people would be poorly educated or illiterate, hungry, and ill.

Most of the Americans would be so busy watching television and playing golf and raising their kids and making money they would be unaware of the plight of their townspeople.

This was understandable years ago when the town was spread out and communication was difficult. But today no part of the town would be beyond rifle shot of any other part.

Second Career

The *Chicago Tribune* had mandatory retirement at sixty-five, but they asked me to stick around a couple of years more, I think because another columnist left, and they didn't want it to look like an exodus.

I didn't really mind leaving after 8,000 columns. I was beginning to think I'd said everything I had to say, and it was time to give somebody else a chance. I also was itchy for a different line of work.

Beware of generalizations about retirement. How it is enjoyed, or disliked, depends a lot on how much the retiree felt about the job he or she is leaving. My first boss retired and took up painting, and I never saw him happier. But I think he hated his job as editor because of the heat he got from above. Another *Tribune* friend of mine spends most of his time since retiring happily sailing around the world on freighters. I would go batty in either activity.

I am one of those nuts who has to stay busy, at real work, not make-work. I have to feel useful. The ingredients for a full life, my wife has told me, are someone to love, something to do, and something to look forward to.

After five years, do I miss the newspaper work? No. I do miss my friends, the camaraderie of the newsroom, and the friends I never met—*Tribune* readers who wrote or called, or one way or another let me know they found our daily communication worthwhile.

I hope to renew many of these friendships with this book.

In my final column at the *Tribune* I said the newspaper could get along without columnists, but it could not survive without the printers and pressmen, the advertising staffs, the circulation drivers, the mailers, the accountants, the thousands of people who work together every day to produce a metropolitan newspaper.

If it weren't for them my forum would have been a soapbox in Bughouse Square. We got the glory, they got the work. Newsprint handlers and maintenance personnel and want ad sales persons and security guards and librarians and payroll staff and artists and copy editors. And even some of the bosses contributed, too.

Some of the things about columning I did not miss were getting up at five o'clock every morning. Commuting. Worrying about the next column every time I put "30" on one column. Lying awake at night writing columns in my mind. Pursuing the unattainable goal, to make my latest column better than any I had ever written.

Just as a shortstop lives in fear of booting a ground ball and a football end of dropping a pass, I worried endlessly about writing a lousy column. I think this made me try harder to be as good as I could be.

The big retirement shindig at the *Tribune* was, at my request, a noontime open house in my office with six-hundred corned beef sandwiches and a lot of brownies my wife cooked.

Then I went home and formed a corporation and set out to help disprove the notion that when you reach sixty-five a button pops and you immediately become less useful. I would try to emulate my role models—George Halas, Grandma Moses, A. N. Pritzker, Clem Stone, Claude Pepper, and Maggie Kuhn.

I was ghosting a speech for a business executive recently and found a new word—new to me, anyway. Chiliasm. Belief in the coming of the millennium. Millennium—a period of 1,000 years; any period of great happiness, peace, prosperity; imagined golden age.

The year 2000 marks the end of one millennium and the beginning of another. I believe we aren't going to blow the human race off the planet, and that we will control our technological miracles, and have a fighting chance at a period of happiness, peace, and prosperity. I am chiliastic.